Sacred Snakes

Orthodox Images of Indian Snake Worship

Laurie Cozad

Contexts and Consequences:
New Studies in Religion and History

Cathy Gutierrez and Lisa Poirier, Series Editors

This series provides a forum for scholarship at the nexus of religion and history in which the contexts and consequences of change are examined. Forthcoming titles will explore pivotal historical moments, or propose alternative readings of history.

Authors are invited to submit works to the series that employ innovative methods in the study of religion. Projects accepted in the series will be marked by originality and creativity and, while maintaining the standards required in scholarly research, will be accessible, engaging, and suitable for use across disciplines.

Proposals should be prepared in duplicate and directed to:

Cathy N. Gutierrez
Department of Religion
Sweet Briar College
Sweet Briar, VA 24595

Lisa J. Poirier
Department of Comparative Religion
Miami University
Oxford OH 45056

Questions may be emailed to cgutierrez@sbc.edu, or to
poirielj@muohio.edu

Sacred Snakes

Orthodox Images of Indian Snake Worship

Laurie Cozad

A volume in the series
Contexts and Consequences:
New Studies in
Religion and History

Cathy Nora Gutierrez and
Lisa J. Poirier, Series Editors

The Davies Group, Publishers *Aurora, Colorado*

Address all requests to:

The Davies Group, Publishers
PO Box 440140
Aurora CO 80044-0140
USA

Library of Congress Cataloging-in-Publication Data

Cozad, Laurie.
Sacred snakes: orthodox images of Indian snake worship / Laurie Cozad.
p. cm. - (Contexts and consequences: new studies in religion and history)
Includes bibliographical references and index.
ISBN 1-888570-72-5 (paper)
ISBN 1-888570-79-2 (hc)
1. Serpent worship—India—History. 2. Serpents—Religious aspects—Hinduism.
3. Serpents—Religious aspects—Buddhism. I. Title. II. Series.

BL2015.S4C69 2004
294.5'212-dc22

2004007193

Printed in the United States of America
Published 2004. The Davies Group Publishers, Aurora CO 80044-0140

For Winston McNulty,
the pride and joy of my life

Contents

Textual Timeline *viii*

Chapter 1 Introduction: Snake Worshippers, Orthodox Redactors and Their Contextual Tug-of-War 1

Chapter 2 The *Ṛg Veda* and the Threat of the Sovereign Snake 13

Chapter 3 The Late Vedas: Revering the Snake's Power and Preserving Snake-Centered Rituals 23

Chapter 4 The *Ādi Parvan* of the *Mahābhārata*: The Epic Redactors Take On the Snake 49

Chapter 5 The Pāli Texts: The Buddhist Redactors [c]Harm the Snake 81

Chapter 6 The *Mahāvastu*: The Buddha Shares in the Snake's Largess 107

Chapter 7 Conclusion: It is Hard to Keep a Good Snake Down 141

Bibliography 153

Notes 165

Index 185

Textual Timeline

HINDU TEXTS

Ṛg Veda: c. 1200 BCE

Late Vedas
Atharva Veda: c. 900-600 BCE
Śatapatha Brāhmaṇa: c. 900-600 BCE
Pañcaviṃśa Brāhamaṇa: c. 900-600 BCE
Sāmavidhāna Brāhmaṇa: c. 900-600 BCE
Gṛhya Sūtras: c. 600-400 BCE

Ādi Parvan of the *Mahābhārata*: c. 300 BCE-300 CE

BUDDHIST TEXTS

Mahāvagga: c. 0-100 CE
Jātaka Tales: c. 0-450 CE
Mahāvastu: c. 100-400 CE

Acknowledgments

I want to thank Mr. William Gresham, Jr. and the College of Liberal Arts, Dr. Michael Metcalf and the members of the Croft Institute for International Studies as well as Dr. Michael Harrington and the members of the Department of Philosophy and Religion at the University of Mississippi for their generosity and enthusiasm, and Dr. Wendy Doniger, Dr. Frank Reynolds, Dr. Norman Cutler and Dr. Lawrence McCrea at the University of Chicago for their invaluable advice and direction during the initial stages of this project. I would also like to thank Winston McNulty, Shirley Cozad, Dale Cozad, Doug Cozad, Christie Cozad Neuger, Zinnia Drennen, Elisabeth Cozad, John Indellicate, Kim Fleming, Kirsten Dellinger, Jeff Jackson, Gina Godalia, Tracy Wascom and Bruce McNulty for their loving support.

1

Introduction: Snake Worshippers, Orthodox Redactors and Their Contextual Tug-of-War

> "It is well done for you lay brothers to abide by the *Uposatha* vows.[1] Wise men of ancient times, having abandoned the fortune of the *Nāgas* (snakes), abide by the *Uposatha* vows."[2]

While the Buddhist authors of this verse enjoin us to abandon the "fortune of the Nāgas," we shall ignore their injunction and focus our gaze on the centuries-old grass-roots tradition they found so threatening: snake worship. Our historical analysis of this tradition, however, will not be devoted to ancient ethnographies, archaeological remains, or ritual texts written by snake worshippers, for in large measure, snake worshippers did not attract the attention of explorers, build grand structures, or document their own practices. Rather, this rich tradition remains manifest within the pages of an unexpected source: the texts of Hindu and Buddhist redactors. Redactors are those priests and monks who, over the centuries, have collected, edited, and amended the myths and rituals that comprise the building blocks of their traditions. We will refer to the texts established by these redactors as "orthodox" texts, for this term reflects that they were generated and preserved by priests and monks for the purpose of codifying and institutionalizing the parameters of "right teaching." On the other hand, we will refer to the figures, practices, and sites established by snake worshippers as "grass-roots" elements, for this term reflects that they were generated and preserved by ordinary people for the purpose of meeting their own religious needs. And what we find as we examine these orthodox texts is that some of the mythic/ritual elements used to construct the building blocks of these orthodox traditions derive from a grass-roots tradition of snake worship. Therefore, not only is it useful to read these texts for an understanding of snake worship, it is essential to understand snake worship if one is to make sense of these orthodox traditions.

Rituals devoted to the propitiation and supplication of snakes, *Nāgas*, that are perceived to be endowed with supernatural powers have been practiced on the Indian sub-continent for more than two millennia, and these ritual practices remain relevant for people in India today. During *Nāga Pañcamī*, the annual festival devoted to the supernatural snakes in Banāras, for example, thousands of people crowd into the area around the Nāga kuān, or snake pool, that is situated in the northwest sector.[3] At this festival, which takes places during the rainy season in the month of *Śrāvana* (July/August) bathers are drawn to the deep, dark pool believed to provide access to the Nāgaloka, the magnificently luxurious underwater world of the Nāgas. According to Diana Eck, during this festival "thousands of people bathe in the deep well, honor its serpent deities, and watch the dare-devil young men from this district plunge from the top of the wall surrounding the well into the waters some thirty feet below."[4] Worshippers honor these supernatural snakes in order that these deities might ensure a variety of things, mostly related to human and earthly fertility, such as the birth of healthy children and the provision of bountiful harvests. While Nāgas are specially equipped with supernatural powers, any snake can potentially be a Nāga. Thus, Nāga worship also involves an acknowledgement of the ubiquitous snake's dangerous power and a plea to keep loved ones safe from its poisonous bite.[5]

In present times, women, particularly those desiring to become pregnant, worship Nāgas. As part of these devotional rituals, supplicants cover Nāga statues with fresh flowers or sprinkle them with water. In Banāras, one site that is very popular for such activities is at the top of Caukī Ghāt in the southeast sector of the city where there are several Nāga statues situated beneath a huge tree. In conjunction with my observations that women are the primary practitioners of these types of rituals, I also noted that women dominate the ritual spaces associated with these practices. For example, on Saturday evenings, the Nāga temple—site of the *Nāga Pañcamī* annual festival—is filled with women who, according to first-hand reports, have been coming to the temple every Saturday night for decades, as had their mothers before them. The temple operates both as a place where women might propitiate these divine sovereigns (usually in order to facilitate healthy pregnancies) and as a place where women would gather together to sing *bhajans,* listen to stories, and socialize.[6] In fact, on the occasions when I visited the temple, only women were in attendance, and I was told that these gatherings traditionally involved only women.

I found the phenomenon of a public temple filled exclusively and regularly with women a rare happening in my experience of temple activities in India. Yet, it provided a clue about the longevity and richness of a tradition which ranges as far north as Himachal Pradesh and as far south as Tamil Nadu: snakes, as ubiquitous, powerful denizens of the earth's surface provide constant and easy access to anyone who might wish to approach them as objects of religious devotion. Snake worship can thus be seen as a form of religiosity created and maintained by those most often disenfranchised by orthodox religion, for example, women.

While first-hand observation is one means for identifying those groups involved in the worship of the supernatural snake, that method does not help us compose a historical picture of these various practitioners. What little historical information we have is as follows. The earliest ethnographic evidence we have of snake worship is documented in conjunction with the 4th C. BCE visit of Alexander the Great to India: "When Alexander was assaulting some of the cities in India and capturing others, he found in many of them, besides other animals, a snake which the Indians, regarding as sacred, kept in a cave and worshipped with much devotion."[7] *Tīrthas* and *caityas* are the sites traditionally associated with snake worship, as well as with the worship of other deities. *Tīrthas* are places where one might literally *tṝ* or "cross" a body of water, and thereby gain access to the supernatural snakes living in the waters or underneath the earth's surface. *Caityas*, on the other hand, are "ancient places of worship marked by a tree, stone altar, pool, or stream, and a railing to designate sacred territory."[8] Unfortunately, the natural contours of these sites traditionally do not leave much in the way of archaeological traces. Therefore, very little exists to mark the historical worship of snakes.

Ancient texts of both the Hindu and Buddhist traditions, however, provide us with a glimpse into the religious life of the ancient world, and while a variety of divine animals play a role in these texts, supernatural snakes abound as do ritual practices and sacred sites associated with the worship of these creatures. The supernatural snake makes its first appearance in the *Ṛg Veda*, c. 1200 BCE, and maintains a central role throughout the late Vedas, c. 900-400 BCE, and into the epics, c. 300 BCE-300 CE. Moreover, in both the Pāli literature, c. 1-400 CE, and Buddhist Hybrid Sanskrit texts such as the *Mahāvastu*, c. 100-400 CE, one finds a full cast of snake characters from the evil-minded reptile to the devoted snake king.

The redactors of these orthodox texts have tremendous influence over the ways in which audiences perceive characters, and their influence is especially profound when the texts at issue are both widely dispersed and generally accessible. They exert this influence through the creation of various scenarios that function to render their protagonists sympathetic and their antagonists diabolical, or put more succinctly, through contextualization. When engaged in contextual analyses, scholars often treat orthodox texts as self-contained entities, thus decreeing that the issue of context pertains only to the internal logic of the text itself. While choices concerning the ways in which a character might be contextualized obviously stem from the redactors' narrative goals, sometimes these goals extend well beyond the limits of the page.

What we will discover, therefore, as we examine these snake characters throughout this survey is that the narrative decision to feature an evil-minded reptile over a devoted snake king, for example, is a very intentional one: the redactors of certain orthodox texts found the phenomenon of snake worship to be threatening to their ideological agenda, and as a result, used context as a weapon to portray the snake and its associated ritual tradition in a very negative fashion. Thus, throughout this book, we will examine the complex and shifting role of the supernatural snake in both Hindu and Buddhist texts in order to delineate some of the historical and political struggles between those who create and engage in the rituals associated with snake worship and those who seek to coopt this practice for their own religio-political ends.

This textual analysis will thus focus on two distinct discourses: the loud and clear discourse of the orthodox redactors, and the subtle—sometimes buried—discourse of snake worshippers who have contributed to the development of this grass-roots movement over the centuries. We will understand both of these groups to be engaged in the building of a religious structure; one which reflects their respective fears and experiences, hopes and dreams. As we will see, this building process involves the construction of a contextual framework within which each group will center its chosen divine champion amidst a matrix of contextual details. Context is defined here as the assortment of narrative elements that are woven into a pattern in order to clothe a character and render it sensible to the reader. Such elements include, but are not limited to, the scope of powers granted, the props supplied, the descriptive labels attached, the degree of respect given, the types of colleagues and associates provided, and the range of behavior allowed. Context thereby functions to reflect the intrinsic worth of a character through a frame of refracting details. And as we will see throughout our analysis, both orthodox redactors and snake worshippers function as 'context constructors', for each promotes the intrinsic worth of its chosen divine champion through the construction of a contextual framework.

The creative efforts of these 'context constructors' reflect a desire to center themselves in a context that works for them; to create a context wherein both the world and their place in the world makes sense. According to Charles Long, this is a religious task, one that at times is not carried out in a conventional institutional setting:

> As a historian of religions I have not defined religion in conventional terms. To be sure, the church is one place one looks for religion.... But even more than this, the church was not the only context for the meaning of religion. For my purposes, religion will mean orientation—orientation in the ultimate sense, that is, how one comes to terms with the ultimate significance of one's place in the world.[9]

I would agree with this statement, particularly Long's emphasis on a strategy that allows him to focus on the myriad alternative avenues through which human beings enact their own religious agency. I would argue, however, that it is not always necessary to resort to non-conventional locations in order to see non-conventional forms of religious agency. In fact, what makes an analysis of snake worship as refracted through the lens of these orthodox redactors so interesting is that it provides us with an opportunity to see the ways in which an institutional setting provides evidence of alternative modes of religious agency. In other words, through this analysis we are able to observe the religious agency of those who practice snake worship as both Hindu and Buddhist redactors have incorporated these practices into their orthodox texts.

In addition to having been guided by the work of Charles Long, I am also indebted to historians of religion such as Wendy Doniger, J.Z. Smith, and Bruce Lincoln, all of whom highlight alternative modes of religiosity and, more importantly, recognize those who constructed these alternative modes. I am also grateful to another set of scholars not for their methodological contributions but rather for their fascination with snakes and snake worship. These include particularly J. Ph. Vogel, whose wonderful text, *Indian Serpent-Lore*, first sparked my interest in snake worship. Also, the work of contemporary scholars such as Lowell Bloss, Christopher Minkowski, and Andrew Rawlinson has proved extremely valuable as I have explored the relationship between the contextual frameworks created by orthodox redactors and those created by snake worshippers.

This relationship is complex; for while in certain texts these respective contextual frameworks conflict, in other texts they are compatible. In other words, while some redactors use context to divest the snake of those elements that originally prompted its worship, others, proceeding from a different agenda, preserve the snake and its ritual tradition within its preestablished contextual frame. As a weapon, then, context might be likened best to a double-edged sword: one that might be used either to damage or to defend. These contextual shifts are best observed as we employ a comparative methodology, for it is in the spaces in between—in the shifting, or recontextualizing process perceived as we compare one text to another—that the redactors allow us to see their various reactions to snake worship. Thus, as we move from text to text within this survey, we will see the contextual transformation not only of particular snake figures but also of particular rituals that centralize the snake as an object of worship.

Those texts which do not attempt to obscure the practice of snake worship provide us with a great deal of material about this tradition; relaying information such as what ritual elements comprised these practices, what social groups may have been involved in these practices, and what brought them to choose the snake as an object of religious devotion. Even a cursory examination of the Hindu and Buddhist textual traditions goes a long way toward answering this last question, for from its earliest appearance in the *Ṛg Veda*, the snake consistently displays the following three features: it is portrayed as an earthly sovereign; it is endowed with supernatural powers over earthly elements; and it responds (both positively and negatively) to human desires. Moreover, texts of the late Vedic period as well as the texts of the Buddhist-Hybrid Sanskrit tradition, such as the *Mahāvastu,* give us a great deal of information as to how snake-centered rituals were conducted and possibly by whom, thus contributing to and preserving the ritual tradition associated with snake worship.[10]

Now, while both the late Vedic texts and the *Mahāvastu* promote the divine efficacy of particular figures, none of these texts are concerned with establishing one particular person or one particular social group as exclusively powerful. This is not the case with the *Ṛg Veda*, the *Ādi Parvan* of the *Mahābhārata,* or the Pāli literature. In fact, the *Ṛg Veda*, the *Ādi Parvan,* the *Mahāvagga*, and the *Jātaka Tales* all strive to promote specific candidates as embodying ultimate religious authority. Given their agendas, the redactors of these texts perceive snake worship as a particularly dangerous religious phenomenon, for it centralizes a multitude of earth-bound, and thus accessible, deities with supernatural powers over the natural world. In so doing, snake worship obviates the possibility of a singular figure claiming exclusive divine power and authority; a singular figure, moreover, whose accessibility and ritual efficacy might be controlled by a particular group of humans. As a result, the redactors of these texts expend a great deal of energy in their efforts to contextualize the snake in a negative fashion.

The redactors achieve this goal through both subtle and obvious means. Their more subtle maneuvers include curtailing the snakes' territorial sovereignty by removing their established regional place-names; [11] transforming the snakes from sovereigns to the servants of sovereigns; [12] and reconfiguring *tīrthas,* not as sites devoted to snake worship but rather as sites devoted to asceticism.[13] Their more obvious maneuvers include condemning all practices associated with the worship of snakes;[14] transforming the snake sovereign into a malevolent figure bent on withholding the earth's bounty from human supplicants;[15] and classifying snakes as threatening, demonic creatures that deserve to die in an enormous *Sarpasattra* or snake sacrifice.[16] Therefore, it is my contention, and will be throughout this book, that in each instance wherein the redactors demonize the snake, they are reacting to a preestablished tradition of snake worship that they perceive as a threat to their primary agenda: that of establishing the religious supremacy of their chosen champion.

Taken as a whole, however, the texts in our survey demonstrate that when the redactors engage in this process of negative contextualization, they do so not only to stamp out the snake as a religious rival, but also to coopt the snake's powers in order that they might be transferred to their chosen champion[s]. In the case of the Hindu texts, these champions include specific deities, such as Indra, that are then ritually controlled by the brahmin priests. In the case of the Buddhist texts, these champions include the Buddha and various Buddhist saints. There is thus an intrinsic relationship between the redactors' desire to affect the hierarchical positioning of specific people, such as brahmin priests, Buddhist saints, and the Buddha, and their treatment of the supernatural snake. This relationship hinges on the following: because the snake is associated with supernatural powers over the natural world, he who has access to these powers is powerful and he who has exclusive access to these powers is exclusively powerful. As a result, in each of the texts in which the redactors are attempting to elevate one particular figure or one particular group as having exclusive religious authority, the snake will operate not only as a *threat* to their religious domination but also as an *opportunity* to advance their objective of religious domination. The demonization and subsequent cooptation of the supernatural snake's powers can therefore be seen as an attempt on the part of the redactors to own exclusively a religious figure that endows its keepers with power over the natural world.

Paradoxically, it is precisely in taking advantage of this opportunity to coopt the snake's powers that these redactors may be contributing inadvertently to the promotion of snake worship. For in attempting to coopt and exclusively own the snake's powers, its sacred sites, and its ritual practices in order to empower their own champion, the redactors highlight these things as valuable and thereby invigorate the image of the snake. Thus, whether these orthodox redactors are attempting to steal the snake's powers and suppress this tradition or to share in the snake's powers and preserve this tradition, they end up encompassing within their texts an enormous amount of material concerning the development of snake worship over the centuries.

I begin my textual analysis in chapter 2 with the *Ṛg Veda* because it is the earliest Indian text that refers to a supernatural snake. In this text, we see the redactors responding to a preestablished tradition of snake worship. This occurs as Indra, chief of the Vedic gods revered by the brahmin-led Āryan people, and Vṛtra, a supernatural snake associated with the indigenous peoples of India are pitted against each other in a fight to the death for exclusive divine authority.[17] The object of this myth is thus to kill Vṛtra in order to transfer exclusive authority to Indra and those with exclusive access to Indra: the brahmin priests.

The supernatural snake and its associated ritual tradition rebound with a vengeance in chapter 3. For unlike the *Ṛg Veda*, the late Vedic texts are not attempting to elevate one person or group of people as having exclusive divine authority and power over the natural world. Rather, the late Vedic redactors are interested in, among other things, compiling all of the various ritual means available for controlling nature and valorize the supernatural snake as one of those means. As a result, these late Vedic texts not only elevate the image of the supernatural snake and maintain it as a powerful, accessible deity but also preserve and formalize a number of rituals that speak to the development of snake worship in the centuries prior to the Common Era. It is also in the late Vedic texts that one sees the redactors focusing on the hybrid nature of this figure, for while it is a snake, it yet comes equipped with supernatural powers. The late Vedic redactors thus highlight the fact that it is precisely its hybrid nature that prompts its worship: as a real snake, it has the distinction of being a ubiquitous denizen of the earth's surface, and thus constantly accessible to those who would propitiate it; as a supernatural snake it has the power to supernaturally affect earthly elements, such as rain, that are so crucial to the livelihoods of agrarian peoples.

As we turn to the *Ādi Parvan* of the *Mahābhārata,* the subject of chapter 4, it is the Nāgarāja's or "snake king's" role as an accessible object of religious devotion that is imperiled. For while the textual redactors and the ritual practitioners of the late Vedic period succeeded in elevating and promoting this ritual tradition, the same cannot be said of the epic redactors. Like the redactors of the *Ṛg Veda*, the redactors of the *Ādi Parvan* are attempting to elevate one particular group as having exclusive control over the natural world: the brahmins. In juxtaposition to this brahminic agenda, snake worship represents both a threat and an opportunity. In terms of a threat, the primary ritual activities associated with snake worship obviate the necessity of a brahmin officiant. As such, the snake king constructed during the pre-epic period possesses the capacity to deprive the brahmin of his very *raison d'être*, and as a result, the redactors of the *Ādi Parvan* wish to dethrone the snake king. This also results in a subordination of those religious practices associated with the supernatural snake's sovereign power such as the *Sarpasattra* ritual. In terms of an opportunity, the redactors of the *Ādi Parvan* attempt to take advantage of the sovereign snake's powers in two ways: first, to insinuate a brahmin into the snake king's ritual role; and second, to incorporate the snake into the brahminic fold, thereby diverting its powers to the brahmin class.

In chapters 5 and 6 we move on to the Buddhist texts, which afford us the opportunity to look at the same four stories as told from two very different perspectives. In chapter 5, we will examine two of the early Pāli texts, namely, the *Mahāvagga* and the *Jātaka Tales.* These texts share the same orientation toward the snake and its associated ritual tradition as the *Ṛg Veda* and the *Ādi Parvan*, namely, they subordinate the snake in order to transfer its powers to an alternative figure. While both the *Ṛg Veda* and the *Ādi Parvan* attempted to subordinate snake worship in order to elevate brahmins, these Pāli texts attempt to subordinate snake worship in order to elevate the Buddha and the developing Buddhist tradition.

Like the Hindu redactors of the late Vedas, the Buddhist redactors of the *Mahāvastu*, the subject of chapter 6, are not attempting to establish one person or one group of people as embodying exclusive religious power. Rather, they focus on natural phenomena and the supernatural snake's capacity to control such phenomena to provide an earthly helpmate for an increasingly otherworldly Buddha. They construct this role for the snake kings as the Buddha is made to receive counsel from the snake kings; as he is made to visit the snake kings at their sacred sites; and even as he promotes the dharma at festivals devoted to snake worship. This results not only in the preservation of the snake king and his ritual tradition but also in the construction of an accessible, transcendent Buddha. The redactors' agenda is illuminated by a comparison of the tellings of the four stories reviewed from the Pāli texts—the Nāgarāja of Uruvelā, the Nāgarāja Kāla, the Nāgarāja Mucalinda, and the Nāgarāja Campeyya—with their tellings in the *Mahāvastu*.[18]

In light of the fact that snake worship remains relevant for people in India today, it would seem that victory must be awarded to those 'context constructors' who worked to valorize the snake as an accessible divine figure. Victory or defeat aside, as we focus our attention on the context constructing efforts of both snake worshippers and orthodox redactors within the *Ṛg Veda*, the late Vedas, the *Ādi Parvan*, the *Mahāvagga*, the *Jātaka Tales*, as well as the *Mahāvastu*, we will see a broader picture: the process by which these religious traditions come to be, the motivations of those engaged in the construction of these religious traditions, as well as the contextualizing strategies employed to assert one tradition over another. This textual analysis thus allows us to mount a methodological strategy through which we are able to use a conventional religious setting to provide evidence of alternative avenues of religious agency.

2

The Ṛg Veda and the Threat of the Sovereign Snake

We will begin with the *Ṛg Veda*, because it is here, with the appearance of Vṛtra, that we find our first reference to a supernatural snake. Dated at approximately 1200 BCE, the *Ṛg Veda* is the most sacred narrative of brahminical Hinduism and is believed to be divine revelation. Consisting of 1,028 hymns, the *Ṛg Veda* tells us, among other things, the proper course of various sacrificial rituals, the myths of numerous gods and goddesses, several stories about how the cosmos first came into being, as well as the story of how Indra, the divine king of the Āryans, came to defeat the supernatural snake, Vṛtra.

The term Āryan denotes a language affinity rather than a discrete ethnicity, and refers to those peoples whose language is of Proto-Indo-European descent and who originally migrated south from what is thought to have been present-day Russia near the shores of the Black and Caspian seas. The Āryans made their living primarily from herding cattle and horses, and they also engaged in agriculture to a limited extent. At some point between 2000 and 1500 BCE, these nomadic herdspeople split into two groups, one moving west into present-day Iran, where they founded Zoroastrianism, the other moving further south to establish themselves on the Indian sub-continent.

Part of their several centuries-long process of establishment in India is chronicled in the *Ṛg Veda* wherein both a divine order and a hierarchical social order are enunciated by the priestly redactors of the text: the brahmins. The social order, not surprisingly, is led by the brahmins who are positioned as the first class, endowed with not only the highest authority but also exclusive access to the gods through their ritual activities. The primacy of their role is made abundantly clear in the *Ṛg Vedic* myth of the Cosmic Giant Puruṣa. In this myth, the Cosmic Giant is dismembered to create all the things of this world. The brahmin class is created from his mouth, and thus it is literally proclaimed to be the mouth of the divine.[1]

The divine order is led by "he who wields the thunderbolt," Indra, who is declared to be king of the Vedic gods.[2] In order to legitimate Indra as exclusive controller of the natural world, however, Indra must prove himself. This occurs as Indra is pitted against an opponent characterized as having dominion over earthly and atmospheric elements: Vṛtra, a supernatural snake.[3] Within this myth, the brahmin redactors render Vṛtra as a demonic character in order to legitimate his defeat at the hands of the heroic Indra. This results in the transference of exclusive control over earthly resources to Indra and those who worship Indra: the brahmin-led Āryans. I would argue that with the narrative demonization, defeat, and subsequent cooptation of Vṛtra's powers, the redactors are not merely telling the tale of Indra's heroic rise to power. Rather, they are demonstrating the narrative process by which a divine figure is made to rise to power: a process through which a preestablished contextual framework centralizing a supernatural snake is dismantled in order to construct one centralizing a brahmin-controlled deity.

Vṛtra: The Demonization of the Sovereign Snake

Vṛtra is so named because he *vṛ* "encloses" or "covers up" things, particularly water, for in several hymns he is called *apo vṛtvī* "the encloser of the waters" and *nadī vṛt* "the encloser of the rivers."[4] Hymn 1.32 extends this association as it positions Vṛtra as the *gopa*—protector or shepherd—of the waters. Vṛtra is also depicted as having "the lightning and thunder, rain and hail" at his command.[5] In addition to controlling both earthly and atmospheric waters, Vṛtra maintains the highest point of the earth as he "lay on the mountain."[6]

It would also seem that Vṛtra is the primary possessor of cows, which are the ultimate resource in the *Ṛg Veda*, for having defeated Vṛtra, Indra "won the cows."[7] In fact, Vṛtra's mother, Dānu, is a cow, who, like Vṛtra, is often associated with water in the Vedas. A. A. MacDonell states, "This name [Dānu] seems to be identical with the word *dānu*, which is several times used as a neuter meaning 'stream' and once as a feminine to designate the waters of heaven."[8] In sum, the mighty Vṛtra, as he appears in the *Ṛg Veda*, marks the textual debut of a sovereign snake endowed with supernatural powers over earthly elements, particularly water.

While the *Ṛg Veda* marks the textual debut of a sovereign snake, I would argue that the construction of this supernatural figure predates the incursion of the Āryans and reflects an indigenous tradition of snake worship. MacDonell supports this hypothesis, noting that snake worship "has been found prevailing very widely among the non-Āryan Indians. The Āryans doubtless found the cult extensively diffused among the natives when they spread over India, the land of serpents."[9] The preexistence of snake worship, moreover, helps to explain what the brahmin redactors are doing in their contextualization of Vṛtra; for while he is first introduced as a sovereign figure with supernatural control over various earthly and atmospheric resources, he is quickly rendered as a malevolent figure bent on withholding these resources from the Āryan people. It would seem then, that the redactors render Vṛtra as a demonic character because they are responding to a rival religious tradition that blocks the ascendancy of their chosen champion. I maintain, moreover, that the redactors' desire to effect in narrative form the ascendancy of Indra over Vṛtra marks not only a religious agenda but also a political agenda. This occurs as the hierarchical elevation of Brahminism over snake worship is perceived as helping to achieve the hierarchical elevation of the brahmin-led Āryan people over the indigenous inhabitants of India.[10]

The redactors demonize Vṛtra, who controls the life-giving waters, mountainous territory, and crucial resources such as cows, as he is said to be Indra's "greatest enemy."[11] And throughout the *Ṛg Veda*, Vṛtra is contextualized as a malevolent creature. In hymns 1.32 and 1.2, wherein the name Vṛtra is used interchangeably with the term *ahi* "snake,"[12] Monier-Williams tells us that the term *ahi* is not merely descriptive but rather carries a negative connotation: it comes from the verb, *aṃh*, meaning "to press together, to strangle," and which forms other words such as *aṃhati* and *aṃhas* which mean "anxiety or distress."[13] While Vṛtra is depicted as "the first-born of the *ahis*,"[14] he is not the only destructive snake in the *Ṛg Veda*. The most memorable of Vṛtra's *ahi* brethren is Arbuda Kādraveya, whom we shall encounter again in the late Vedas. In the *Ṛg Veda*, Arbuda Kādraveya is similarly characterized as a supernatural snake representative of the demonic forces of darkness and chaos.[15] The *Ṛg Veda* briefly mentions one other shadowy figure, Ahi Budhnya, who is said to be born in the celestial waters,[16] and who is invoked in several hymns and asked to refrain from causing injury.[17]

Because the malevolent Vṛtra "had barricaded those waters with his earthly powers,"[18] the redactors of the *Ṛg Veda* establish a context in which it is necessary to kill Vṛtra for Āryan civilization to proceed. Vṛtra, however, is very powerful and not easy to overcome, and Indra must call on other divine Vedic luminaries such as Viṣṇu and the Maruts to help him defeat Vṛtra.[19] Indra is ultimately victorious and his conquest of the demonized sovereign snake leads to a demonstration of Indra's exclusive right to rule over India's earthly resources, expressed through exclusive control over the earth's waters, mountains, and livestock.

> No use was the lightning and thunder, rain and hail that he [Vṛtra] scattered about, when the *ahi* and Indra fought. Indra the Generous was made the victor both for now and for the future.... Indra, who raises up the thunderbolt in his hand, is the king of those that journey and those that rest, of the tame and of the horned. He rules over the people as king, encompassing everything as a rim encompasses spokes.[20]

The demonization and subsequent eradication of Vṛtra, moreover, allows the redactors to take advantage of the opportunity to transfer the snake's powers to Indra. This occurs as Indra coopts the powers through which Vṛtra is known—he who "scattered about" the "lightning and thunder, rain and hail,"[21]—to become the supreme god "who wields the thunderbolt."[22] Therefore, while the *Ṛg Veda* tells us that, having been defeated, "the body lay hidden in the middle of the currents...and the waters flow over Vṛtra's secret place as he lies in long darkness,"[23] Vṛtra, in absentia, continues to legitimate Indra. This occurs as the story of his defeat is repeated up through the *Purāṇas* as the act that defines Indra as the supreme controller of earthly elements and the King of the Gods:[24] "Let me proclaim the heroic deeds of Indra, that which the thunderbolt-wielder did first: he killed the snake."[25] Thus, as seen in the *Ṛg Veda*, Vṛtra operates not only as a threat to the brahminic agenda of religious domination but also as an opportunity for the brahmins to achieve religious domination through their champion Indra.

The defeat and subsequent cooptation of Vṛtra's powers by Indra has further consequences, for it represents the construction of a contextual framework in which an earthly, supernatural snake is first demonized and then defeated in order to secure the reign of a heavenly, warrior god. As a result, divine control over earthly elements is removed to a separate, heavenly realm, one that might be accessed only by a sanctioned group of people, namely, brahmin priests. As divine constructs go, then, Indra and Vṛtra are very different figures, for while the supernatural snake is grounded in a real animal, and thus virtually available to anyone who might wish to approach it as an object of worship, Indra is the exclusive property of a particular group of people: the brahmin-led Āryans. A group of people, moreover, who exclude all but Āryans from their hierarchical social system, thus positioning the indigenous peoples of India and their divine figures outside of this system altogether.[26] The *Ṛg Veda* thus marks our first encounter with redactors who wish to dismantle a preexisting contextual framework, one which centralizes the supernatural snake and the desires of indigenous snake worshippers in order to use the pieces to build up their own framework, one which centralizes Indra and the desires of the brahmin-led Āryans. The assertion of the redactors' framework over that of snake worshippers is made explicit in a comparison of hymn 1.32 with hymn 10.43: in the former, Vṛtra and the indigenous peoples of India are called the masters of the waters, while in the latter, the Āryans, through their God Indra, have usurped this position and the waters are now to be designated as *Āryapatnīs*, "having the Āryans as the masters."

The Buried Elements of the Snake Worshippers' Buried Discourse

Just as the redactors of the *Ṛg Veda* explicitly bury the snake under the waters that he once protected, they implicitly bury the discourse that centralized the snake as an object of religious devotion. It is possible to speculate, however, that certain elements retained and re-signified by the redactors pertain to the snake's original context. It would certainly appear that the supernatural snake is originally empowered to protect the waters. And as he is said to have "the lightning and thunder, rain and hail" [27] at his command, it would also seem that he functions as a rainmaker. As we will see in relation to the late Vedas, the *Ādi Parvan*, and the Pāli texts, this association between supernatural snakes and water is expanded over the centuries to include control over many aspects of both earthly and human fertility.

The earliest representation of a snake comes from the Indus Valley civilization in the form of a pottery tablet found at Harappa, c. 2300-1750 BCE.[28] On this tablet there are painted two snakes that are poised behind two kneeling men, each flanking a seated figure. Mahalingam refers to the seated figure as a "seated deity," but from the evidence it could just as easily be a royal personage.[29] Other archaeological artifacts from the Indus Valley civilization include pottery pieces painted with snakes; the carved figure of a snake; a clay amulet with a snake situated in front of a stool on which there appears to be an offering of some sort; and an amulet picturing two snakes and a bird.[30] From this evidence, what can be said about the representation of snakes during the pre-Vedic period is that they seem to be associated at times with divine and/or sovereign power and they seem to be objectified in a positive fashion. We cannot tell from this evidence, however, which segments of society particularly associated themselves with snakes.

During the *Ṛg Vedic* period, the redactors associate Vṛtra with those people they call the Dāsas. Dāsas is the pejorative word meaning "slave," used by the Āryans to signify the indigenous peoples of India. It also suggests a possible play on words, as the term Dāsas is related to another word oftentimes used to signify snakes, *daṃś*, meaning "biter."[31] According to the *Ṛg Vedic* myth of the Cosmic Giant Puruṣa, the Dāsas are positioned outside of the Āryan social hierarchy.[32] Positioned as the enemy and separated from the Āryans both linguistically and socially, this group "frequently rises to the mythological rank in the *Ṛg Veda* as the line between what is historical and mythical is not clearly drawn."[33]

In hymn 4.18, Vṛtra is called a Dāsa: "At one time Generous Indra-the shoulderless one [Vṛtra] pierced you, and although pierced, you over-powered him and ground up the head of the Dāsa with your weapon."[34] The reference to Vṛtra as "shoulderless" or *viaṃsa* is repeated in hymn 1.32, and is a wonderful descriptor of the snake's serpentine form.[35] In hymn 1.32, Vṛtra is linked with the Dāsas, as both appear in a compound modifying the waters: "the waters had the *ahi* as their protector and the Dāsas as their husband."[36] Thus in light of this linkage, it would seem that the indigenous peoples of India were originally responsible for constructing a contextual framework around the snake; a framework which would allow this figure to address their fears, desires, hopes and dreams.

Conclusion: Redactors and Rival Traditions

Clearly, the brahmin redactors of the *Ṛg Veda* are troubled by the phenomenon of the supernatural snake as they position this figure as a rival that remains just outside of their control; a rival who is perceived as so powerful that Indra alone is not able to defeat him but rather must call on Viṣṇu and the Maruts for help.[37] This rival, moreover, is perceived as so ubiquitous that the redactors' narrative vitriol must extend beyond Vṛtra to characterize other snakes, such as Arbuda Kādraveya and Ahi Budhnya, as malevolent creatures. I have argued that the redactors are contextualizing the supernatural snake in this fashion because they are shadowboxing with a preestablished tradition of snake worship; a preestablished tradition that is perceived as threatening to their religio-political agenda.

Snake worship is perceived as threatening because it is antithetical to the establishment of exclusive control over the natural world. This is due to the fact that a snake, endowed with supernatural powers over natural elements, provides constant access to anyone who might wish to propitiate it for the purpose of effecting abundant rainfall, a bountiful harvest, or any other condition related to earthly fertility. Thus, a religious paradigm featuring sovereign snakes functions to deconstruct the possibility of exclusive human control over the natural world as it centralizes an endless array of accessible, supernatural, sovereign figures.

Given this fact, snake worship will appear as both a threat and an opportunity to those redactors working to establish the exclusive religious authority of one figure; and as a result, they will make every effort to demonize the snake and coopt its power. This is precisely the scenario we have just seen enacted within the *Ṛg Veda*, wherein the redactors view the sovereign snake as Indra's "greatest enemy."[38] The real power of the snake to operate both as a threat to the redactors' agenda as well as an opportunity to achieve their agenda, moreover, derives from other people's recognition of the snake's power. In other words, it is only as those people outside of the Āryan social structure first, attribute supernatural powers to the snake and second, enjoy access to those powers that the snake functions both as a threat to Indra's superiority and as a means for empowering Indra. As a result, in successfully taking over the supernatural snake, the redactors succeed in narratively constructing a world in which access to the snake and thus power over the natural world is taken away from those who may have formerly enjoyed it—the Dāsas—and placed squarely in the hands of the brahmin-led Āryans.

If we understand the snake as having had a preestablished role as an accessible supernatural sovereign, then we can see that the demonization of Vṛtra represents a struggle between two groups (the brahmins and the Dāsas) over a religious figure that endows its holders with power over the natural world. As we will see as we continue with our survey, such a conclusion is further substantiated as we find a similar struggle between two historical groups (those who wish to control exclusive access to the snake's powers versus those who wish to enjoy unrestricted access to these powers) made evident in every other text that demonizes the snake. Moreover, in those orthodox texts that are not attempting to promote one particular figure as having exclusive religious authority, the supernatural snake is not demonized, but rather is maintained as an efficacious deity along with the ritual tradition with which it is associated.

The depth and diversity of the supernatural snake's ritual tradition is particularly clear as we turn to the late Vedas, the subject of our next chapter, for the late Vedic texts have preserved a variety of supernatural snake figures and myriad ritual practices for honoring these creatures. It is interesting to note, moreover, that the late Vedic redactors are not expressly attempting to promote snake worship, but rather are attempting to list all of the various means available for controlling the natural world and valorize the supernatural snake as one of those means. Therefore, given the fact that the late Vedic redactors are not actively constructing a tradition of snake worship, the late Vedic texts testify to the historic longevity of this tradition. It would be extremely unlikely that these supernatural snake figures and their associated ritual practices would appear in the late Vedas with such depth and diversity unless they were part of an established religious movement that managed to retain its integrity regardless of the *Ṛg Vedic* redactors' machinations. And in fact, by recognizing the snake's powers (if only to coopt these powers) it is possible that the *Ṛg Vedic* redactors may have inadvertently given a boost to the very figure they were attempting to stamp out. Thus, as we will see in the late Vedic texts, not only is the snake revered for the very powers for which it is reviled in the *Ṛg Veda*, but particular snakes such as Arbuda Kādraveya are recontextualized as objects of religious devotion.

3

The Late Vedas: Revering the Snake's Power and Preserving Snake-Centered Rituals

As revealed through our exploration of the *Ṛg Veda*, the narrative decision to contextualize Vṛtra as an evil-minded reptile was an intentional one and points to the following: the *Ṛg Vedic* redactors found snakes—constructed as supernatural sovereigns over the natural world—threatening to their ideological agenda. As a result, they used context as a weapon not only to portray the snake in a very negative fashion but finally to stamp out the snake and transfer its powers to their chosen champion, Indra.

Unlike the brahmin redactors of the *Ṛg Veda*, however, the brahmin redactors of the late Vedas seem unconcerned with positioning themselves as exclusive controllers of the natural world. One might speculate that by the time of the late Vedas, more than three centuries after the establishment of the *Ṛg Vedic* social order, brahmins felt their power as the top class to have been sufficiently consolidated. As a result, the redactors of the late Vedas neither express a narrative agenda aimed at elevating their own role in society through the promotion of a singular divine champion nor respond in a negative fashion to alternative modes of religiosity such as snake worship. Rather the late Vedas, more than any other texts in our survey, preserve and formalize the figures, sites and rituals central to snake worship. There appear to be several reasons why the redactors are doing this. For one thing, various snake-centered ritual practices such as the *Sarpasattra* and the *Sarpanāma* function to empower brahmins and help them to carry out their own ritual activities. However, given the fact that most of the snake-centered rituals included in these texts are not reserved for brahmins but may be conducted by anyone, we must turn to the following to explain their inclusion: these redactors seem most interested in compiling all of the various ritual means available for controlling nature and valorize the supernatural snake as one of those means. While this agenda is certainly different than that of the *Ṛg Vedic* redactors, it is hardly surprising; one of the primary jobs of these learned brahmin priests was that of sorting out and recording the correct manner in which rituals were to be performed, thereby establishing an orthodox canon of ritual activities. Toward that end, the late Vedic redactors not only preserve and formalize a variety of snake-centered rituals but also use context as a weapon to defend rather than damage the snake as an accessible, if dangerously powerful, earthly sovereign.

The textual preservation of snake-centered rituals along with the contextual transformation of the supernatural snake into a powerful, earthly sovereign is best observed as we explore the following texts: the *Atharva Veda*, the *Śatapatha Brāhmaṇa* attached to the *Yajur Veda*, the *Pañcaviṃśa* and the *Sāmavidhāna Brāhmaṇas* attached to the *Sāma Veda*, and lastly, the *Gṛhya Sūtras*. The *Atharva Veda* and the *Brāhmaṇas* are dated from c. 900-600 BCE and the *Gṛhya Sūtras* are dated from c.600-400 BCE. All of these texts are classified as ritual texts for they function as "ceremonial guides or didactic manuals"[1] on various ritual practices ranging from the formalistic *Śrauta* rituals of the *Pañcaviṃśa Brāhmaṇa* to the domestic rituals of the *Gṛhya Sūtras*. The purpose of these texts is thus to preserve, formalize, and valorize various ritual activities.

I use the terms "preserve", "formalize", and "valorize", very intentionally, for while the priests were responsible for compiling these rituals and sometimes creating these rituals, Indologists generally agree that the late Vedic redactors were also drawing from sources outside of the priestly tradition. In relation to the *Atharva Veda*, for example, Wendy Doniger notes:

> These three texts, [the *Ṛg Veda*, the *Sāma Veda*, and the *Yajur Veda*] intimately connected, were the original corpus of Vedic literature and are still often referred to as 'the

> three Vedas.' But a fourth text, the *Atharva Veda*, was composed a century or two after the first triad. This is a text of an entirely different nature; although 1,200 of its 6,000 stanzas are taken from the *Ṛg Veda*, the great bulk of the work is a collection of magic spells and incantations, drawing upon ancient folk materials.[2]

Now we cannot say for certain who these "ancient folk[s]" were, but we can speculate along the following lines. First, many of these snake-centered rituals deal with ordinary, domestic issues such as the proper siting of a foundation stone for a new house, the protection of the family from poisonous snakes, or the provision of a good harvest. Second, most of these rituals can be conducted by anyone and require neither the presence of a priest nor elaborate preparations. Given these facts, we can say that those who would stand to benefit most from such rituals would be neither kings nor brahmins but rather ordinary people: those engaged in building their own homes; those responsible for protecting their families, oftentimes women; and those interested in a good harvest, primarily agriculturists. In other words, it would seem that these "ancient folk[s]" were none other than ordinary men and women who constructed the snake as an object of religious devotion in order to create a sacred being relevant and responsive to their fears and hopes, experiences and desires. Seen in this light, the supernatural snake both reflects and represents the lived reality of those who revered it.

We will view these late Vedic texts as an amalgam of snake-centered myths and rituals from both priestly and grass-roots sources, all of which share a common objective: to position the snake as a powerful nature deity accessible to all. Snake worship thus rebounds with a vengeance in the late Vedas. For while the redactors of the *Ṛg Veda* engaged in a contextual tug-of-war with snake worshippers, one which resulted in pulling Vṛtra into the waters where his "body lay hidden in the middle of the currents,"[3] the late Vedic redactors are constructing a contextual framework that is compatible with this grass-roots movement. This is particularly clear as we examine the frame of refracting details through which the late Vedic redactors contextualize the supernatural snake. This frame can be divided into the following categories: deifying the powerful snake; reconfiguring the *Ṛg Vedic* snake, Arbuda Kādraveya; and valorizing regional snake deities such as Dhṛtarāṣṭra Airāvata, Takṣaka Vaiśāleya, and Vāsuki. Moreover, throughout this chapter, we will discuss not only a variety of ritual practices but also a variety of myths that function to position the snake as a powerful, autonomous sovereign. We begin, however, with a look at the archaeological and ethnographic data describing snake worship in India during these centuries.

Snake Worship During the Late Vedic Period

As noted in chapter 1, the earliest evidence we have for the worship of the supernatural snake is documented in conjunction with the 4th C. BCE visit of Alexander the Great to India: "When Alexander was assaulting some of the cities in India and capturing others, he found in many of them, besides other animals, a snake which the Indians, regarding as sacred, kept in a cave and worshipped with much devotion."[4] And Richard Gombrich states that there is

> epigraphic and archaeological evidence for the worship of nāgas, supernatural snakes, in shrines and temples. Härtel has excavated a nāga temple at Sonkh, near Mathurā, which he dates to the Kuṣāṇa period. He considers that the area round Rājagṛha had a long history of nāga worship. A structure at Rājagṛha known as Maṇiyār Maṭha has been securely identified by excavators as a nāga shrine; its oldest strata are dated to the second or first century B.C.... [I]t is about as old as the evidence for any Indian shrine or temple, so it seems reasonable to extrapolate by projecting the cult back a couple of centuries....[5]

The excavation and dating of such places is essential because the sites traditionally associated with the worship of the supernatural snake are either *tīrthas* or *caityas*, neither of which leave much in the way of archaeological traces. *Tīrthas* are places where one might literally *tṝ* or "cross" a body of water, and thereby gain access to the deities living in the waters or across the waters on the metaphysical "other side." *Caityas*, on the other hand, are sacred spots marked by a pool, a tree, or perhaps a stone altar.[6] Given the natural contours of such sites, very little exists to mark the historical worship of these figures. It is useful, however, to see the ways in which the late Vedic texts expand upon this archaeological and ethnographic evidence to enhance our picture of snake worship in the late Vedic period.

The Deification of the Powerful Snake

While the *Ṛg Vedic* redactors constructed powerful snakes as demonic beings, the late Vedic redactors have taken the opposite tack: they construct powerful snakes as divine beings. In fact, the late Vedic redactors go out of their way to detail the snake's inherent powers as a reptile, the snake's enhanced powers as a supernatural being, and thus, the snake's deserved status as a divine being. They begin this process by shifting the terms used to signify powerful snakes. Thus, the negative signifier used by the *Ṛg Vedic* redactors, *ahi*, is first shifted to the neutral *sarpa* and later shifted to the positive *Nāga*; the latter signifying a divine snake.

Snakes in the *Ṛg Veda* were consistently designated by the term, *ahi*, a word stemming from the verb root *aṃh* and denoting both physical and mental distress.[7] In contrast, snakes in the late Vedas are most often designated by the term *sarpa*—a term that comes from the verb *sṛp*, to glide. We thus see a shift in focus from a negative, malevolent characterization of the snake to a neutral, descriptive characterization of the snake; one which focuses on the snake's reptilian being. This shift in signifier, however, does not signal the snake's impotence, for in these texts, a constant association is made between snakes and their inherent power. Not surprisingly, the snake's capacity to render a poisonous bite is highlighted as the ultimate source of its power. In the *Śatapatha Brāhmaṇa*, for example, poison is declared to be the snake's divine essence: "The snakes meditate on the divine person as poison."[8]

Beyond their poisonous prowess the late Vedic snakes are depicted as capable of such amazing feats as stopping the world from spinning on its axis and protecting the four corners of the earth. In the *Sarpanāma*, or snake-name mantras, snakes are said not only to rule the worlds but also to be able to control the earth's motion. As the *Sarpanāma* is one of the few snake-centered practices used exclusively by priests in the course of a sacrifice, it provides us with an occasion to view the ways in which the brahmin redactors take advantage of or perhaps enhance the supernatural snake's powers in order to help them conduct their ritual activities.

> Now he [the god of fire] approaches with the *Sarpanāma* (those snake-name mantras), for these worlds are ruled by snakes. They glide (*sarp*) along with all that there is. This one [god], namely fire, is the soul of all the gods. Having laid him down [on the fire altar] the gods were afraid that these worlds would glide away with their soul. They recited the *Sarpanāma* [mantras] as they approached [the altar], and these formulas stopped the worlds for him....
>
> And again, the god of fire approaches with the *Sarpanāma,* because these worlds are ruled by snakes, since all things that glide, glide in these worlds. And since he approaches with the *Sarpanāma*, whatever destructive force there is, whatever piercing thing there is, whatever demonic thing[9] there is, he causes all of this to be calm.
>
> 'Let us honor the snakes on the earth along with those that are in the atmosphere and those that are in the heavens. Honor to those snakes!' This honors those snakes wherever they are in these three worlds. 'To those snakes who are the arrows of demons,' some of them bite for they have been sent by demons, 'to those snakes who are in the trees or who lie in holes—honor to those snakes!' This honors those who are in the trees and those who lay in holes. 'To those

> snakes who are in the shining sky, or those who are in the rays of the sun, or those whose home is in the water. Honor to those snakes!' Wherever they are, this honors them. One does this by saying '*nāma, nāma*' for honor is sacrifice.[10]

We can see in the above passage that one of the reasons why the late Vedic redactors are intent upon contextualizing the snake in a positive manner is that it allows them to collect a share of the snake's powers. In other words, as snakes are depicted both as capable of stopping these worlds and as responsive to ritual invocation, they are available to assist the priests in carrying out their primary task of successfully enacting the sacrificial ritual. It is possible then, that this ritual derives from priestly sources and the brahmin priests' recognition that the supernaturally powerful snake is a very useful creature.

The details through which the redactors promote the snakes' positive image are evident not only through their enhancing of the snakes' supernatural powers, as the snakes are now said to control the earth's motion, but also through their extending of the snakes' sovereignty, as the snakes are now said to rule these worlds. Moreover, the snakes are able to perform these fantastic feats precisely because they are *sarpas*—gliders. Thus, according to the *Sarpanāma,* snakes are worthy of great honor due to their essential nature as snakes.

In hymn 12.3 of the *Atharva Veda,* the redactors again enhance the snake's supernatural powers over the entire earth as they portray snakes as guardians of the four quarters: the Eastern quarter has Asita as protector; the Southern quarter has Tiraśchirāji as protector; the Western quarter has Pṛdāku; and the Northern quarter has Svaja. Each of these names, moreover, describes their reptilian characteristics: Asita—"black," Tiraśchirāji—"striped-across," Pṛdāku—"adder," and Svaja—"viper." In the same manner as the *Sarpanāma*, then, this hymn highlights the fact that the snake's power, its capacity to act as a world protector, is grounded in its reptilian being; for while functioning as a celestial guardian, each of these creatures is characterized first and foremost as a snake.

Having made a strong association between snakes and their inherent powers, and having enhanced the snakes' supernatural powers, the redactors make a further assertion: because they are powerful, snakes are worthy of deification. In another hymn from the *Atharva Veda*, it is stated that snakes, again named for their reptilian characteristics, should be regarded as gods because of their mordacious powers.

> May the snake not kill us along with our children and our people. If its jaws are closed, let them not open, if they are opened, let them not close. Honor to the god-people. Honor to Asita, honor to Tiraśchirāji, honor to Svaja, [and] honor to Babhru, honor to the god-people. I seal up your teeth, your jaws, your tongue, and your mouth.[11]

Anyone who has ever had a snake drop out of a tree onto her or looked down to see a snake slither into his path knows that snakes possess something that is also always associated with divinity: the capacity to engender an immediate response which provokes an instantaneous apprehension of what Rudolf Otto called, "the Wholly Other."[12] According to Otto, this experience of "the Wholly Other" is endlessly mysterious and ineffable; it defies rational explanation as it transcends the boundaries of a human-centered, socially constructed worldview. Given their capacity to engender such a response, it is not surprising that snakes are represented within these texts as divine beings.

The *Śatapatha Brāhmaṇa* also speaks to the divinity of snakes as it states that "the *sarpavid* (one who has knowledge of snakes) should meditate on the divine person as a snake."[13] The idea that divine snakes might be useful in managing their more unruly brethren is an important idea to which we will return for it highlights an assumption that forms the foundation of many snake-centered rituals: it is possible to control dangerous snakes through the ritual propitiation of a divine snake by a person (a *sarpavid*) who is knowledgeable about such things.

The equation of immanently powerful things, such as snakes, with divinity is a common occurrence within the religious sensibility of India. Susan Wadley, an anthropologist who has focused her work in rural north India, speaks to this point:

> First, living human beings can be, and often are, deities in Karimpur, as are plows, snakes, bullocks, and wheat seedlings, in addition to the normally recognized pantheon of mythological gods and goddesses. The basic rule is that any being that a person considers more powerful than himself or herself in any particular realm of life can become an object of worship.... Moreover any action that is undertaken because of another being's power (*shakti*) is religious action.[14]

Such a sensibility leads to a religious landscape populated with hybrid beings; immanent things charged with supernatural powers. For as the redactors characterize snakes both as gods (*deva-jana*) and as reptiles (Pṛdāku, Svaja, etc.) they both highlight and value their hybrid nature; a nature that allows these figures to be both divinely powerful yet fully accessible. In fact, the supernatural snake's genesis in the powerful reptile is what drives its elevation to sacred status, for it is the fact of its ubiquitous, uncontainable presence that not only necessitates its appeasement but also facilitates its accessibility as an object of religious devotion. Moreover, as an uncontainable yet accessible object of religious devotion, the snake cannot be exclusively claimed or contained within any one religious framework but rather crosses over ideological boundaries. This fact is attested to in that the supernatural snake appears not only throughout the early texts of both the Hindu and Buddhist traditions but also in ritual practices, which, as we have seen, extend beyond the parameters of these textual traditions.[15]

The *Śatapatha Brāhmaṇa* further elaborates on the hybrid nature of the snakes as it sets out to explain why various hybrid figures, such as a long-haired man, are needed to ward off snakes:

> As for what it [the *Yajur Veda*] says of a long-haired person: He is neither a woman nor a man since he is long-haired. Since he is a man, he cannot be a woman, since he is long-haired, he cannot be a man. And this red metal is neither iron nor gold, and these biting ones are neither worms nor non-worms. Red metal is used because these biting things are reddish. This is the reason you put it [red metal] in the mouth of a long-haired man [to ward-off snakes].[16]

Given the *Śatapatha Brāhmaṇa's* explicit acknowledgment that a deified snake is a hybrid creature, it makes sense that this text attempts to redress the inadequate modifiers so far imposed on this supernatural creature. We thus see in this text the first use of a word that comes to define the snake's dual nature: Nāga. "The wise Śvetaketu Āruṇeya said, 'To the one who will know the splendor of the preliminary offerings, people in future days will come in droves as if desiring to see a great Nāga.'"[17] While the term Nāga is also sometimes used in these texts to signify an elephant, the *Śatapatha Brāhmaṇa*'s commentary explicitly states that the Nāga in question is a *mahāsarpa*—great snake.[18] What is striking about the term 'Nāga' as it is first employed in the above passage is that unlike *ahi* or *sarpa* it signifies a snake that is differentiated explicitly from the average reptile: a snake that is exceptional due to its great size, its great powers, or perhaps both. This term thus captures the dual nature of the late Vedic snakes as they are valorized both as immanent and as exceptional beings. This image, moreover, of people coming "in droves as if desiring to see a great Nāga," is reminiscent of that described in relation to Alexander the Great's 4th C. BCE visit to India, in which it was observed that people would come to see a "sacred" snake, "kept in a cave and worshipped with much devotion."[19]

The late Vedic texts include one other reference to a Nāga as it signifies a divine snake and this occurs in the *Āśvalāyana Gṛhya Sūtra*.[20] In these verses, the term appears within a long list of "*devatās*" or demi-gods which include, among others, Gandharvas, Apsarasas, Yakṣas, and Nāgas.[21] This is clearly a reference to a divine snake rather than to an elephant, for not only do we find divine *sarpas* listed along with Yakṣas, Apsarasas and Gandharvas in the *Atharva Veda*[22] but also, only another demi-god would be at home in such supernatural company. Thus, building on the first reference to a Nāga in the *Śatapatha Brāhmaṇa* in which this term is used to distinguish a reptile of gargantuan proportions and/or powers, both of these textual references use this term to mark a snake explicitly classified as an extraordinary being.

Arbuda Kādraveya: The Transformation and Anthropomorphization of the Ṛg Vedic Snake

The process by which the redactors contextualize the snake through a frame of refracting details is particularly clear as we look at Arbuda Kādraveya. For rather than viewing an accumulation of singular narrative elements such as the scope of powers granted or the degree of respect given, which are then attached to a general population of snakes, a look at Arbuda offers us a new opportunity: to view the centering of one particular snake in its own descriptive framework as well as the recontextualization of one particular snake as it is shifted from the *Ṛg Veda* (in which it has only a brief appearance) to the late Vedas.

We know two things about Arbuda Kādraveya as he is featured in the *Ṛg Veda.* First, like Vṛtra, Arbuda Kādraveya is depicted as an enemy of Indra: "Having strengthened himself, [Indra] killed Arbuda."[23] Second, like most *Ṛg Vedic* snakes, Arbuda Kādraveya is characterized as a supernatural snake representative of the demonic forces of darkness and chaos.[24] In contrast, the late Vedas present Arbuda as a wise and powerful earth deity. We come to know a great deal about him, moreover, through the following vehicles: first, the chronicle of the *Sarpavidyā*, literally, the knowledge or science of snakes, in which Arbuda stars as the king of the snakes; and second, the myth of the *Sarpasattra*, which explains the origins of powerful, sovereign snakes such as Arbuda Kādraveya, Takṣaka

Vaiśāleya, and Dhṛtarāṣṭra Airāvata. In examining the late Vedic Arbuda Kādraveya, we also learn something about the function and importance of snake names as they explicitly represent these creatures as earth deities. Lastly, the late Vedas give us a glimpse of Arbuda's snake family, and in looking at his sons, presented as friends of Indra, we see the degree to which this snake has been transformed from his *Ṛg Vedic* roots.

The Sarpavidyā: The Science of Snakes

It is in the *Śatapatha Brāhmaṇa* that we first hear of the *Sarpavidyā*, or the science of snakes, which features Arbuda Kādraveya as the king of the snakes. "Arbudya Kādraveya (the son of Kadrū) is King. And his people are the snakes, and they are sitting here, both snakes and snake-knowers have come together and [the King] teaches them: 'The *Sarpavidyā* is the *Veda*.'"[25] As stated in the *Śatapatha Brāhmaṇa*, then, Arbuda Kādraveya has been anthropomorphized in that he is made to function as both a king and a teacher. As king, he rules over the population of snakes. As teacher, he conveys the science of snakes, which is said to be as sacred as the Vedas. He teaches this science, moreover, both to snakes and to specific people: those "knowers," *vidaḥ,* of "snakes," *sarpas*, or those who have proved they have the capacity both to understand and to control snakes.

It makes perfect sense that the original "knower of snakes" and the only one qualified to teach this material is King Arbuda. For there would be none better qualified to understand the power of snakes and techniques for controlling them than the king of all snakes. We see particular assumptions in this positioning of Arbuda that form the basis of many ritual activities: the deification of a powerfully dangerous, earthly being constructs an instrument through which the rest of those immanent beings might be controlled. In other words, it is through the construction and ritual propitiation of a powerful supernatural snake sovereign that the real snake's dangerous tendencies might be ameliorated. These assumptions are held to be true for two reasons. First, only an anthropomorphized, supernatural snake, one perceived as amenable to human desires, might be able to act as a mediator between the natural world of the snake and the civilized world of the human. Second, and more subtly, only the supernatural snake might be used to control the elemental dynamism of the real snake as the powerful, yet propitiated, essence of King Arbuda Kādraveya is ritually merged with the real snake.[26] In fact, we will remember that this idea is referenced in verse 10.5.2.21 of the *Śatapatha Brāhmaṇa*, in which the divine person is conflated with the snake through the machinations of the *sarpavid*: "the *sarpavid* (one who has knowledge of snakes) should meditate on the divine person as a snake."

In a further examination of King Arbuda Kādraveya's *Sarpavidyā,* the *Śāṃkhāyana Śrauta Sūtra* lists it along with various other types of knowledge that the Vedic student was required to know. Moreover, according to this text, the Kādraveyas, the snake citizens of King Arbuda Kādraveya, were to be taught the *Sarpavidyā* so that it might be recited on the fifth day of the horse-sacrifice.[27] As noted by Christopher Minkowski, however, the bulk of the material further elaborating the *Sarpavidyā* remains unchronicled as it lies outside of the Vedic textual tradition:

> The text of the *Sarpavidyā* is not provided in the *śrauta* texts. The commentators, who appear not to have had access to a continuous commentorial tradition, suggest that *Sarpavidyā* is the same as *viṣavidyā*, and that the *Sarpavidyā* must therefore refer to charms against snakebite. In making this identification, the commentators are linking the ritual *Sarpavidyā* with the vast network of Indian snake lore, the science of how to avoid harm from snakes, which escapes the limits even of Sanskrit literature.[28]

Given the on-the-ground reality of poisonous snakes in India, it is expected that others, in addition to the redactors (possibly farmers tending their fields or women tending their homes) would have been interested in the issue of controlling them. So it would seem that the *Sarpavidyā*, in part or in whole, derives from a grass-roots tradition of snake-worshippers. Thus, just as the *Śatapatha Brāhmaṇa* states that "people come in droves" when "desiring to see a great Nāga,"[29] Minkowski suggests that a variety of people, in addition to the redactors of the late Vedas, might have had an interest in generating information about snakes.

The Sarpasattra: The Sacrifice Performed by the Snakes

Like the *Sarpanāma*, the *Sarpasattra* is a ritual originally intended to be enacted by priests exclusively. Given its purpose, I would suggest that like the *Sarpanāma*, the *Sarpasattra* derives from priestly sources and reflects the fact that the priests of this period found supernaturally powerful, divine snakes to be useful. First, they are useful in the enactment of their ritual activities, for the sole purpose of the *Sarpanāma*, as we will recall, is to invoke the snakes to stop the earth from turning in order to enable the priests to complete the sacrifice. Second, they are useful in the obtainment of various boons; for as we will soon see, several benefits accrue to brahmin priests who would conduct the *Sarpasattra* ritual. Thus, as the priests' agenda proved compatible with those engaged in the grass-roots worship of these creatures, the priestly redactors of the late Vedas not only preserved but also may have contributed to the growing tradition of snake lore with such rituals as the *Sarpanāma* and the *Sarpasattra*.

The term *Sarpasattra* literally means "snake sacrifice", and in the late Vedic version of this ritual, this term denotes a sacrifice performed by snakes functioning in the role of brahmins. The late Vedic version of the *Sarpasattra* also incorporates a cosmogonic myth explaining how snakes became both powerful biters and wonderfully heroic. Arbuda Kādraveya is one of several snakes featured as a participant as are two other snakes whom we will be discussing shortly, Takṣaka Vaiśāleya and Dhṛtarāṣṭra Airāvata.[30] Minkowski notes the following in relation to the *Sarpasattra*: "As are all *sattras*, it is subject to unusual rules. Only brahmins are eligible to perform it; there is no separate *Yajamāna* or sponsor; no *dakṣiṇā*, or sacrificial fee is given."[31] A *sattra* is set up in this way because it is above all a ritual by and for the brahmin officiates, who collectively accrue the benefits of their own endeavor. Thus, in accordance with the rules, "[t]he first offerers of the *Sarpasattra* were the snakes themselves,"[32] who, according to the *Baudhāyana Śrauta Sūtra*, became endowed with the power of a poisonous bite "*daṃśuka*" as a result of completing the ritual.[33]

In addition to their boon of becoming "*daṃśuka*"—biters—the completion of the *Sarpasattra* also causes these snakes to become "*daṃśuvīrya*"—wonderfully heroic, powerful, and virile. And it would seem from the sense of the verse that they are wonderfully "*vīrya*" precisely because they are "*daṃśuka*;" a natural development given that the late Vedic redactors consistently prize the snake's inherent powers. Moreover, beyond the boons awarded to the original snake officiates, the *Sarpasattra,* according to the *Baudhāyana Śrauta Sūtra,* promises benefits such as sons, cattle, and snake-bite protection to those human brahmins who would perform this ritual.[34]

The *Baudhāyana Gṛhya Sūtra* documents what might be seen as a grass-roots intervention as it amends this ritual practice: rather than performing the entire ritual, one need only recite the names of Arbuda and the other original snake officiates saying, "Let there be homage paid to the snakes," to be protected from dangerous snakes.[35] The alternate version of this ritual practice thus allows the average householder to benefit from the *Sarpasattra's* promise of protection from snakes.

As more and more rituals and mantras are developed—from both priestly and grass-roots sources—which focus on the supernatural snake as a protector of humans, supernatural snakes such as Arbuda Kādraveya can be seen to undergo a process by which they become increasingly anthropomorphized. For example the *Śatapatha Brāhmaṇa* has Arbuda Kādraveya functioning as a king privy to the special knowledge of the *Sarpavidyā*, whereas in the *Sarpasattra* ritual, Arbuda Kādraveya, Takṣaka Vaiśāleya, and Dhṛtarāṣṭra Airāvata are made to function as brahmin priests engaged in an esoteric sacrificial ritual. Moreover, these are not the only allusions to Arbuda Kādraveya in anthropomorphized roles: as noted by Minkowski, in the *Aitareya* and *Kauṣītakī Brāhmaṇas* as well as in the *Āpastamba* and *Śāṃkhāyana Śrauta Sūtras*, Arbuda Kādraveya is said to be the *ṛṣi* or divinely inspired sage responsible for *Ṛg Vedic* hymn 10.94.[36]

As we will see in chapter 4, this process of anthropomorphizing the supernatural snake only goes further as in the epic texts, these snakes are able to transform themselves into humans at will. And in almost all post-BCE plastic representations of Nāgas, they are represented as mostly human but with some remnant of the snake remaining such as a cobra hood or snake tail. This anthropomorphizing process might be explained, however, by the fact that these supernatural snakes are made to function as mediators; for while figures such as Arbuda Kādraveya are first and foremost snakes, their human supplicants must be sure that they will be inclined to protect them against snakes. And how better to achieve this goal than to make these supernatural snakes as human-like as possible?

Arbuda Kādraveya and his Family

The anthropomorphization of the supernatural snake continues as Arbuda Kādraveya is presented as a family snake. In this context, the late Vedic redactors focus on three members of Arbuda's family: his mother and his two sons. The texts' focus on Arbuda Kādraveya's mother, moreover, is helpful for it allows us to see the way in which snake names function to represent these creatures specifically as earth-gods.

The name, Kādraveya, is a matronymic. That means that it functions to identify Arbuda as the son of a particular mother: Kadrū. And while Arbuda carried this name in the *Ṛg Veda*, it is not until later that the name Kadrū is defined as denoting "this earth."[37] Positioning Arbuda as the son of the earth contextualizes this snake in two very specific ways: first, as a divine figure, for he is the son of the earth personified as a goddess; and second, as explicitly linked to the earth as the direct progeny of the earth herself. Thus, the late Vedic redactors have taken pains to represent Arbuda Kādraveya specifically as an earth-god. As we will see in chapter 4, this explicit role of earth-god is further extended in the epic text, the *Mahābhārata*, wherein all snakes are said to be the sons and daughters of Kadrū.

The late Vedas also introduce two sons of Arbuda, Arbudi and Nyarbudi, both of whom are depicted as powerful warlords and compatriots of Indra.

> The god named Arbudi, and the lord named Nyarbudi, by whom the atmosphere and this great earth are covered *(vṛ)*, I follow the conquered one with my army and with these two companions of Indra.
> Stand up you, O god Arbudi! Breaking the army of the enemies, surround them with your coils.[38]

It is here in this *Atharva Vedic* verse that we can really see the resignification of crucial details that allows these redactors to recontextualize the *Ṛg Vedic* snake. This occurs particularly as the late Vedic redactors resignify the term *vṛ*, "to cover." In the *Ṛg Veda*, the snake was perceived as evil precisely due to its capacity to *vṛ* or cover the earth and thereby control precious earthly resources such as water. And in fact, the text's primary snake antagonist, Vṛtra, was so-named to highlight its malevolent nature: Vṛtra, he who has "the lightning and thunder, rain and hail" at his command "had barricaded those waters with his earthly powers."[39] In contrast, the late Vedic redactors celebrate the snake's capacity to cover the earth and name both Arbudi and Nyarbudi as "god" and "lord" respectively because of the fact that they are the ones "by whom the atmosphere and this great earth are covered (*vṛ*)...."

Another crucial departure from the *Ṛg Veda* occurs as the late Vedic redactors present Arbudi and Nyarbudi as friends of Indra. Given the fact that "Arbuda in the *Ṛg Veda* is a demon-serpent whom Indra is bound to slay," it is strange, notes Bloomfield, that there is a "friendly relation of Arbudi and Nyarbudi, as ancillary war gods, with Indra, notwithstanding Indra's hostility to Arbuda in the *Ṛg Veda*."[40] And indeed it does seem strange except for the following: while the *Ṛg Vedic* redactors found it necessary to stamp out the snake and transfer its powers to Indra, the late Vedic redactors found a means by which to control and to utilize the powers of the snake through the vehicle of a supernatural snake. Therefore, while Indra acted as a divine protective force against snakes such as Arbuda Kādraveya in the *Ṛg Veda*, Arbuda's sons are presented as friends of Indra and divine protective forces in their own right here in the late Vedas.

The friendship of the supernatural snake with Indra, moreover, signifies a tremendous shift in the religious significance of the supernatural snake, for it signals that the supernatural snake is no longer viewed by the redactors as a demonic power and opponent of Āryan civilization, as was Vṛtra in the *Ṛg Veda*. Rather, the supernatural snake is now viewed as a true and efficacious deity. The late Vedic redactor's willingness to employ this strategy—that of *using* the snake's powers rather than *eradicating* the snake's powers—derives from the fact that they, unlike their *Ṛ g Vedic* counterparts, did not feel their religio-political position to be threatened by alternative modes of religiosity such as snake worship. Moreover, as these redactors value rather than fear the snake's powers, they expand upon the uses to which these powers might be put. In other words, these redactors not only see these supernatural snakes as protecting humans against dangerous snakes, but also as protecting humans against any and all dangerous foes.

"Stand up you, O god Arbudi! Breaking the army of the enemies, surround them with your coils."[41] It makes sense, however, that the late Vedic redactors would come to appreciate these snakes for the very powers for which they were condemned in the *Ṛg Veda.* For in attempting to stamp out Vṛtra and Arbuda Kādraveya and transfer their powers to Indra, the *Ṛg Vedic* redactors did these snakes a favor: they highlighted their powers as valuable.

Dhṛtarāṣṭra Airāvata, Takṣaka Vaiśāleya and Vāsuki: The Valorization of Regional Snakes and the Formalization of Land-Related Rituals

Both Takṣaka Vaiśāleya and Dhṛtarāṣṭra Airāvata make their textual debut in the late Vedas, and both will make a return appearance in the *Ādi Parvan* of the *Mahābhārata.* As noted, both of these snakes appear alongside Arbuda Kādraveya in the *Sarpasattra* ritual wherein they become not only "*daṃśuka*"—biters—but also "*daṃśuvīrya*"—wonderfully heroic, powerful, and virile. And like Arbuda Kādraveya, both Takṣaka Vaiśāleya and Dhṛtarāṣṭra Airāvata possess family names as well as the ability to protect humans from dangerous snakes. Takṣaka Vaiśāleya and Dhṛtarāṣṭra Airāvata, however, differ from Arbuda in two important ways: They are both regionalized and ritualized to a far greater extent than Arbuda Kādraveya. In other words, not only do their family names tie them to a particular region and its inhabitants but also they are worshipped, along with a third snake, Vāsuki, in conjunction with important land-based rituals such as the *Sarpabali* and the *Vāstupraśamana* that do not require the presence of a priest.

Names and Localized Sovereignty

Like Arbuda Kādraveya and all of the other snakes so far reviewed from the late Vedas, Takṣaka Vaiśāleya and Dhṛtarāṣṭra Airāvata are configured as powerful, divine figures with sovereign control over earthly domains. And in *Atharva Veda* 8.10.29, both Takṣaka Vaiśāleya and Dhṛtarāṣṭra Airāvata are listed as the primary sovereigns of the divine race of supernatural snakes. While Arbuda Kādraveya's name ties him to the earth in its entirety, both Takṣaka Vaiśāleya and Dhṛtarāṣṭra Airāvata have names that associate them with particular regional locations. Connecting these supernatural snakes nominally with a specific spatial territory is not surprising given that the custom of endowing a human child with the name of its birthplace as part of its permanent title is a traditional practice that persists up to the present time in both India and Sri Lanka. More importantly for our purposes, the fact that these snakes are named as the sovereign deities of a particular regional locale links them historically to the people of that region.

Vaiśāleya and Airāvata respectively could either be patronymics (identifying a father) or matronymics (identifying a mother). If we take Airāvata as a matronymic, the parent is Irāvatī, thus indicative of the Irāvatī River region located in the Punjab; as a patronymic, it is Irāvant, and according to Monier-Williams, Irāvān was the original name of the Irāvatī River.[42] If we take Vaiśāleya as a matronymic, the parent is Viśālā, and again indicative of a river mentioned in both the *Mahābhārata* and the *Rāmāyana*; as a patronymic, it is Viśāla, and Vaiśāla is both the name of a town that was founded by a certain Viśāla and the name given to one who is from the town of Vaiśalī. The name Vaiśāleya also turns up in the *Karṇa Parvan* of the *Mahābhārata* to signify a tribe of Nāga people—those who took the divine snake as a totem or who believed themselves to be descendants of divine snakes.[43]

Whether they are matronymics or patronymics, these names are indicative of a particular region. If one looks at a list of divine snakes, such as that in the *Pañcaviṃśa Brāhmaṇa*,[44] more than one-third of them have a patronymic or matronymic that was at one time most probably associated with a particular locale. For example, Timirgha Daureśruta, "son of Dūreśruta,"[45] a snake named as the *Āgnīdhra* in the *Pañcaviṃśa Brāhmaṇa's Sarpasattra* ritual, has a name that means literally "far-hearing."[46] While this in and of itself would seem to indicate an attribute rather than a place name, the *Mahābhārata* tells us that far-hearing is one of the benefits that will be received by worshippers bathing at a particular *tīrtha*, a site on a river oftentimes associated with the worship of Nāgas.[47] Unfortunately, as noted by Lowell Bloss, many of the original names of these *tīrthas* are no longer known to us because "these sites now have such names as Kṛṣṇanāga (Kṛṣṇa + Nāga) and Jyeṣṭheśa (a name of both a nāga and Śiva), [and] perhaps point to another interaction between more universally known deities and a local sacred place."[48] As the transformation of sites and rituals from their original role in a grass-roots tradition to an incorporated role in an orthodox, Sanskritized tradition drives much of the epic redactors' agenda, we will return to this subject in chapter 4.

The family names attached to Takṣaka Vaiśāleya and Dhṛtarāṣṭra Airāvata respectively emphasize the landed nature of these creatures, linked not merely to a vague notion of earthly sovereignty or territoriality (as in the case of Arbuda Kādraveya or as they are in the *Sarpanāma* mantras in which they inhabit every corner of the earth's surface) but rather to a specific parcel of land. Dhṛtarāṣṭra Airāvata and Takṣaka Vaiśāleya are thereby constructed as *localized* sovereigns, figures that might be charged by the local inhabitants with maintaining the prosperity of their domains.

Snake Rituals: Protecting the Populace and Insuring Prosperity

The ways in which snakes and snake worshippers maintained the prosperity of their region was through the practice of particular rituals. And when we view the rituals with which these snakes are associated, we get a much better feel for why these snake regents were and continue to be valued by local inhabitants: they guard the populace from dangerous snakes; they purify the earth; they insure a solid foundation for a new house; and they protect the house and all who are in it.

Takṣaka Vaiśāleya appears in the *Śāṃkhāyana Gṛhya Sūtra.*[49] *Gṛhya* literally means that which belongs to a house, and the spoken formulas associated with these domestic rituals were usually composed in prose and much less formal and less stylized than those of the *Śrauta Sūtras.* Within the *Śāṃkhāyana Gṛhya Sūtra,* Takṣaka Vaiśāleya is addressed in a ritual known as the *Sarpabali,* in which offerings are made to three classes of snakes: the earthly, the atmospheric, and the heavenly. The *Pāraskara Gṛhya Sūtra* further informs us that these three classes should be broken down as follows:

> This offering goes to the king of the snakes associated with Agni and to the yellowish, earth lords.
> This offering goes to the king of the snakes associated with Vāyu and to the white, atmospheric ones.
> This offering goes to the king of the snakes associated with Sūrya and to the overpowering, heavenly ones.[50]

We see in these verses the supernatural snake's explicit connection to all three realms conceptualized within the Vedic tri-world scheme: earth, atmosphere, and heaven. The "yellowish, earth" snakes are associated with the earthly element of fire (Agni); the "white, atmospheric" snakes are associated with the atmospheric element of the wind (Vāyu); and the overpowering, heavenly snakes are associated with the heavenly body of the sun (Sūrya). In addition to their *Ṛg Vedic* association with water, an association maintained by the late Vedic redactors, the snakes are represented here as ubiquitous in that they reside in all three realms of the universe. These verses are therefore designed to pay homage to and thereby propitiate all snakes, wherever they may live.

The *Sarpabali* is to be conducted every day from the month of *Śrāvana* to the month of *Agrahāyaṇa* (mid-July to mid-November), or in other words, during the rainy months when the snakes come out of their holes to show up in gardens, porches, and rooms. The ritual of the *Sarpabali* as encompassed in the *Gṛhya Sūtras,* particularly the *Śāṃkhāyana Gṛhya Sūtra*, the *Āśvalāyana Gṛhya Sūtra*, and the *Pāraskara Gṛhya Sūtra*, has two main purposes. First, it lists those items that are to be offered to the snakes in order that they might be propitiated; and second, it lists various precautions that should be taken to avoid their fangs.

The process of anthropomorphization, noted in relation to Arbuda Kādraveya, also occurs in conjunction with Takṣaka Vaiśāleya and the *Sarpabali*. For example, most of the items offered for the snake's benefit assume a creature with human habits, most probably to render it amenable to human desires: in *Khaṇḍa* 15 of the *Śāṃkhāyana Gṛhya Sūtra,* Takṣaka Vaiśāleya is given water with which to wash himself, combs with which to groom himself, flowers with which to adorn himself, clothes with which to cover himself, and even make-up for his eyes; while the last verse advises the worshipper to "climb upon the highest couch" at night time in order to escape the notice of Takṣaka Vaiśāleya's less sophisticated brethren.[51] In this ritual, just as in the *Sarpavidyā*, the supernatural snake, constructed in a very human-like fashion, operates as a boundary-keeper between humans and real snakes.

Like the *Sarpavidyā*, the *Sarpabali* uses a supernatural snake as an intermediary between humans and poisonous snakes. Also like the *Sarpavidyā*, the *Sarpabali* was not restricted to brahmins but could be practiced by anyone; it does not utilize a sacrificial fire, "but merely the placing on the ground of the oblations destined for the divine powers."[52] The *Sarpabali*, over the centuries, was probably linked up with other *bali* rituals such as "agricultural rites, often accompanied by charms to promote the growth of the crops...."[53] Given that snakes are perceived as insuring "abundance and health to a region through their control over water and its essences, such as semen and sap,"[54] this would be a natural linkage to make. Moreover, it would explain the fact that snakes, up to the present time, are worshipped by agriculturists to promote the growth of crops. Gonda notes that "many elements of the agricultural rites...date from hoary antiquity. In course of time...cases of incorporation of non-Aryan practices did not fail to occur."[55] Thus, along with the redactors' inclusion of this local snake deity comes the inclusion of a ritual useful in several ways to the local populace.

The sense of the snake as an independent *deva-jana* explicitly identified with the earth and its elemental forces is further reinforced in the *Sāmavidhāna Brāhmaṇa*, in which we are first introduced to the supernatural snake Vāsuki, a figure who will also reappear in an altered role in the *Ādi Parvan*. Like Arbuda Kādraveya and Takṣaka Vaiśāleya, Vāsuki functions as a boundary-keeper between humans and destructive snakes. Unlike the other two, however, Vāsuki is particularly portrayed as the supernatural sovereign of the subterranean realm.

In the *Sāmavidhāna Brāhmaṇa*, Vāsuki is invoked during a *Vāstupraśamana*, a ceremony specifically designed to insure a solid foundation for a new house.[56] Within this ritual, Vāsuki is depicted as having the capacity to purify the earth and make it fit for human habitation. Vāsuki appears in the same capacity in the *Gobhila Gṛhya Sūtra*, as he is asked to ensure the propitious setting of a foundation stone for a new house.[57] In this ritual, Vāsuki is specifically portrayed as the deity of the earth and an offering is thrown down upon the ground where the foundation stone is to rest.[58] In the *Kauśika Sūtra*,[59] both Takṣaka Vaiśāleya and Vāsuki are invoked as protectors of the house, as the supernatural snake stands on the *limen* between the civilized world and the natural world.

Conclusion: Revering the Sovereign Snake as an Independent, Approachable Deity

From the *Ṛg Veda* to the late Vedas, the religious significance of the supernatural snake has undergone an enormous shift. No longer viewed as a rival sovereign and opponent of both priest and god alike, as was Vṛtra in the *ṚgVeda*, the supernatural snake is now viewed as an efficacious nature deity. Clearly, the late Vedic redactors were working from a different ideological agenda than that of their *Ṛg Vedic* counterparts: seemingly less concerned with promoting their role in society, the late Vedic redactors legitimate forms of religiosity, such as snake worship, that do not require the participation of a priest. As a result, the late Vedic redactors contextualize snakes as inherently potent, supernaturally powerful, divine creatures. They live under the earth, on the earth, in the waters, and in the heavens; but wherever the snakes reside, they are worthy of reverence.

The late Vedic redactors' sanctioning of the snake's divinity led them to preserve and formalize a variety of snake-centered, earth-related rituals, many of which may derive from a grass-roots tradition of snake worship. For example, rituals such as the *Sarpabali* and the *Vāstupraśamana* do not require the presence of a priest nor do they list any special qualifications for would-be practitioners. In fact, these rituals centralize the supernatural snake as a powerful sovereign whom anyone might efficaciously propitiate for such things as a well-secured cornerstone, a purified building site, or protection of the house and its inhabitants from biting snakes.

The textual preservation of such rituals expands our view of snake worship in late Vedic times beyond the limited archaeological and ethnographic data available. These texts allow us to see features of snake worship that would otherwise have been lost as they are erased in later texts, such as the fact that both Dhṛtarāṣṭra Airāvata and Takṣaka Vaiśāleya are originally characterized not as universal figures but as local ones. This indicates that they and the rituals connected with their worship were associated with a particular region and its inhabitants, and again, may very well derive from a grass-roots tradition of snake worship. Also associated with a grass-roots tradition, we have the *Sarpavidyā*, or the science of snakes, for as noted by Minkowski, this too "escapes the limits even of Sanskrit literature."[60] Clearly, then, these very early orthodox texts seem to have preserved religious practices constructed and enacted by those most often disenfranchised by the redactors of orthodox texts: women, lower castes, and basically anyone who was not a brahmin or a king.

The contextual frame in which the snake is centered within these texts reflects a larger contextual frame: the lived reality of those who constructed the snake as an object of religious worship and were interested in such things as keeping their families safe and sheltering themselves from nature. While not actively engaged in the promotion of snake worship, the late Vedic redactors' interest in contextualizing the snake as a powerful, divine figure stems from a compatible set of motivations: to compile a complete canon of ritual activities as well as to avail themselves of the benefits accruing from a powerful snake deity who could both enhance their ritual efficacy and provide them with various boons. As a result, these late Vedic redactors may not have been mere conservationists; they might actually have further enriched this tradition with mantras and rituals such as the *Sarpanāma* and *Sarpasattra* that were relevant to their fears and hopes, experiences and desires. Seen in this light, the supernatural snake possibly mirrors the lived reality of the late Vedic redactors and the larger context in which they were trying to center themselves.

As we will find when we turn to the *Ādi Parvan* of the *Mahābhārata* in chapter 4, however, the boost given to snake worship in the late Vedas spelled nothing but trouble for the epic redactors. For compared to their predecessors, they were not as confident of their position as ritual specialists charged with controlling nature, and at times responded in a very negative fashion to alternative modes of religiosity. In fact, certain portions of the epic seem to reflect that these redactors were as threatened by the phenomenon of supernatural snakes and snake worshippers as were the *Ṛg Vedic* redactors. As a result, we will find in the *Ādi Parvan* many of the same tactics used in the *Ṛg Veda* to quash this grass-roots tradition. Thus, much of the contextualizing frame built-up by the late Vedic redactors, which served both to elevate the supernatural snake and to formalize rituals designed to show it reverence, will be demolished when the epic redactors take on the snake.

4

The Ādi Parvan of the Mahābhārata: The Epic Redactors Take On the Snake

As seen in the previous chapter, the snakes of the pre-epic period are noble yet fearsome creatures. They are said to inhabit every corner of the earth's surface, to control the earth's motion, to affect the earth's weather, and to guard the four quarters; their poisonous fangs ever-ready to defend their birthright. Explicitly named in the late Vedic texts as snake kings, some, such as Vāsuki, are said to control the entire earth, while others such as Dhṛtarāṣṭra Airāvata and Takṣaka Vaiśāleya are endowed with names that connect them with particular regional domains.

As recounted in the late Vedas, the snake kings are worshipped through a variety of rituals designed to secure such things as a bountiful harvest, a host of healthy sons, a solid foundation for a new house, and freedom from snakebite. These rituals form the foundation of a contextual framework that centralizes the supernatural snake as a powerful sovereign whom anyone might efficaciously propitiate, for these ritual activities do not require the presence of a priest nor do they list any special qualifications for would-be practitioners. Moreover, as we have speculated as to what groups might have been most interested in constructing this contextual framework around the snake, we have examined the following: travelers' reports and archaeological evidence from the late Vedic period that serve to confirm the actual practice of these ritual activities as well as the various purposes served by these rituals. From our examination of this evidence, it would seem that those 'context constructors' most involved in building a tradition of snake worship were probably ordinary people: farmers hoping for a good harvest, women concerned with giving birth, families involved in building homes, and parents worried about poisonous snakes. While the late Vedic redactors maintained and even advanced the contextual framework that centralizes the supernatural snake as an efficacious deity, the same cannot be said for the epic redactors. Thus, as we turn to the *Mahābhārata*, it is the snake king's role as an accessible object of religious devotion that will concern us.

The *Mahābhārata*, the great epic of India, was redacted over a period of several centuries and is dated from c. 300 BCE to 300 CE. Like all epics, the *Mahābhārata*, to use Levi-Strauss' term, is a *bricolage*: a narrative conglomeration of recycled bits and pieces. According to van Buitenen, its compilation might be understood as having occurred in three phases: "*The Bhārata* of 24,000 couplets grew to *The Mahābhārata* of 100,000. The original story was in the first phase of complication expanded from within, in the second phase mythologized, in the third phase braminized."[1] And the *Ādi Parvan*, literally, the "beginning section" of the *Mahābhārata* but clearly a later addition, particularly demonstrates the mark of the brahmin priest, for in this section the redactors are concerned with insuring the superior position of brahmins over all others.[2]

While we lack specific sociological data as to why brahmins, as a class, might have felt the need to shore up their role in society, we can speculate along the following lines. Many passages within the *Ādi Parvan* focus on the denigration of the kṣatriya class, which as we will recall is made up of kings, warriors, and noble land-holders. In fact, much of the first three sections of the *Ādi Parvan* is centrally concerned with portraying a particular king, King Janamejaya, as a vengeful ruler who must be brought under control.[3] At the same time that the redactors are critiquing the kṣatriya class, they are making a great effort to exalt the brahmin class in what appears to be an attempt to reassert the social order as it was first established in the *Ṛg Veda*. This social order positioned brahmin priests as the first class, endowed with the highest authority, and kṣatriyas as the second class, endowed with the power to uphold that authority. From a sociological perspective, this social structure is inherently unstable, for while the brahmins' authority is granted *de jure*, the kṣatriyas' authority is granted *de facto*, as they are the only class endowed with the means to enforce social order. It is possible, then, that approximately eight centuries after the original proclamation of this social structure in the *Ṛg Veda*, brahmins might feel the need to reassert their claim of social primacy. That claim is reestablished in this text as the brahmin redactors construct a contextual framework centralizing the religious practices of brahminism, and by extension, the exclusive religious authority of the brahmin class. Like the redactors of the *Ṛg Veda*, then, the redactors of the *Ādi Parvan* enact a political agenda through a religious agenda as the hierarchical elevation of brahmins occurs through the hierarchical elevation of Brahminism.

In relation to this brahminic agenda, the redactors of the *Ādi Parvan* perceive snake worship as both a tremendous threat and a tremendous opportunity. In terms of a threat, the supernatural snake and its accompanying ritual practices have only grown in stature over the intervening centuries, especially with the narrative assistance of the late Vedic redactors. Moreover, people worship these snake kings as insurers of what brahmins, through their sacrificial ritual activities, are supposed to provide: prosperity, posterity, and longevity. And to add insult to injury, the primary ritual activities associated with snake worship obviate the necessity of a brahmin officiant. As such, the snake king constructed during the pre-epic period possesses the capacity to deprive the brahmin of his very *raison d'être*, and as a result, the redactors of the *Ādi Parvan* wish to dethrone the snake king.

In terms of an opportunity, the late Vedic redactors make it abundantly clear that he who controls the snake's powers is powerful while the *Ṛg Vedic* redactors make it clear that he who controls the snake's powers exclusively is singularly powerful. Thus, having worked to suppress the sovereign snake the epic redactors attempt to control the snake exclusively. They do this not only as they move in on its ritual territory through insinuating a brahmin into the snake king's ritual role but also as they incorporate the snake into the brahminic fold and thereby divert its powers to the brahmin class. For as stated in the late Vedas, the sovereign snakes are wonderfully mighty, powerful, and virile, and brahmins, as we will see in this text, are particularly in need of these qualities. Thus, in the same manner as the *Ṛg Veda*, the *Ādi Parvan* uses context as a weapon in order to achieve a narrative objective in which the snakes are first dethroned and second supplanted. The *Ādi Parvan's* redactors then go one step further as they incorporate the snake into their ritual/theological framework. They achieve this three-pronged objective as they deconstruct the contextual framework within which the supernatural snake is centered in order to reconstruct a new framework; one within which brahmins are centered as "the first eater of all beings, the first of all classes, the father, the guru."[4]

The Dethronement of the Late Vedic Snakes

The redactors of the *Ādi Parvan* use a variety of means to recontextualize and thereby disempower the pre-epic snake kings, including the following: the snakes are made to behave as troublesome and deceptive creatures; they lose their regional place names; they lose their spatial sovereignty as they are removed to the Nāgaloka (the world of the snakes); they lose their status as independent demigods as they are made dependent on established gods such as Indra; their powers over the natural elements are diminished; they are provided with an overpowering natural enemy in the form of the great Garuḍa bird; and finally, they are presented as a threatening, multitudinous force that deserves to die.

The three sections of the *Ādi Parvan* with which we will concern ourselves include two of the so-called "minor" books,[5] namely, the book of *Pauṣya* and the book of *Puloman*, followed by the much longer book of *Āstīka*. The book of *Pauṣya* gives us our first glimpse of a recontextualized late Vedic snake king in an encounter between the brahmin Utanka and Takṣaka, wherein the brahmin requests the following: "Let the Nāgas be in my power." The story begins with the brahmin Utanka, who has ventured forth from his guru's house in order to procure his "guru gift," a payment given to one's guru upon completion of one's training. But having disguised himself as a wandering ascetic, the snake king Takṣaka hinders the brahmin's progress.

> Then he [Utanka] saw a naked mendicant coming down the path, who was first visible and then invisible. Having put the earrings [his guru gift] on the ground, Utanka went for water.[6] In that interval, the mendicant, having hastily drawn close and seized the earrings, ran away. Utanka caught-up and grabbed him. Relinquishing the shape [of the mendicant] and resuming his natural form as Takṣaka, the snake entered a great hole that had suddenly opened-up in the ground, and he went to the Nāgaloka, his natural habitat.[7]

Utanka follows Takṣaka into the Nāgaloka, and in an attempt to retrieve the earrings, praises the snakes in verse.

> 'The snakes whose king is Airāvata shine in battle, and are like rain clouds streaked with lightning and driven by the wind.
> Beautiful and ugly with speckled coils, the ones who arose from Airāvata shine like the sun in the vault of the sky.
> The Nāgas have many paths on the north bank of the Ganges.
> Who would wish to march against the rays of the sun without Airāvata in their army?
> Twenty-eight thousand and eight hundred snakes set out when Dhṛtarāṣṭra stirs; to those who march close to him, and to those who march as fore-runners, I give honor to the elder brothers of Airāvata.
> To Takṣaka, who dwells always in the field of the Kurus in the Khāṇḍava Forest, I praise him, son of Kadrū, for the sake of the earrings.[8]

The snakes are not alone in the Nāgaloka. The other residents include two goddesses, Dhātā and Vidhātā, Indra, presented as Parjanya—god of rain, and a magical horse capable of some rather disconcerting antics.[9] Utanka's poetry finds favor with Indra, who is described further as "[t]he bearer of the lightning bolt, the protector of all living creatures, [and] the killer of Vṛtra [the snake]."[10] Indra agrees to help Utanka:

> 'Your song of praise pleases me. What favor can I do for you?' Utanka said to him: 'Let the Nāgas be in my power.' Indra spoke to him again. 'Blow into the anus of this horse.' Utanka blew into the horse's anus and flames of fire flew out from all of its orifices. He thus fumigated the Nāgaloka. Then Takṣaka, confused, worn-down with fear from the powerful fire, grasped the earrings and immediately ran out from his palace and said to Utanka: 'Sir, take back these earrings....'
> And Utanka, having procured his guru's gift, returned to his guru's house.
> Once there, Utanka saluted his teacher, and the teacher said to him: 'Dear Utanka, welcome to you. What took so long?' Utanka replied, 'The snake king Takṣaka impeded me.'[11]

It is not surprising that Takṣaka would be the first supernatural snake to be encountered in the *Mahābhārata*, since the late Vedic texts refer to him three times as often as either Dhṛtarāṣṭra Airāvata or Vāsuki—two of the other snakes that make the leap from the Vedic texts to the epic. And in one respect, Takṣaka and his brethren appear in a manner familiar to us from the late Vedas: they are characterized as kings. "The snakes whose king is Airāvata, shine in battle." However, unlike the snake kings of the late Vedas that were portrayed as both noble and benevolent, snakes in general and particularly Takṣaka are portrayed as troublesome, fearful creatures that tend to wreak havoc in the lives of brahmins.[12]

As Takṣaka appears in this passage, and in fact, as he appears throughout the *Ādi Parvan*, he has lost the matronymic Vaiśāleya, a term that relates him most probably to the kingdom of Vaiśālī.[13] These place names are very important for they emphasize the landed nature of these creatures, linked not merely to a vague notion of earthly sovereignty or territoriality but rather to a specific parcel of land and its inhabitants. Dhṛtarāṣṭra Airāvata has undergone a similar name-change, for he has been split into two separate beings: in this passage we find an Airāvata who is king of the snakes and a Dhṛtarāṣṭra who stirs the snakes to action. Moreover, this is not just some kind of narrative confusion, for Dhṛtarāṣṭra and Airāvata also are listed as separate beings in the list of chief Nāgas.[14] In splitting up this single entity into two separate figures, the redactors of the epic again cancel out the Vedic snake's matronymic, Airāvata, which indicates his association with the Irāvatī River region located in the Punjab.[15] Thus, while contextualized in the late Vedas as *localized* sovereigns charged with maintaining the prosperity of their local domains, the epic redactors, in removing their place names, remove them from any direct relationship with the land and its people.

However, we also see in this passage three elements that reflect, I would argue, the development of snake worship up to and during this historical time period: the prevalent use of the term Nāga, the highlighting of the Nāgaloka, and the full anthropomorphization of the snake. As we saw in relation to the late Vedic texts, the term Nāga, as it was applied to a supernatural snake, occurs only twice. And as we will recall, this term functions to emphasize the hybrid nature of the supernatural snake, one that is simultaneously earthly yet divine. In fact, it would appear that it is the snake's hybrid nature that drives its elevation to sacred status for it allows this figure to be both fully accessible and supernaturally powerful. Given the importance of a modifier that reflects this dual nature, it is not surprising that the term Nāga would have been central to a tradition of snake worship and slowly but surely makes its way into these orthodox texts as the dominant signifier of supernatural snakes.

While snakes such as Arbuda Kādraveya showed a tendency to become increasingly anthropomorphized throughout the late Vedas, the transformation of Takṣaka into a "naked mendicant" and thus an anatomically correct human being most likely marks the first textual instance of the full anthropomorphization of the supernatural snake. This is not an unexpected development given that snake worshippers construct these supernatural snakes to function as mediators between the natural world of snakes and the civilized world of humans. As a result, it makes sense that over time snake worshippers would further embellish this figure to be as human-like as possible, for it would help to insure the Nāga's allegiance to the human race over that due to its coiled brethren. Thus, just as the late Vedas preserve the first phase of this process of anthropomorphization, the epics preserve the full realization of the Nāga's capacity to transform into a human. As the *Ādi Parvan's* narrative agenda is not conducive to valorizing those elements of snake worship which promote the snake's powers, it is not surprising that they contextualize the snake's transformative agility as a negative thing; one that is used in this case merely to fool the brahmin Utanka and jeopardize his mission.

Upon resuming his natural reptilian form, Takṣaka disappears into the Nāgaloka, literally, the 'world of the Nāgas,' taking the brahmin Utanka's earrings with him. The *Ādi Parvan*'s reference to the Nāgaloka marks the first reference to such a locale in a Hindu text.[16] And as described here, the Nāgaloka is a subterranean world, accessed by a hole in the earth, which is said to be the Nāga's "natural habitat." The Nāgaloka is also called Bhogāvatī, which represents a wonderful play on words for *bhoga* signifies both a snake's hood and or its coils as well as all manner of sensual pleasures. Given that reptiles primarily live in holes in the earth, it is to be expected that an oral tradition involving the worship of this creature would highlight the snake's subterranean habitat. In fact, the late Vedas preserved this aspect of snake worship in their depiction of Vāsuki as both the *devatā* (demigod) of the subterranean realm and the sovereign lord of the earth's surface.[17] And over time, it is also to be expected that snake worshippers would weave a richly textured narrative around the hidden world of the Nāgas; especially as the sacred sites associated with the worship of these creatures are expressly situated to allow access to these nether regions. While the *Ādi Parvan* brings up the Nāgaloka only to disenfranchise the snake, we will learn much more about this aspect of snake worship in chapter 5, for the Pāli redactors spend almost as much time highlighting the Nāgas' luxurious world as they do criticizing it.

In the *Ādi Parvan*'s depiction of the Nāgaloka, however, we learn very little about this place except for the following two details: the Nāgaloka is said to be a world that is inhospitable to humans, and the supernatural snake is presented as a second-class citizen in its own "natural habitat." The inhospitable atmosphere of the Nāgaloka is emphasized as we are told that the brahmin Utanka, upon entering this place, has to take a special elixir, and as told to him by his guru: "It was because of that elixir that you were not overcome in the Nāgaloka."[18] The *Ādi Parvan's* depiction of the Nāgaloka, like the removal of their place names, thus functions to separate the snakes from their human populations.

The supernatural snakes are disenfranchised in the Nāgaloka as they are not situated there as independent figures, rather they are accompanied by Indra, as well as the two supernatural women, Dhātā and Vidhātā. "As regards those two women, one is the creator, and the other is the arranger."[19] These two might be seen as the general contractors in charge of the whole operation. According to Monier-Williams, both Dhātā and Vidhātā signify an "[e]stablisher, founder, creator, bearer, supporter...presiding over generation, matrimony, health, wealth, time and seasons."[20] Unlike their role in the Vedas wherein the snakes had control over such things as the seasons and the earth's bounty, here they are second to Dhātā and Vidhātā.

The fact that Indra is down there as Parjanya, the god of rain and "bearer of the lightning bolt," is a further blow to the snakes' stature. For operating as the god of rain in the Nāgas' "natural habitat," Indra is made to usurp the snakes' power over the waters; a power not only attributed to the snakes as early as the *Ṛg Veda*, but also functioning as their most essential attribute. In demoting the snakes in relation to these alternative controllers of nature, the epic redactors attempt to strip the snakes of the very powers for which they are worshipped. And having revoked the bulk of their divine powers, the *Ādi Parvan* revokes their divine status as the redactors never refer to the snakes as *deva-jana* (divine beings) nor do they associate them with other *devatās* such as Apsarasas or Gandharvas, as the late Vedic redactors do.[21]

While placed in a position once removed from their late Vedic control over the waters, these creatures display a brand new attitude toward one of the other natural elements: a strong antipathy toward fire and heat in general. We see this first in the threat of marching "against the sun," and much more explicitly in the verse in which Takṣaka returns the earrings because he is "worn down with fear from the power of the fire." The rather shocking activity in which the brahmin Utanka is made to engage, namely, blowing into the horse's anus, highlights this fiery motif as it produces the flames that frighten Takṣaka into submission.

While the late Vedas portray the snake kings as divine, accessible sovereigns, we know from our examination of the *Ṛg Veda* that there is a literary precedent for the negative portrayal of these creatures. In fact, the brahmin redactors of the *Ṛg Veda* present Vṛtra not only as a malevolent snake sovereign but also as one who "had barricaded those waters with his earthly powers."[22] As such, the reference in this passage to Indra as "the killer of Vṛtra" is telling for it testifies to the snake's long history as both a controller of the waters and a forceful rival threatening to brahminic power.

In the next set of passages we revisit Kadrū, the earth personified as a goddess and the mother of the late Vedic snake king Arbuda Kādraveya. These passages represent an epic recontextualization of a story from the *Yajur Veda*. In its original form in the *Yajur Veda*, it recounts the exploits of Kadrū and her sister Suparṇī—a bird Goddess—as they wager over who is to fetch the *soma*:[23]

> Kadrū and Suparṇī [she with good wings] wagered [with each other]...Kadrū beat Suparṇī and said: 'The *soma* is in the third heaven from here, bring it, and by this means redeem yourself.' Kadrū is this (earth) and Suparṇī is that (heaven), the descendants of Suparṇī are the meters. 'For this reason,' Kadrū said, 'parents bear children; the *soma* is in the third heaven from here, bring it, and by this means redeem yourself.'[24]

Several new elements are incorporated into the epic version of this tale. Kadrū is presented as the mother of all supernatural snakes, while her sister (now named Vinatā rather than Suparṇī) is presented as the mother of the snakes' greatest enemy, the supernatural bird—Garuḍa:

> Long ago, in the age of the gods, faultless brahmin, there were two brilliant sisters, the daughters of Prajāpati, who were endowed with beauty and supernatural powers. These two, Kadrū and Vinatā, were both wives of Kaśyapa. Their husband Kaśyapa...gave a boon to these two lawful wives...Kadrū chose 1,000 Nāgas for her sons, all equal in brilliant energy (*tejas*). Vinatā chose two sons [Garuḍa and Aruṇa]....
>
> In the course of a great long time, Kadrū gave birth to 1000 eggs. Then Vinatā gave birth to two eggs, great Brahmin....
>
> Just at the appropriate time, Garuḍa was born—he who destroys snakes—and directly after his birth, he abandoned Vinatā and entered the sky. And when he was hungry, he ate the food [snakes] that was ordained for him by the creator, O tiger of the Bhṛgus.[25]

David Knipe notes that this story, as recontextualized by the epic redactors, now serves to reinforce the savage potential of the sovereign snakes, for as Kadrū gives birth to "1,000 Nāgas...all equal in brilliant energy," while Vinatā gives birth to only two sons, the Nāgas appear right from the start as an overpowering, multitudinous force.[26] Regardless of their numbers, however, the Nāgas are set up from the beginning to be overcome by Garuḍa, a contextualization that highlights the supernatural snake as chaotic yet ultimately defeatable.

As featured in the epic, Garuḍa attends to his task with zeal. For example, in one episode Garuḍa attempts to annihilate the Nāgas by flying them into the sun's rays, and they must rely on Indra to make it rain and thus effect their rescue.[27] Garuḍa's role is not without precedents, for the enmity between snakes and birds is mentioned as far back as the *Ṛg Veda*,[28] and both the *Atharva Veda*[29] and the *Gṛhya Sūtras*[30] mention a particular Garutmat (literally, one who has wings) who is depicted as a happy imbiber of poison in a hymn devoted to Takṣaka Vaiśāleya. The epic Garuḍa, who is also called Garutmat[31] and Suparṇa,[32] is lauded as a new and improved Indra: "There shall be another Indra among all the Gods, displaying heroism at will and coming and going as he pleases, who shall inspire fear in the king of the Gods."[33]

While the text explicitly states that no one is to exceed this bird in power, there is one group who exceeds him in authority, and that is the brahmins. Vinatā makes that point very clear to her son in the following statement: "Among all beings, a brahmin should never be killed, for a brahmin is like fire. An angry brahmin is a weapon, a poison, a sun, a fire. A brahmin is the first eater of all beings, the first of all classes, the father, the guru."[34]

As the epic story of Kadrū and Vinatā continues, we find the two sisters gambling as in the *Yajur Veda*. The epic redactors present a new twist, however, for this time Kadrū introduces her snake sons into the action, and as they fail to please her, she curses them. The mother of the snakes, and the earth herself, thus provides the catalyst for the snakes' genocide, as she decrees that they are to be burned in the *Sarpasattra* (snake sacrifice) ritual.

> The Bard said: But in that time, O ascetic, these two sisters saw the horse Uccaiḥśravas approach, that ultimate jewel

of a horse, born when the elixir was being churned, the one that all of the hosts of the gods revered, thrilled with happiness. It was the greatest of horses, best of the swift ones, splendid, never aging, divine, and marked with all the [auspicious] marks....[35]

Having observed that [horse], Kadrū said to Vinatā, 'My dear, what color is Uccaiḥśravas—judge without delay!' Vinatā said, 'This kingly horse is white, O beautiful one, or what do you think? Say the color and we'll wager on it.' Kadrū said, 'I think this horse has a black tail, bright-smiling one. Come wager with me for the prize of slavery, you hot-tempered thing.'

The Bard said: 'Having made this mutual agreement, through which one would be forced to become the slave [of the other], they returned to their homes saying, 'We will look tomorrow.' Then Kadrū, desiring to make her 1,000 sons crooked, ordered them to do the following: 'Become black tail-hairs so that I will not have to be a slave.' They did not follow her instructions so she cursed the snakes: 'The fire will burn you when the snake sacrifice of Janamejaya, the wise sage king of the Pāṇḍavas, takes place.'

The Grandfather [Brahmā] heard Kadrū's curse; a curse that was extremely cruel and exceeded what had already been fated. However, along with all the hosts of gods, he allowed the curse to stand, for having seen the multitude of snakes, he wanted to preserve all of the other creatures. Indeed, the snakes are tremendously powerful, they are biters (*dandaśūka*), and they are sharply and mightily poisonous (*tigmavīryaviṣa).* Because of their sharp poison, he [Brahmā] gave to the great-souled Kāśyapa,[36] knowledge of anti-poison for the benefit of all creatures.[37]

The fact that the earth itself is made to curse the snakes is a very clever strategy, for what better way to dethrone the earth's original sovereigns. Even more savvy, though, is the use of the late Vedic *Sarpasattra* ritual to effect the snakes' demise, for it allows the redactors an opportunity to invalidate the ritual tradition associated with the snakes. As we saw in the last chapter, the late Vedic *Sarpasattra* ritual is a sacrifice conducted by the snakes for their own benefit. In fact, it is as a result of the late Vedic *Sarpasattra* that the snakes became so wonderfully mighty and virile in the first place. However, as recontextualized in the epic, the *Sarpasattra* has taken a nasty turn—at least from the snakes' perspective—because rather than being a sacrifice *for* snakes as it was in the *Brāhmaṇas*, it is now a sacrifice *of* snakes.

While Kadrū's curse is the catalyst for the new *Sarpasattra*, we see in this passage that Brahmā lets it stand for one reason: to undo the results of the original *Sarpasattra*. This sense of reversal and undoing is achieved by the fact that almost exactly the same words are used here as in the original ritual, albeit with slight alterations. Thus, while the snakes were previously made *daṃśukā* and *daṃsuvīryā,* "biters and wonderfully mighty" it is now *because* they are *dandaśūkā* and *tigmavīryaviṣā*, "biters and sharply, mightily poisonous," that they are to be sacrificed. Moreover, the above passage implies that the Vedic *Sarpasattra* has not only backfired, as it has allowed for the proliferation of powerful, biting snakes, but now is completely useless in managing this multitude of snakes. For while the *Baudhāyana Gṛhya Sūtra* states that one should recite the list of the original snake officiates of the *Sarpasattra* in order both to praise the snakes and to protect oneself from snake-bite,[38] the last sentence of the above passage tells us that now the knowledge of anti-venom is one's only recourse. We will recall from chapter 3, moreover, that prescribing that one should merely recite the list rather than perform the entire ritual seemed to be a grass-roots intervention, for it allowed not just brahmins but rather anyone to benefit from the supernatural snake's protective propensities. Thus, the *Sarpasattra*, a ritual that in Vedic times allowed the snake to be both revered and managed, now becomes, through the medium of Kadrū's curse, a ritual in which the snakes are to be destroyed. And in one fell swoop, not only is the supernatural snake disempowered but so too is the snake worshippers' ritual tradition.

King Takṣaka and King Vāsuki: The Redactors Take Aim

Recontextualized from a noble figure to a savage figure who commits the sin of regicide, Takṣaka is the main target of the snake sacrifice:

> 'Takṣaka, the most vile of those who creep low, crazed with pride-of-strength, committed an evil act when he bit your father, protector of a lineage of sage kings, best of those who resemble the immortals. He killed the king and even turned back Kāśyapa—an evil act! Oh great king, you must burn this wicked thing in a flaming sacrificial fire, in a snake sacrifice.'[39]

In setting the scene for Takṣaka's "evil act," the redactors of the *Ādi Parvan* again borrow a ritual from the late Vedas, a ritual also designed both to revere and to control snakes. As stated in the *Śatapatha Brāhmaṇa*, the verses read: "And this red metal is neither iron nor gold, and these biting ones [divine snakes] are neither worms nor non-worms. Red metal is used because these biting things are reddish."[40] In the *Śatapatha Brāhmaṇa*, these verses serve to valorize the hybrid snake, whose divine yet reptilian nature transcends classification. In the *Ādi Parvan*, however, they are used to illustrate the transformational threat of the hybrid, as Takṣaka transforms himself into a worm the color of red metal and sequesters himself inside a piece of fruit in order to kill King Parikṣit, father of Janamejaya.

> As the king picked up the fruit, a worm appeared, O Śaunaka, tiny, black-eyed, and the color of red metal. Having grasped it, the king said to his ministers, 'The sun is setting, so I no longer fear death from poison today. But in order that the sage may have spoken truthfully, let this

> worm bite me, having become Takṣaka in name, so that a lie should be avoided.' His counselors, convinced by the timing, applauded him. And having spoken, this Indra of the kings, insensible and about to die, placed the worm on his neck and laughed. He was still laughing when Takṣaka encircled him with his coils....[41]

This attack on the transforming hybrid is repeated in two other Takṣaka-related stories. The first we have already seen, for it occurs as Takṣaka transforms himself into a wandering mendicant in order to steal the brahmin Utanka's guru gift.[42] The second story also occurs as Takṣaka takes on the form of a brahmin to fool a brahmin; and in this instance, he tricks the brahmin Kāśyapa into turning back from his mission to save Janamejaya's father, King Parikṣit.

> Takṣaka, the king of the snakes, having become an aged brahmin, spoke to Kāśyapa, bull among sages: 'Where are you going and what task do you wish to fulfill?' Kāśyapa said: 'Today, Takṣaka, chief of the snakes, will try to destroy the king with his fiery poison, the victorious King Parikṣit, who came forth from the family of the Kurus. I am going, good Sir, to heal the fever of the almighty king of the Pāṇḍava lineage, after he has been bitten by the king of the snakes, whose heat is equal to Agni.'[43] Takṣaka said, 'I am Takṣaka, O brahmin, and I will set that great king on fire. Turn back! You are not able to medically treat one that has been bitten by me.'[44]

This short passage perfectly exemplifies the narrative fate of the late Vedic snakes, for while Takṣaka remains a king, and in fact is referred to as such three times in the above passage, he is characterized as a malevolent force bent on deceit and destruction. Moreover, as the kingly snake consistently assumes the form of a brahmin for the sole purpose of blocking a brahmin's appointed task, the redactors characterize the kingly snake as one who corrupts the brahmins' dharma. Dharma is best defined here as one's religiously designated social duty, and it is said in the *Ādi Parvan* that the brahmin's dharma is "the paramount dharma known to all breathing things."[45]

In the passage below, Vāsuki convenes a king's council in order to discuss the *Sarpasattra*. Depicted in the late Vedas as both a devatā of the subterranean realm and a purifier of the earth's surface,[46] he loses this role in the epic. Unlike Takṣaka, however, Vāsuki is usually spared the vilification process imposed by the epic redactors. His brothers do not escape this fate as they are associated below with destruction and sacrilege. "Vāsuki said: You know, my blameless brothers, that a curse has arisen over us. Having taken counsel, let all of us join forces in order to free ourselves from this curse."[47] A discussion ensues that revolves around the merits of various plans concocted in order to free them from their present predicament, and their plotting reaffirms Brahmā's pronouncement as it emphasizes the fact that "they are biters (dandaśūkā) and they are sharply and mightily poisonous."[48]

> 'Or let the snakes bite the people at the Sacrifice, by the hundreds and thousands, so that there will be great terror. Or let the snakes defile the sacrificial food with urine and shit, which will destroy all the food....' There were other snakes there, righteous ones, who said, 'Let us grab hold of him [King Janamejaya] and bite him once, and it will be done. Once he is dead the root of our misfortunes is cut. This is the final judgment, with which we all agree.' And having spoken, they all looked at Vāsuki, king of the snakes.[49]

Myths—among other things—are models of reality, or in other words, they narratively reflect the actual aims of human actors. The above passages skewering Takṣaka and his brothers particularly illustrate this dynamic. In both passages, snakes, whose actual worship is perceived by brahmins to threaten their religious hegemony, are contextualized as obstacles to the brahmins' "paramount dharma" and defilers of the sacrifice—the centerpiece of Vedic orthodoxy.

Śeṣa/Ananta: The Supplantation of the Sovereign Snake

In order that the brahmins might supplant the sovereign snake, a mechanism had to be constructed through which the brahmins might interpose themselves between the snake kings and their worshippers. And for the redactors of the *Ādi Parvan*, this mechanism took the form of a new liminal being: a devout brahmin snake. Top of the line of this new model is Śeṣa. As Śeṣa does not appear at all in the Vedic texts, this set of passages offers the first look at this figure as well as the first etymology of the alternative name for Śeṣa: Ananta—"the one whose coils are *ananta* or endless."[50]

> Śaunaka said: 'So, those snakes had become mighty and inviolable, dear one. Now that the snakes know about this curse, what were they doing about it?'
>
> The Bard said: 'The greatly famous and blessed Śeṣa, having abandoned Kadrū, performed abundant austerities, for his vow was harsh and he ate the wind. Having gone to Mount Gandhamādana, he remained addicted to his austerities, and so too at Badari, Gokarṇa, the forests of Puṣkara, and the slope of the Himālayas. At each of these places, *tīrthas* and sanctuaries, where people made merit, he was solely devoted to his discipline and his senses were always conquered.'[51]

Śeṣa is so successful in his practice, however, that he generates too much *tapas* "inner heat" and is burning up the local populace. The god Brahmā thus attempts to woo him away from his excessive discipline with the promise of a boon.

> The Grandfather saw him practicing the ascetic's dreadful austerities, wearing bark and a knot of braided hair, with his flesh, skin, and tendons dried out. And the Grandfather spoke to the ascetic, whose motivation was sincere: 'Śeṣa, what are you doing? Act kindly toward all of the creatures, O faultless one. Due to your excessive asceticism, the creatures are being burned. Tell me, Śeṣa, what is your long-held, heart-felt desire?'

> Śeṣa said: 'All of my maternal brothers are dull-witted. I cannot bear to live with them. Sir, grant me this wish. Like enemies they are always angry. So I practice austerities so that I do not have to see them.... And having practiced austerities, I will release my body so that even in death I will not be reunited with them.'
>
> Brahmā said...'Choose a boon from me Śeṣa, whatever you desire. Indeed, I want to give a boon to you, for I am highly pleased with you. Luckily, your mind is set on dharma. May your mind be well-grounded in dharma to an even greater degree.'
>
> Śeṣa said: 'The boon that I desire, Grandfather, is this: Let my mind delight in dharma, in tranquility, and in austerities, my lord.'[52]

Śeṣa's choice of a boon allows him not only to be separated forever from his brothers but also to be enveloped fully within his ascetic discipline. Brahmā readily agrees to this but exacts a further price from Śeṣa.

> Brahmā said: 'I am pleased with the way you have tamed yourself and made yourself tranquil. Let your desire be fulfilled at my command, for the benefit of all creatures. This earth, covered with forests and mountains, with her oceans, jewel-mines, and people, Śeṣa, you must properly grasp this moving earth and stand so that it will be immobile.'
>
> Śeṣa said: 'Just as the boon-granting God Prajāpati says, I will bear the earth so that she is motionless. Place her on my head, Prajāpati, Lord of the Earth, Lord of the Creatures, Lord of the Universe....'
>
> The Bard said: 'Having made this speech and having entered the hole, he stands there, first-born of the snakes, Lord of the world. And having encompassed this ocean-encircled earth all around, he bears this earth—a Goddess—on his head. '

> Brahmā said: 'You are Śeṣa, the best of Nāgas, god of dharma. As the one whose coils are endless, you alone bear this earth, encompassing her completely just as Indra or I might do.'
>
> The Bard said: 'So, the glorious, endless Nāga lived under the ground, bearing the good earth alone as per the order of the omnipresent Brahmā. And the Grandfather, the Blessed Lord who is the best among the immortals, gave Suparṇa [Garuḍa] the son of Vinatā, to Ananta as a friend.'[53]

It is a particularly effective technique to use a snake to castigate the members of his own snake family as he denounces them as dull-witted, unremittingly angry, and so unbearably awful that he never again wants to see them, not even after death. Śeṣa highlights the destructive nature of the sovereign snake, as he is positioned as the exception that proves the rule. In fact, the name Śeṣa, from the verb root *śiṣ*—to remain, literally means 'the remainder' or that which is separated out from the rest. He is, moreover, the only one of his family never once referred to as a king or associated with autonomous sovereignty. Rather, this Nāga is constructed as a brahmin ascetic said to have *pariśuṣkamāṃsatvaksnayum,* literally, "flesh, skin, and tendons dried-out"—due to his severe austerities. Custom-designed, this brahmin snake demotes his sovereign brothers as he is consistently promoted over them.

The text further emphasizes Śeṣa's exalted status by stating that he is the "first-born of the snakes," thus granting him instant superiority regardless of the fact that his textual debut post-dates several of his brethren, such as Takṣaka Vaiśāleya, Vāsuki, and Dhṛtarāṣṭra Airāvata. However, Śeṣa's superiority extends only as far as other snakes, for just as Takṣaka is positioned in a subordinate role in relation to the Vedic god Indra, Śeṣa is positioned in a subordinate role in relation to the Vedic god Brahmā.

The redactors necessitate Śeṣa's subordination as his austerities are said to be causing "the creatures [to be] burned." Thus, while separated out from his brothers, he is likened to his brothers as he is portrayed as a threat to the local populace; a threat, moreover, which must be contained. Brahmā gives Śeṣa a hint as to the way in which his fierce energy might be contained: "May your mind be well-grounded in dharma to an even greater degree." In other words, be less of a snake and more of a brahmin. Śeṣa, ever compliant, follows-up on Brahmā's directive: "The boon that I desire Grandfather is this: Let my mind delight in dharma, in tranquillity, and in austerities, my lord." Thus, Śeṣa is not only recognized as a true brahmin ascetic and "god of dharma," but also rendered as a harmless, fully controllable being; so harmless that he is given Garuḍa, "the destroyer of snakes," as a friend and protector.

Having modified this snake into a submissive brahmin, Śeṣa is ready to fulfill one of the redactors' primary objectives: to insinuate a brahmin-like figure into the sovereign snake's usual role. This occurs not only as Śeṣa is made to bear the earth on his head with his coils "encompassing her completely," but also as an austerity-practicing brahmin snake is situated at a tīrtha. The idea of a snake or snakes encompassing the earth is hardly new. The *Sarpanāma* mantras from the *Śatapatha Brāhmaṇa* were chanted precisely in order to control the movement of the earth that *sarps*/glides because of the snakes within and around it,[54] while the *Sāmavidhāna Brāhmaṇa* and later the *Kauśika Sūtra* praised Vāsuki as the subterranean sovereign and purifier of the earth's surface.[55] However, as Śeṣa follows Brahmā's decree to "live under the ground, bearing the good earth alone," he is made to usurp Vāsuki's former role as subterranean sovereign and controller of the earth. This brahmin snake is thus singled out as the only snake in the text to retain a direct connection to the earth; a point highlighted within this passage as it is twice-stated that he bears this earth "alone." In relation to this point, Vogel notes the following: "It is obvious that in the *Mahābhārata* version of the myth the old world-snake has been strangely brahmanized: he has been made into a pious ascetic after the heart of the priestly compilators of the great epic."[56]

The redactors are careful, however, that their attempt to supplant the sovereign snake with a brahmin functionary might not be compromised. In other words, they take added precautions to guard against the possibility that Śeṣa might be perceived as an end in himself and confused with the "old world-snake," whose recognized sovereignty established him as an autonomous object of religious devotion. The redactors accomplish this objective as they bring up the snake's presence at "tīrthas" only to make Śeṣa unavailable to potential supplicants, for "[a]t each of these places, tīrthas and sanctuaries, where people made merit, he [Śeṣa] was solely devoted to his discipline and his senses were always conquered." The portrayal of an unavailable brahmin snake at these tīrthas is telling, for as discussed in the preceding chapter, tīrthas are historically linked to the worship of earth deities such as Nāgas.

> In mythology the nāga is, however, more often said to have control over the terrestrial rather than the celestial waters. In this capacity of the controller of the waters of the earth, the nāga is believed to abide in a pool, tank or cistern, or a specific portion of a river. These watery abodes are labeled tīrthas, an appellation no doubt coming from the Sanskrit root, *tṛī*, 'to cross' or 'to ford'.
>
> Within these pools and positions on rivers, the nāga might reside both in the mind of the worshipper and more concretely in the form of a statue. In both ancient and contemporary India, statues of nāgas are placed in cisterns, tanks, and pools. Vogel reports that one of the many nāga statues found near Mathurā bears a Brahmin inscription which translates, 'In the fortieth year, 40, of the king, king of kings Huviska...on this date...erected this nāga at their own tank. May the Lord Nāga be pleased.'[57]

The practice of worshipping Nāgas and other deities at tīrthas is not a foreign element in the *Mahābhārata*, for the *Tīrtha-Yatra Parvan* goes into great detail on this subject. In this *Parvan*, which extends for more than 70 sections,[58] we learn about not only all of the different tīrthas of the east, south, west, and north but also the benefits that accrue from bathing at these sites, such as the capacity to hear far-distant sounds, the knowledge of all the worlds, freedom from snake-bite, and, at the tīrthas called Nāgobheda and Sarpadarvī, the capacity to cross over to the Nāgaloka.[59] It would seem then, that in this section of the epic (a text, we will recall, that was redacted for as many as six centuries) the redactors are not attempting to suppress the worship of snakes and other earth deities. Rather, the redactors are comparing *tīrtha* worship to sacrificial rituals and lauding the former as a type of religiosity that might be more generally accessible to a broader range of people. "One might wish to sacrifice with the 'Praise of Agni' ritual[60] or with other rites that require extensive fees, yet not obtain the reward [that accrues] from visiting the tīrthas."[61]

The *Ādi Parvan*, as we know, displays a different orientation toward the worship of sovereign snakes; an orientation expressed as the redactors bring up tīrthas in order to introduce a brahmin snake into the sovereign snake's usual realm. Thus, having interposed a brahmin-like figure between the sovereign snake and its human supplicants, the redactors of the *Ādi Parvan* are well situated to infiltrate the snake's ritual domain.

Āstīka: The Incorporation of the Snake

While the supplantation of the sovereign snake with a brahmin-like snake positions brahmins to take a piece of the snake's ritual action, the incorporation of the snake positions them to fulfill another objective: to take a piece of the sovereign snake—the piece that is "*daṃsuvīrya*," wonderfully mighty and virile. The incorporation of the snake occurs as Jaratkāru, "best of the twice-born, beget[s] a brave and heroic son on an unmarried female of the same name,"[62] an unmarried female who is also a snake. The product of this union is the half snake, half brahmin Āstīka. Like Śeṣa, Āstīka appears for the first time in the *Ādi Parvan*, and these two figures are constructed as mirror images of each other, for while Śeṣa is a brahminicized Nāga, Āstīka is a nāganized brahmin. However, unlike Śeṣa, who has forsworn any kind of relations with his family members, Āstīka explicitly functions as "the salvation of the frightened snakes,"[63] as his ostensible raison d'être is to stop the annihilation of the snakes in the grisly *Sarpasattra.*

Āstīka's snake mother is none other than Vāsuki's sister, who, as fate has ordained, bears the name Jaratkāru. The story of Jaratkāru and the Nāgī princess[64] is an early literary example of a human/Nāgī inter-marriage. Another example from the *Mahābhārata* is that of Arjuna and the Nāgī princess Ulūpī.[65] Kālidāsa's *Raghuvaṃśa* also includes a Nāgī/human inter-marriage: the union of Kuśa and the Nāgī princess Kumudvatī.[66] Several *Jātaka* tales also preserve this theme, as in the *Bhūridatta Jātaka* with the marriage of a Nāgī princess and the exiled Prince Brahmadatta.[67] And the poet Guṇāḍhya, purported author of the *Bṛhatkathā*, is said himself to be the progeny of a mortal mother and a Nāga. All of these texts portray Nāgī women in a similar fashion: they are of royal heritage; they are fabulously beautiful and sexually irresistible; they have healthy sexual appetites and are often driven to find a mortal man in order to satisfy these cravings;[68] and they are forever fertile, often giving birth to a host of sons.

The association of Nāgas with human fertility begins in the *Ṛg Veda*, where the supernatural snake is constructed as a rainmaker and hence a controller of earthly fertility. It is the perception of the snake's control over life-giving waters—*rasa*—that leads to this further association with human fertility. Coomaraswamy notes, *rasa* is much more than mere water, rather it is "that essence (rasa) in the waters which is one with the sap in trees, with the amṛta or elixir of the devas, especially Agni, with the *soma*, and with the seed in living beings."[69]

The matrimonial union between a mortal and a Nāgī crosses the line from the mythological to the historical (a more or less invisible line in the context of Indian literature) as a large number of royal dynasties claim a Nāgī ancestress somewhere in their lineage. Having a Nāgī in one's genealogical history is seen as an exceptionally desirable thing, for it conveys not only a sense of sovereignty but also a promise of perpetual progeny. Thus as chronicled by Vogel, the kings of Udyāna (Swāt Valley), of Kashmīr, of Bhardarvāh, of Chutia Nāgpur, of Maṇipur (between Bengal and Myanmar), of Bastar and of Gonds (Central Provinces), of Cholas and Pallavas (Coromandel),[70] and also from as far afield as Cambodia and China all claim a Nāgī ancestress somewhere in their family tree.[71]

As we turn to the denouement of the *Āstīka Parvan*, namely, the *Sarpasattra*, the brahmin snake Āstīka is cast in the role of heroic savior; stopping the genocide of his mother's species in the nick of time. As noted by Christopher Minkowski, the text reveals the darkness of the *Sarpasattra* by describing it almost as a ceremony of black magic.[72]

> The performance unrolled in accordance with the precepts of a *Sarpasattra*. Each of the sacrificers went about their own task according to the rules. Having put on black robes and with eyes red from the smoke, they spoke the mantras and made the offerings into the fire. Then, they offered all of the snakes into the mouth of the fire, causing terror to roil in the minds of all those snakes. The snakes fell into the blazing fire, coiling around themselves, weeping, and crying out to each other. Falling heavily into the lustrous fire they died, trembling and hissing, writhing about with their heads and their tails. White, black, blue, old, and young, screeching horrible screams, they fell into the radiant flames. Hundreds of thousands and millions and tens of millions of snakes were destroyed completely against their own will.[73]

This is a horrific scene, as millions of snakes are burned alive. It has been prophesied, however, that a brahmin will save the snakes,[74] and Āstīka manages to evade the host of guards set up around the ritual grounds. Having penetrated this unholy precinct, he proceeds to praise the *Sarpasattra* of King Janamejaya with passion and eloquence. "Thus praised, all were soothed, the king, the *sadasyas*, the priests, and the offering fire."[75] The last is described as a particularly dynamic substance for it is said to have "golden-sperm" and to "eat all things."[76] Yet Āstīka's words work to tame this fire because he is the perfect man for the job: a half Nāga and half brahmin, who combines the elements of both the dynamic and the quiescent, and is thereby equal to the offering fire that combines "the cosmic/human power of fire and plant, Agni as life-maintaining, and *Soma* as life-transcending."[77]

King Janamejaya is so soothed by Āstīka's song of praise that he is about to grant him a boon. However, the *hotṛ* speaks up and reminds the king that Takṣaka has not yet arrived at the *Sarpasattra.*[78] As it turns out, Takṣaka is sequestered in the robe of Indra, for Indra has promised that he will hide Takṣaka from the flames. Indra's protection of Takṣaka enrages Janamejaya, and he orders both Tak ṣaka and Indra to be hurled into the fire. Having issued that order and flushed with his success, King Janamejaya grants Āstīka his boon.

> And when Takṣaka, the Indra of the Nāgas, was falling into the fire, at that moment, Āstīka spoke: 'Janamejaya, if you give me a boon, then I choose that your sacrifice should come to an end and no more snakes should fall.' This having been said, O brahmin, the king, son of Parikṣit, said to Āstīka, none too happily, 'Gold, silver, or cows, or any other treasure that comes to mind, O brahmin, will be given to you as a boon, but you should not stop my sacrifice.' Āstīka said, 'I do not choose gold, silver, or cows, O king. Your sacrifice must stop so that the race of our mother is maintained....' Then the *sadasyas*, who know the *Veda*, said altogether to the king, 'Let the brahmin take his boon.'[79]

And quite a boon it is, for in one fell swoop the hybrid Āstīka saves not only the Nāga King Takṣaka but many other Nāgas as well, for while "millions and tens of millions" of Nāgas have been killed, many more were left alive.

While Āstīka is able to save the most prominent among the snakes, such as King Takṣaka and King Vāsuki, the threat of a repeat performance hangs forever over their heads with only a brahmin positioned to stand between them and the destruction of their species. Given the redactors antipathy toward the snakes, it may seem odd that some of them, especially Takṣaka, are rescued at the very last minute. However, Takṣaka is the object of salvation that defines Āstīka as "the great dharma-minded" brahmin.[80] Seen in this light, the killing of snakes has only been a means to an end; a point the redactors' illuminate as Takṣaka's escape is hailed with "the joyous sounds of celebration."[81] The ultimate aim of the epic *Sarpasattra* is thus to save the snakes, for it positions the half snake, half brahmin Āstīka as the hero of the *Ādi Parvan*: "Greatly delighted, the king sent a highly honored Āstīka back to his home."[82]

Having positioned Āstīka as the heroic savior of the *Sarpasattra*, Āstīka is upheld as the new ideal: the mighty brahmin through whom the dynamic energy of the snake might be channeled to future brahminic generations. Brahmins are particularly in need of this energy, for as they are associated with ascetic life, they are liable to the withdrawal of procreational life force. The story of the brahmin Jaratkāru particularly highlights the problem of the non-dynamic, non-generative ascetic figure. The etymology of his name stems from the following: "*Jarā*, it is said, means 'wasting away,' and *kāru*, it is agreed, means 'frightful.' Thus, this wise man had a body that was wasted away, and it withered little by little."[83] Jaratkāru devotes his life to his ascetic practice with no thought toward the body, but only toward the spirit; and the idea of finding himself a wife and settling down is completely foreign to him. This behavior continues until one day he sees the following distressing scene: "his ancestors hanging face-down in a cave."[84] When Jaratkāru offers his assistance, they reply to him:

> 'You are an elderly celibate ascetic, and you desire to rescue us from here?! Indeed, religious austerities are not able to benefit us, this is the result of religious austerities, O preacher and friend. Our family line is broken, O brahmin, and we are falling into a foul hell!'[85]

Jaratkāru, prostrate with grief over the way in which his actions have affected his ancestors, promises to remedy the situation by marrying and producing an heir who might continue his family line. However, Jaratkāru artfully constructs a series of caveats into his agreement that would seem to preclude any possibility of its fulfillment; for he will only marry if a freely given, consenting virgin who shares the name of Jaratkāru presents herself.[86] But Jaratkāru has not counted on the strange merging of his destiny with that of the Nāgas; and the next thing he knows there is a freely-given, consenting virgin by the name of Jaratkāru standing on his door-step. The Nāgī Jaratkāru, Vāsuki's sister, is duly accepted by Jaratkāru, and their union produces the procreative/dynamic brahmin—Āstīka.[87]

The physical merging of these two species into the hybrid Āstīka acts as a link between two worlds: the physical and the metaphysical, the elemental and the spiritual, the dynamic and the quiescent. Āstīka is merely the first of this new model, for the text states that this new pattern of association between snakes and brahmins will be extended into future brahminic generations. "Having released the snakes from the *Sarpasattra*, the best of the brahmins, whose mind was suffused with dharma, went in the course of time to his destiny, leaving sons and grandsons behind him."[88] Thus, Āstīka solves the problem of the non-dynamic brahmin by transferring to him his capacity to be wonderfully heroic, powerful, and virile. This is made particularly clear in the following passage.

> A brahmin, as it is said in the highest sacred sources, is born to be gentle, knowledgeable of the Vedas and Vedic materials, and one who offers security to all beings. It is said that non-injury, truthfulness, and tolerance are without

> doubt, a higher dharma for a brahmin even than maintaining the Vedas.... Hear it from me Ruru, one who is dedicated to dharma, the ancient slaughter of the snakes by Janamejaya, and the rescue of those terrified snakes from his *Sarpasattra* came from a brahmin! One who possessed strength, heroism, and inner heat, and who had mastered the Vedas and Vedic materials—Āstīka, best of the brahmins.[89]

A brahmin, as defined here, is one who possesses "strength" and "heroism." This speech thus represents the crowning touch of a narrative objective in which brahmins, through the auspices of Āstīka, are made to incorporate the sovereign snake's heroic powers.

The redactors, however, are not quite through with Āstīka; for as he embodies the powers of the sovereign snake, he is positioned, like Śeṣa before him, to take over the sovereign snake's ritual role. This point is highlighted as the snakes, having been saved by Āstīka, grant him a boon.

> And the snakes said, 'Choose the boon that you most desire.' Āstīka said, 'All the brahmins and people in the world, with their minds at ease, should tell my tale of dharma morning and evening, and in so doing they should never have reason to fear you.'[90]

The recitation of the tale of Āstīka is now to be used as a ritual formula to ward off snakes. This is the third such formula we have encountered. The first, as we recall, was discussed in relation to the late Vedic *Sarpasattra*, and proclaims that the naming of the original snake officiates will effectively neutralize the snakes' mordacious tendencies as it calls up the snakes' heroic tendencies.[91] It would appear that this ritual, moreover, was custom-designed in order that it might be practiced by all people, not merely brahmins. This unrestricted ritual, one which maintains a respectful orientation toward the snakes, is twice-shifted by the epic redactors, both times to the detriment of both snakes and snake worshippers: first, as it is stated that anti-venom alone might counter-effect their inevitable damage,[92] and second, as it is stated here that the tale of a hybrid brahmin rather than that of heroic snakes is the new means that might control the snakes. The brahmin Āstīka is thus made to usurp the sovereign snakes' preestablished role as an object of religious devotion as the redactors dismantle the contextual framework centralizing the sovereign snake in order to use the pieces to construct their own: one in which the snake's supernatural powers and ritual practices are transferred to brahmins.

Conclusion: The Upside of the Downtrodden Snake

The supernatural snake's sovereign role vis-à-vis the earth and her natural processes, one that was established by snake worshippers and preserved in the late Vedic texts, is consistently encroached upon in the *Ādi Parvan.* While still associated with the atmospheric elements, the snakes have lost their power to control water, the primary power for which they are worshipped. The severing of their place-names also has important ramifications from this perspective, for it removes the snakes from a direct association with a particular regional area and, more importantly, its inhabitants. The redactors also strive to invalidate snake-centered ritual practices; and when not invalidating the snake's ritual tradition, the redactors are reconfiguring it to position a brahmin or a brahmin-like figure as the reverential object. Thus, using context as a weapon to dethrone, supplant, and incorporate the snakes and their associated ritual practices, the redactors of the *Ādi Parvan* launch a narrative assault directed toward stamping out a rival tradition of snake worship and simultaneously elevating brahmins and brahminically sanctioned forms of worship.

As the redactors of the *Ādi Parvan* attempt to coopt the snake's powers and ritual practices in order to elevate Brahminism, however, they also end up preserving important pieces of information that speak to the evolution of this grass roots tradition. For example, it is in the *Mahābhārata* that we first here of the Nāgaloka, the "natural habitat" of the snakes. Additionally, the term Nāga comes to be standardized in this text, thus reflecting the importance of the supernatural snake's hybrid nature. Finally, we see a fully anthropomorphized Nāga in the *Ādi Parvan* as Takṣaka is capable of transforming himself into a human being at will. Thus, as the redactors highlight the supernatural snake as a religious rival, they also preserve elements of this tradition that contribute to our understanding of snake worship during these centuries.

Just because a figure is demonized within one narrative context does not mean that it is forever fixed in that role. In fact, the preceding pages have demonstrated how a character's image will shift as the details through which it is contextualized are shifted. If we look outside of the *Ādi Parvan*, we find that Śeṣa's image has undergone just such a reversal of contextual fortunes. For while the redactors of the *Ādi Parvan* restrict Śeṣa's role to that of a brahminicized snake subordinate to Brahmā, a recent ethnography reports that Śeṣa has been shifted out of that role for the following reason: to function as an independent, accessible earthly sovereign, propitiated to facilitate the digging of a foundation, which in turn is thought to ensure prosperity for the family.

> *yadi śeṣnāg ke sir par khudvāve, to mātā-pitā ki hāni hoy aur pīṭh par*
> *khudvāve, to bhay rog pīṛā ho, pū̃ch par khudvāve, to tīn gotra kī hāni*
> *hove aur jo khālī jagaj par khudvāve, to strī, putra, dhan ityādi kā lābh ho.*

> If one digs over Śeṣnāg's head, there will be harm to one's parents; and if one digs over the back there will be fear, disease, and pain; and if one digs over the tail there will be harm to the three *gotras*.[93] But whoever digs over an empty space will obtain the benefits of wife, sons, and wealth.[94]

Gloria Goodwin Raheja recorded the preceding verses in her 1977 to 1979 study of the North Indian village, Pahansu. In relation to this study, she states the following:

> In order to determine exactly where the digging and the placing of the foundation stone should be done, the position of Śeṣnāg beneath the earth...is mapped onto the plot of land on which the house is to be built. During each three-month period, Śeṣnāg moves ninety degrees clockwise, and the 'empty space,' where the digging should always be done, changes accordingly. The consequences of not taking the movements of Śeṣnāg into account are generally thought of, by ordinary villagers, in terms of failure to produce offspring, particularly sons.[95]

In this recontextualization of Śeṣa, the villagers of Pahansu have reassigned the *Ādi Parvan's* "god of dharma," to Vāsuki's late Vedic role, for as presented in the *Sāmavidhāna Brāhmaṇa,* as well as in the *Gobhila Gṛhya Sūtra,* it is Vāsuki who is to be invoked during a *Vāstupraśamana*, literally, a ceremony specifically designed to insure a solid foundation for a new house.[96] Thus, while the redactors of the *Ādi Parvan* seem to have been somewhat successful in displacing Vāsuki as an independent deity worthy of propitiation, they were less successful in restricting Śeṣa to his brahminic role, as this popular narrative reconfigures him as an accessible, autonomous sovereign.

Given the *Ādi Parvan's* narrative agenda, it is unlikely that this recontextualization would have found favor with the redactors. But to give the redactors of the *Ādi Parvan* their due, it is difficult to suppress a centuries-old tradition that centralizes an accessible sovereign figure perceived to be responsive to the needs of the general populace. And while the Buddhist-Hybrid text of chapter 6 celebrates this figure, the Buddhist Pāli texts of chapter 5 once again use context as a weapon to wage war against the snake in the grass roots movement.

5

The Pāli Texts: The Buddhist Redactors [c]Harm the Snake

As we continue to traverse the Indian religious landscape, we leave Hinduism in order to explore the great ascetic movement that emerged in the 5th century BCE: Buddhism.[1] In this chapter, we will focus on two of the early Buddhist texts, the *Mahāvagga* and the *Jātaka Tales.* Both of these texts belong to the canon preserved by the Theravādin School,[2] the entirety of which is written in Pāli, a literary language deriving from western India. These Pāli texts share the same orientation toward the supernatural snake as the *Ṛg Veda* and the *Ādi Parvan*: they work to subordinate the snake in order to transfer its powers to alternative figures. While both the *Ṛg Veda* and the *Ādi Parvan* attempted to subordinate the snake in order to elevate brahmins and the gods of brahminic Hinduism, these Pāli texts attempt to subordinate the snake in order to elevate the Buddha.

While there at one time may have been several different canons belonging to different Buddhist schools, each claiming to encompass best the words of the Buddha, only one, that preserved in Pāli by the Theravādins, exists in its entirety. Divided into three major parts or Piṭakas, the Pāli canon consists of the Sutta Piṭaka, "basket of discourses," the Vinaya Piṭaka "basket of discipline," and the Abhidhamma Piṭaka "basket of analytic principle." The *Mahāvagga*, literally, the 'Great Division,' is part of the *Vinaya Pi ṭaka* of the Pāli canon.[3] The *Vinaya Piṭaka* is primarily devoted to issues relating to the Buddhist community or *saṃgha*, i.e. monastic discipline, social organization, rituals of initiation, regulations governing rain retreats, etc. The rules relating to these issues are presented in the form of anecdotes, and all are attributed to the Buddha. The classical *Vinaya Piṭaka* preserved by the Theravādins probably takes on its present form in Sri Lanka by the beginning of the common era.[4]

The *Jātaka Tales* form part of the Sutta Piṭaka of the Pāli canon. While the Vinaya Piṭaka was particularly concerned with monastic discipline, the Sutta Piṭaka focuses not only on the teachings of the Buddha but also on the lives of the Buddha and his disciples. The *Jātaka Tales* encompass a collection of approximately 500 stories relating the incidents that transpired during the Buddha's previous lives. The verse portions of each tale are considered to be canonical, while the prose portions are considered to be non-canonical commentaries.[5] There is also a long introduction to the *Jātaka* commentaries known as the *Nidānakathā* that is primarily a biography of the Buddha. The *Jātaka* tradition appears to take on something like its present form in Sri Lanka sometime between the beginning of the Common Era and the 5th century CE.

As noted by Andrew Skilton, the canonical texts preserved by these various Buddhist schools "probably reflected the particular concerns and practices of the community that retained them."[6] The Theravādins, the preservers of the Pāli texts, are likely to have formed in the mid-third century BCE. They are a conservative school and proclaim themselves to be the guardians of orthodoxy. As such, the canon they retained is concerned not only with establishing the bounds of right teaching and right practice but also with presenting a particular image of the Buddha: that of an extraordinary man but a man rather than a transcendent being, nevertheless. As we look at the *Mahāvagga* and the *Jātaka Tales*, moreover, it becomes evident that the members of this school are also concerned with how to recruit converts to Buddhism in the midst of a great deal of ideological competition. For during this time, these early Buddhists had to contend with not only competing ascetic movements from the brahminic as well as the Jain traditions but also Nāga worship.

Given the fact that the supernatural snake has been revered as an object of religious devotion from as early as the Vedas, it is not very surprising that these Pāli redactors might feel the need to grapple with this figure as they attempt to disseminate the Buddha's teachings, establish an institutional framework, and gain converts. And like the epic redactors, the Pāli redactors are masters of contextual manipulation. In other words, context is the narrative strategy they use to divest the snake of the elements pertinent to its role as an object of religious devotion, such as the ability to protect humans from dangerous snakes, to make rain, and to purify the earth. As we have seen throughout previous chapters, however, when the redactors engage in this process of negative contextualization, they do so not only to stamp out the snake as a religious rival but also to coopt the snake's powers in order that they might be transferred to their chosen champion[s]. In the case of these Buddhist texts, such champions include the Buddha as well as various Buddhist saints or "arhats."

The redactors enact this process by contextualizing the supernatural snake as a malevolent figure; one that is made to use its supernatural powers exclusively for purposes of destruction. And, once the destructive snake has been conquered and rendered impotent, its former powers are magically conferred upon the Buddha and his saints. Thus, using a one-two punch, the redactors of these Pāli texts demonize the supernatural snake in order to justify their cooptation of the snake's powers.

As a final touch to insure the Buddha's superiority, the supernatural snake is incorporated into the Buddhist hierarchy either as a convert or as a tutelary deity charged with guarding the Buddha, the latter strategy reminiscent of the *Ādi Parvan's* use of the tamed, brahminicized Nāga, Śeṣa. The redactors of the Pāli texts incorporate the snake into the Buddhist framework in an attempt to carry out the following objectives: first, to sustain the Buddha's presence on this earth as the incorporated snake memorializes the absent Buddha; second, to prove Buddhism's superiority over other religious practices, especially those that revere the sovereign snake as an object of worship; and third, to gain converts, for the incorporation of figures, sites and rituals from a grass-roots tradition may sometimes provide a means for incorporating worshippers into more institutionalized forms of religiosity such as the nascent tradition of Buddhism.[7]

Thus, while concerned with myriad issues, these texts clearly document a struggle between two competing forms of religiosity: Buddhism and Nāga worship. And as such, they demonstrate a contest over which system of values is to be granted preeminent status, that associated with the Buddha's teachings or that associated with the experiences and desires of Nāga worshippers. This struggle between the Buddha and the supernatural snake has an interesting side-effect, moreover, for while the redactors are subordinating the supernatural snake in order to transfer its powers to the Buddha and his arhats, they are also preserving, while usually denigrating, a number of snake-centered ritual practices. To best view the process of demonization, cooptation, and incorporation by which these Pāli redactors attempt to subjugate the supernatural snake, we will focus on four snake figures that will reappear in our discussion of another Buddhist text, the *Mahāvastu*, in chapter 6: the Nāgarāja of Uruvelā, the Nāgarāja Kāla, the Nāgarāja Mucalinda, and the Nāgarāja Campeyya.

The Demonization of the Sovereign Snake: The Nāgarāja of Uruvelā

In each of the texts that we have examined, the supernatural snake is portrayed as a sovereign, and this holds true in the Pāli texts in which the supernatural snake is first and foremost a Nāgarāja or Nāga king. I would argue that the Buddhist redactors maintain the supernatural snake as such in order to be absolutely clear about who they are demonizing, coopting, and incorporating: the central figure within a rival tradition of worship that poses a particular threat as it is supernaturally powerful, always accessible, and open to all who would propitiate it.

The redactors' desire to subordinate the supernatural snake and thereby effect a hierarchy in which the Buddha is made superior first manifests itself as they portray the supernatural snake as both malevolently intentioned and instantaneously destructive. Its destructive capacity extends beyond its ability to deliver a poisonous bite, for while the epic snake was afflicted with a fear of fire, some Pāli snakes are portrayed as masters of fire, a fire that is somehow generated from the supernatural snake's venom. For example, in the *Ghatāsana Jātaka*, the Nāga King Caṇḍa is depicted as one who intends to burn up a flock of birds with his flames merely because they had the temerity to shit in his pool. The name Caṇḍa, moreover, serves to emphasize the redactors' characterization of this figure, for it literally means violent or fierce.

This antagonistic pairing of Nāgas and birds is a familiar motif from the Hindu texts, which hailed Vinatā's son, Garuḍa, the enemy of snakes, as "another Indra among all the gods, displaying heroism at will and coming and going of his own accord."[8] While there was one and only one Garuḍa in the *Ādi Parvan*, however, the redactors of the Pāli texts create a whole new species of garuḍa birds solely devoted to fighting the malevolent Nāgas. Both the Buddha and his arhats will sometimes transform themselves into these birds to protect humans and other creatures from the snakes. For example, the *Bakabrahma Jātaka* depicts the Nāgarāja of the Ganges as a flesh-eater who tries to eat two raftsmen. In order to save them, an arhat transforms himself into a garuḍa to frighten away the predator. In both the *Ghatāsana* and *Bakabrahma Jātakas*, the Nāgarāja, like Vṛtra, maintains control over watery places and threatens any creature who might trespass upon its territory. Therefore, as both the Buddha and his arhats effectively neutralize this character, they, like Indra, are portrayed as heroic saviors.

Nowhere is this theme of the malevolent but ultimately defeatable Nāga more evident than in the story of the Nāgarāja of Uruvelā from the *Mahāvagga*, in which the Buddha encounters a malicious Nāga king, who, again, goes by the name of Caṇḍa. It is said in the prologue that this encounter takes place directly after the Buddha finishes his first sermon at the Deer Park of Sārnāth on the outskirts of Banāras.

> At that time there were three brahmin ascetics,[9] brothers, who lived at Uruvelā and were the leaders of several hundred ascetics. The Buddha, having arrived at the hermitage, spoke to Kassapa, the eldest brother. 'If it is not troublesome for you, Kassapa, allow me to spend one night inside the house where the sacred fire is maintained.' Kassapa answered, 'It is not troublesome for me, Great Monk; however, there is a tremendously potent Nāga king in there whose poison is sharp and terrible. So it would be better not to let him harm you.'
>
> [The Blessed One made his request to Kassapa a second and third time until finally, Kassapa agreed.]
>
> Then the Blessed One, having entered the place that housed the sacred fire, made a mat of grass and leaves and sat down, keeping his back erect, intending to immerse himself in mindfulness. The Nāga, seeing that the Blessed One had entered, became unhappy and aggravated and produced a cloud of smoke. The Blessed One thought, 'What if I were to overcome the fire of that Nāga with my fire, but without injuring his skin, hide, flesh, ligaments, bone marrow, or bones.' Then, the Blessed One through his successful accumulation of miraculous power produced a cloud of smoke. And the Nāga, unable to endure his own anger, blazed up. The Blessed One, having obtained the element of fire, also blazed up. Then the ascetics surrounded the sacrificial fire hut and said, 'Indeed friends, the great monk looks lovely, but he will be harmed by that Nāga.' That night having passed, the Blessed One, without injuring the skin, hide, flesh, ligaments, bone, or bone marrow of that Nāga, and having overcome the Nāga's fire with his fire, threw the Nāga into his alms bowl and showed him to the brahmin

> ascetics: 'Here is the Nāga, Kassapa; his fire has been overpowered by my fire.' Then the ascetic Kassapa of Uruvelā thought, 'That great monk has great magical power and great majesty since he is able to overcome the fire of the Nāga King Caṇḍa with his fire, for that poisonous, fanged snake is magically powerful and terrible. However, he [the Buddha] is still not as saintly as I am.'[10]

Several aspects of the characterization of the Nāga of Uruvelā stand out in this tale. First, while the redactors emphasize the reptilian nature of the Nāga by depicting him as "a poisonous, fanged snake," they nevertheless call him a Nāga king. As noted, the Buddhist redactors have a very specific religious rival in mind; a rival whom the redactors are attempting to supplant with the Buddha and his arhats. Moreover, the illustration of this story on a bas-relief situated over the eastern gate at Sāñchi portrays the Nāga specifically as a multi-hooded cobra. It is possible to correlate this story with the bas-relief at Sāñchi because of the similarities in content such as the presence of fiery flames shooting through the roof of a small structure, the three figures with matted hair standing off to one side representing the brahmin ascetics, the presence of grass huts, and of course, the snake. [11] Thus, while the Hindu tradition allows the supernatural snakes a range of forms as they are variously "black," "striped-across," "adder[s]," and "viper[s],"[12] "some tiny like mice, others fat like elephant trunks,"[13] as well as a range of signifiers and personas, the Buddhist tradition, through both its texts and artistic representations, refines this figure down to a single persona—a king—a single signifier—a Nāga—and a single species—a cobra.[14] Given the specific targeting of this figure, I would speculate that the tradition of snake worship with which these Buddhist redactors were most familiar was one that centralized cobras specifically as objects of religious devotion.

The last line of this story gives us two interrelated reasons why the Nāga is contextualized as an evil character: first, to demonstrate the Buddha's superior powers; and second, to gain potential converts to the Buddha's community. In relation to the first goal, the defeat of the Nāga king allows the Buddha to display his superior magical skills and thereby establish his right to a superior status in relation to this supernatural snake. Since these texts herald the Buddha as an extraordinary man but not as a transcendent figure (a task left for the redactors of the *Mahāvastu*), the establishment of the Buddha's earthly power and authority is one of their essential objectives. The Buddha's demonstration, moreover, is not merely that of an extraordinary man overcoming a supernatural snake; rather, it is portrayed as the force of dharma overcoming the potentially destructive forces of nature. Thus, as the *Ādi Parvan* does for the figure of Āstīka, stories such as these position the Buddha as the better natural sovereign who governs the natural world in accordance with dharma.[15]

The structure of this tale duplicates the pattern in the *Ṛg Veda,* which configured Vṛtra as an evil snake in order that he might be righteously overcome by Indra. This allows Indra to demonstrate not only his superior might but also his legitimate right to take over the powers with which Vṛtra is endowed. Unlike Indra, however, the Buddha cannot fight the Nāga king as a warrior, for as the Pāli canon places a high value on *ahiṃsā,* or non-injury, it would be counter-productive in the extreme to have the Buddha engage in the same destructive behavior as the Nāga. Thus, the actual flames that the Buddha shoots forth are differentiated from those of the Nāga, as they emanate from the fiery purification of his own bodily substances—his *tejo-dhātuṃ*—rather than from the destructive force of the snake's dreadful venom.

Along these same lines, the redactors take great pains to show that while the Buddha might have overcome the Nāga, he has not hurt him. The text states twice that the Buddha has vanquished the Nāga "but without injuring his skin, hide, flesh, ligaments, bone marrow, or bones," merely breaking the Nāga's spirit rather than his body with his superior display. Despite these minor adjustments, the Buddha's display allows him to be associated with the powers of the supernatural snake, a result that Andrew Rawlinson notes, "naturally gives rise to the Buddha as the ultimate magical being: a mahānāga...."[16]

The second reason why this text configures the Nāga as an evil character is that in defeating it and thereby protecting the local populace, the Buddha might impress potential converts to his community, not only snake worshippers but also those engaged in alternative ascetic traditions. Kassapa is the leader of a group of brahmin ascetics, and during this time period, Brahminism along with Jainism were two competing ascetic traditions with which Buddhism had to contend. Kassapa and his followers would need five more miracles before they would be induced to acknowledge the Buddha's superiority. The defeat of the Nāga, however, was the first of these miraculous acts and was obviously considered to be both a heroic and a death-defying feat.[17]

Given this proselytizing emphasis, it is no coincidence that the action takes place in the brahmins' sacrificial hut, the sacred space that houses the brahmin's sacrificial fire. As the Nāga has usurped this sacred place prior to the entry of the Buddha, moreover, the redactors have established a hierarchy of religious traditions in which the Nāga (the central figure in snake worship) overcomes the sacrificial hut (the central space of brahminical Hinduism) while the Buddha overcomes both. The contextual set-up for the defeat of the Nāga is important, for it occurs as the Nāga is made to languish within a primary symbol of the Buddhist tradition—the Buddha's alms bowl, the object most emblematic of the Buddhist vow of poverty and humility. The redactors' use of this bowl as well as their use of the brahmins' sacrificial hut represent brilliant maneuvers in the game of contextual strategizing. For in positioning the Nāga king as having subjugated a primary symbol of Brahminism, the hut, while being subject to a primary symbol of Buddhism, the bowl, the redactors effect their ideological hierarchy with a marvelous economy of detail.

The theme of ideological competition is thus played out in two directions in this story, not only as the Buddha takes on the Nāga in order to convert a whole hermitage full of ascetics but also as the demonization and subsequent defeat of this figure allows the Buddhist redactors to elevate Buddhist practices over those which revere the Nāga. The demotion of snake worship also occurs as the supernatural snake is presented here not as a protector of humans as the late Vedas would have it, but rather as one to be protected against. As noted by Gombrich, "we can surmise that just as Buddhism was competing with brahminism and with other groups of renunciates, it was competing with Nāga worship."[18]

While competing with "Nāga worship," however, the redactors are also using the Nāga, for they do not reject this figure out of hand but rather place it in a religious hierarchy in which the Buddha figures first. It would seem that as the redactors incorporate the supernatural snake into the Buddhist symbolic framework, they are hoping to impress and thereby incorporate not only brahmin ascetics but also those who worship the supernatural snake, the idea being that as this symbol is incorporated so too are those that revere this symbol.[19]

While the other snake stories presented in this chapter are explicit in their incorporation and subsequent use of the supernatural snake, this story's incorporative gesture is very subtle: the Nāga of Uruvelā is captured yet preserved by the Buddha's superior prowess, thus demonstrating that an ascetic tradition dedicated to non-injury might nevertheless quell and contain a destructive nature god. It is in the artistic rendering of this story that we see a related use of the incorporated snake, for the presence of this figure helps to overcome a problem in the artistic representation of the Buddha: the need to highlight the Buddha's absence while recalling his time here on earth.

Stories such as the Nāga of Uruvelā were illustrated in plastic representation throughout India, with correlations between narrative and representation discernible through specific overlaps in content. The Buddha, however, is rarely shown in these artistic renderings. This is because after his *parinirvāṇa*,[20] it is ideologically maintained that his presence is best marked by his absence. This is understandable given the fact that the early Buddhist sects were trying to establish a new soteriological goal—one of full dispersal into everything—in the face of a dominant religious sensibility that predicated reincarnation as the natural follow-up to death. Given this soteriological agenda, the Buddha is indicated not by his likeness but by certain symbols such as a throne or a cakra.[21] In fact, in the previously discussed bas-relief at Sāñchi depicting the story of the Nāga of Uruvelā, the Buddha's presence is marked only by a stone seat situated in the center of the panel along with flames of fire generated, presumably, by the Buddha's ascetically-produced *tejas.* Given this fact, Buddhist ideologues were obviously in need of a way to maintain and to personalize the figure of the Buddha in the minds of worshippers. The Nāga may have offered a partial solution to this problem for, along with the cakra and the throne, the Nāga king provided another symbol by which the Buddha's supremacy might be commemorated.

The Sovereign Snake Becomes a Tutelary Deity: The Nāgarāja Kāla and the Nāgarāja Mucalinda

Having contextualized some Nāgarājas as evil beings who might be heroically overcome, the Buddhist redactors contextualize another set of Nāgarājas as benign and subservient beings who might be more readily and usefully incorporated. Along with the demonized Nāgarāja, then, the redactors of the Pāli texts also construct the disempowered Nāgarāja who is foolish, weak, and timid. For example, the *Kharaputta Jātaka* tells of a Nāga king who is so powerless as to be cowed and subsequently beaten by some village boys. In the *Paṇḍara Jātaka*, an unscrupulous ascetic in league with a Garuḍa tricks the gullible Nāga King Paṇḍara into spilling the secret of how he might best be caught. The *Bhūridatta Jātaka*,a wonderfully rich tale, tells the story of the Nāga King Bhūridatta, who is captured by the greedy snake charmer Ālambāyana. It is said in the tale that Nāgas always scan the crowd to see if there is a Garuḍa in attendance, and if they see one they will be too afraid to dance.

Snake charmers appear regularly in these tales and operate as a means by which the redactors humble the Nāga. As noted by Andrew Rawlinson, the literal translation for this occupation (*ahi-tuṇḍika*) combines *ahi* "snake" and *tuṇḍika*, from the verb root *tuṇḍ* "to hurt"; the meaning is clearly not snake charmer but snake harmer. Rawlinson goes on to report that snakes, at the hands of the *ahi-tuṇḍikas*, "are severely mistreated....Their bones are crushed [and they]...[are] treated in deliberately ignominious ways [such as being] worn as a turban."[22] Thus, in contrast to the late Vedas, which present the snakes themselves as the first masters of snakes, literally, *sarpavids* "snake-knowers," who then pass on their knowledge for the benefit of all,[23] the Pāli texts have depicted the *sarpavid* as the *ahi-tuṇḍika* whose role is not to know snakes but rather to harm snakes.

The Nāga King Kāla, like the Nāga of Uruvelā, is a character who will reappear in a much more full-bodied fashion in the *Mahāvastu*. The Pāli texts, however, portray him as a fearful being who, along with the Hindu gods Indra and Brahmā, cannot withstand the presence of Māra and his army.[24] Thus, although he has been charged with protecting the Bodhisattva[25] (the soon to be Buddha) on the eve of his enlightenment, Kāla nevertheless runs away to the Nāgaloka leaving the Bodhisattva to face Māra on his own. The following is from the *Nidānakathā*, the prologue to the *Jātaka Tales*.

> Kāla, the Nāgarāja, stood there uttering his praises [to the Bodhisattva] that were several hundred verses long....But as the army [of Māra] approached...Kāla, the Nāgarāja, having dived into the earth, went to his palace, Mañjerika, where he covered his face with his hands. [26]

The figure of Kāla represents another modulation in the contextualization of the Nāgarāja, for while the Nāga has been both demonized and disempowered, the redactors portray him here as a tutelary deity and devoted follower of the Bodhisattva, singing verse after verse of praise in his honor. This portrayal of Kāla also points to the redactors' recognition that Nāgas can transform into human shape, for this Nāga has hands. This contextual detail, however, is used to highlight not the Nāga's magical abilities but rather his cowardly behavior. For instead of protecting the Bodhisattva at this crucial moment, the Nāga King Kāla is portrayed as both a weak and impotent figure; one who runs away from his tutelary post and shame-faced, "covered his face with his hands."

One of the most famous stories pairing the Buddha and a Nāga, and one that further exemplifies the characterization of the Nāga as a humble yet devoted subordinate, features the Nāgarāja Mucalinda. In this tale from the *Mahāvagga*, the Nāgarāja Mucalinda shelters the newly enlightened Buddha from rain and winds.

> At the end of a week, the Blessed One, having arisen from the state of *samādhi*, went from the foot of the Ajapāla tree to the foot of the Mucalinda tree. And having reached it, he spent one week there, sitting with his legs crossed and experiencing the happiness of emancipation.
>
> But at that time, a great black cloud arose out of season, and for seven days in a row, there was bad weather—cold, wind, and rain. Then the Nāga King Mucalinda, having come forth from his palace, surrounded the body of the Blessed One seven times with his coils, and having extended his great hood above his [the Blessed One's] head, he thought to himself: 'Let not cold [touch] the Blessed One, nor heat [touch] the Blessed One, nor the biting mosquitoes, wind, hot air, or crawling things touch the Blessed One.'
>
> Then at the end of the week, when the Nāga King Mucalinda found the sky free of rain clouds, he unwrapped his coils from the body of the Blessed One. And changing his own appearance in order to manifest the appearance of a young man, he positioned himself before the Blessed One, lifting his folded hands as a token of respect, and venerated the Blessed One.[27]

The redactors certainly make use of the fact that it is a cobra, specifically, with which they are grappling, for it is the cobra's hood that allows the Nāga king to be contextualized here as a tutelary deity—one that is capable of protecting the Buddha from the wind and rain. As a faithful servant, moreover, the Nāga is called upon to protect the Buddha from the very forces of nature for which the Nāga stands. Vogel notes this strangeness with the following: "It is certainly curious that the great Nāga Mucalinda, instead of withholding the showers of rain which threaten the Buddha with discomfort, has to sit up for a whole week and to use his body as an umbrella."[28] In portraying the Nāga in such a way, however, the Pāli redactors have constructed a figure that is no longer efficacious as an object of worship, for the Nāga king has lost the very powers that elevated him to a deified status in the first place.

While the Nāga is portrayed as having lost these powers, the Buddha and his arhats are portrayed as having gained them, for just as the Buddha bested the Nāga of Uruvelā's fiery powers, the Buddha and his arhats become associated with the Nāga's watery powers. Thus, at Bharhut, Gandhāra, Ajaṇṭā, and Sārnāth the Buddha is depicted with streams of water gushing out of both the upper and lower parts of his body. Reginald Ray writes that "the association of the Buddhist saints with rain and storm is not atypical, particularly through their frequent connection with and power over the Nāgas, who control rain and storm."[29] Thus, it would seem that these early Buddhists are attempting to transfer worshippers' allegiance from the Nāga to the Buddha by transferring over one of the primary powers for which the Nāga is worshipped: the power to make rain. This occurs as the Buddha and his saints are depicted both as rainmakers and as controllers of the original rainmaker, the Nāga.

In the above passage, the redactors associate the Nāga King Mucalinda with a Mucalinda tree, an association not made in later versions of this story. And in fact, this story as told in the *Mahāvagga* is located among several other stories that situate the

Buddha at the foot of a particular type of tree.[30] In relation to the Nāga King Mucalinda and the Mucalinda tree, Vogel notes "there is some connexion between the Nāga Mucalinda and the tree of the same name under which the Buddha was seated. May we perhaps assume that in the ancient story the Nāga was conceived as a tree-spirit?"[31] The supernatural snake is often associated with the Yakṣa, a tree-dwelling deity who is also connected with water and fertility. In fact, this connection between the supernatural snake and the Yakṣa occurs as early as the *Atharva Veda*,[32] and the Nāga is specifically mentioned alongside the Yakṣa in the *Āśvalāyana Gṛhya Sūtra*—one of the first times, we will recall, that the term Nāga is used by redactors to signify a supernatural snake.[33] While the Nāga is historically linked with this tree-dwelling deity, however, the Nāga is never actually conceived of as such, and so it is unlikely that the two figures are being conflated here.[34] The Nāga king is more probably associated here with a *caitya,* a sacred site devoted to the worship of Nāgas that is usually marked by either a pool or a tree surrounded by a railing. I would argue that the redactors here are attempting to resignify such sites as sacred places devoted not to Nāga worship but to Buddhism, a strategy that the redactors of the *Ādi Parvan* applied to Śeṣa and *tīrthas*.[35]

As Mucalinda is conscripted as a tutelary deity, the Nāga king is forced to remain present with the Buddha. Lowell Bloss argues that in the visible depiction of this popular deity side-by-side with the Buddha, Buddhist ideologues may have found a means of reaching an audience that was not naturally inclined toward the meditative and otherworldly nature of the Buddha.[36] The earliest plastic rendition of this story appears on a piece of sculpture from Sāñchi in which an anthropomorphized Nāga with five hoods extending from the back of his neck is pictured in front of a tree. The Buddha's presence is marked by an empty seat situated in front of the tree. [37] At Amarāvatī, the Buddha is shown sitting cross-legged on top of the coils of the Nāga king.[38] Thus, in the same manner as the Nāga of Uruvelā, the Nāga Mucalinda serves both to commemorate the absent Buddha and to provide a potential rallying symbol for the recruitment of new worshippers.

Buddhist Nāgas and the Resignification of Nāga Rituals: The Nāgarāja Campeyya and the Nāga Who Wanted to be a Monk

Given the degree of ideological competition at play in these stories, it is not surprising to find several of these tales devoted to the denigration of Nāga worship.[39] This occurs in the *Campeyya Jātaka*, which is presented as a cautionary tale for those laypeople who—confirming the redactors' worst fears—would forget the subsidiary role assigned to the Nāga and treat him instead as the central object of worship. The tale begins with the following prologue from the Buddha: "It is well done for you lay brothers to abide by the *Uposatha* vows.[40] Wise men of ancient times, having abandoned the fortune of the Nāgas, abide by the *Uposatha* vows."[41] As we will see, however, while the redactors wish to disparage the worship of Nāgas, they also wish to resignify and incorporate Nāga rituals into the Buddhist framework in order to make Buddhism more appealing to potential converts. In this story, then, the redactors will denigrate a ritual reminiscent of the late Vedic *Sarpabali* ritual, yet resignify and incorporate a Nāga-centered fertility ritual.

The story of the Nāga King Campeyya begins with a description of two kingdoms at war: Anga and Magadha. At the culmination of the battle, the defeated ruler of Magadha decides to kill himself rather than be captured by his enemies. He attempts to drown himself in the Campā River, but instead of dying, the king finds himself in the underwater realm of the Nāga King Campeyya, a beautiful place of gem-encrusted lotus pools, fruit trees and flowering trees that blossom in all seasons, palaces made of jewels, a full retinue of ministers and advisors, servants ready to fulfill every need, and a harem full of beautiful, sensual snake women. The Nāga king, feeling compassion for this defeated ruler, offers him not only the throne of his own kingdom but also sovereign rule over both his and his rival's earthly territories. The king of Magadha returns to the surface and finds that the Nāga king's promise has been fulfilled. He is so thrilled that "every year, he caused a pavilion of jewels to be built on the bank of the river Campā, and he made a bali offering to the Nāga king at great expense. Having emerged from the Nāga world along with his great retinue, the Nāga king accepted the bali offering, and all the people observed the Nāga king's splendor."[42]

The story goes on to relate that the Nāga King Campeyya had once been a man, in fact, the Buddha in a previous life, who wanted to be reborn as a Nāga. In due course his wish came true and he was born as the Nāga King Campeyya, but the hedonistic life of the Nāgas did not satisfy him, and so he often left the Nāga world in order to observe the vows of a Buddhist layperson. Because he knew that the world of humans was filled with dangers, he had given the following warning to his chief queen, Sumanā: "If anyone should strike me, good woman, the water in this pond will become dirty. If the supaṃas [garuḍa birds] should seize me, the water will go away. And if a snake harmer should take hold of me, the water will appear blood-red."[43]

Then, as the Nāga king lay on his ant-hill observing the *Uposatha,* "those who came and went by the highway, having seen him, worshipped him with perfumes. And those who lived there on the border, thinking, 'he is a Nāga king of great power,' made a pavilion over him, spread sand for him, and worshipped him with perfumes. Since then, the people have been devoted to the Nāga king and worship him in their desire for sons."[44]

But he was seen by a young brahmin of Banāras who possessed powerful magic spells. Thinking that he could make the Nāga king dance for money, the brahmin grabbed him. Even though the Nāga saw the young brahmin coming, he decided to forgo using his powers even to protect himself, for to practice violence in any form would be to betray his Buddhist vows. The brahmin then proceeded to break the Nāga's teeth, squeeze him to a bloody pulp, and crush his head before stuffing him into a basket.

After the brahmin snake-harmer had made off with the Nāga king and kept him captive for quite some time, the Nāga queen became worried. She therefore went and viewed the pond as her husband the king had told her to do, and sure enough, it was red as blood. Seeing this, she left the Nāga realm in order to consult with the ruler of Banāras, King Ugrasena, who eventually had the Nāga king rescued from the evil brahmin snake-harmer. Upon his rescue, the Nāga king invited King Ugrasena to visit his realm. King Ugrasena was deeply worried about the deadly destructive nature that was attributed to all Nāgas (at least in these texts). He soon acquiesced, however, and duly equipped with elephants, horses, carriages, armies, ministers, servants, and wives, he made his way to the Nāga world. Upon his eventual departure from the Nāga's kingdom, the Nāga king gave him a cartload of precious gems, and, truly impressed with the richness of the Nāga king's realm, which is said to be like that of a god, King Ugrasena asked him why he would leave the world of the Nāgas to observe the *Uposatha* vows. To this question, the Nāga King Campeyya made the following answer: "Purity and self-restraint exist only in the world of human beings. When I have attained rebirth in the realm of human beings, then I will have attained the end of birth and death."[45]

While contextualized in such a way as to disparage the inferior life-style of the Nāga, and more importantly, to disparage the inferior desires of Nāga worshippers such as the desire for "fortune" as stated in the prologue,[46] this tale nevertheless tells us a great deal about Nāgas, the Nāgaloka, and their role as objects of worship, much of which is familiar from the late Vedas. The name of the Nāga King, Campeyya, is clearly derived from his location at the Campā River. Like Dhṛtarāṣṭra Airavata and Takṣaka Vaiśāleya, this Nāga king is tied to a particular locale and its inhabitants. The intrinsic relationship between the Nāga and his territory is particularly emphasized in this tale, as the Nāga's welfare is reflected in the landscape itself. Thus, when the Nāga is injured, the earth is injured as well, its waters turning bloody as the Nāga is bloodied by the evil snake-harmer. The Nāga's role as a sovereign extends to his ability to confer sovereignty on human kings. In fact, numerous *Jātaka* tales encompass this motif,[47] and in ancient times, *caityas* were sites of royal coronations.[48] In the *Campeyya Jātaka,* the king of Magadha receives from the Nāga king not only sovereign control over the kingdoms of both Anga and Magadha but also control over the Nāga king's underwater territory. The Nāga is able to convey such authority as a supernatural sovereign whose very being is intricately connected to the well-being of the earth itself.

The Nāgaloka as described in this tale is a truly splendid place that recalls the alternative name for this world preserved in the *Ādi Parvan*: Bhogavatī. As previously stated, this term represents a play on words, for it signifies not only a snake's coils [bhoga] but also all manner of sensual pleasures. Nāgas are the original and rightful possessors of all the treasures of the earth, such as gemstones and precious metals, a fact alluded to as King Ugrasena departs the Nāgaloka with a cart-load of precious gems. And Nāgas are most usually depicted with a priceless gem set within their hoods, or in the case of the beautiful sensual Nāgīs, set directly in the middle of their foreheads. Beyond these earthly riches, Nāgas are also the owners of a variety of priceless items that they will sometimes give to humans. These items include divine articles of clothing, ornaments, magical wish-granting jewels, musical instruments, magical spells, works of art, thrones, and magical weapons. The recipients of such objects, however, must treat them with care and hold on to them tightly, for if left on a river bank or dropped into the water, these precious items immediately return to the Nāgas.[49]

These early Pāli texts thus further elaborate the reasons for which people worship Nāgas: no longer exclusively dedicated to providing for earthly fertility, or securing a foundation stone for a new house, the Nāgas depicted here are able to provide their worshippers with earthly riches, "the fortune of the Nāgas," as stated in the prologue.[50] In fact, it would seem that the *Sarpabali* ritual has been transformed over the ensuing centuries from its original purpose in the late Vedas to another purpose altogether: the giving and receiving of earthly riches. As we will recall from the *Gṛhya Sūtras*, the *Sarpabali* has two main purposes originally: first, it lists those items which are to be offered to snakes such as Takṣaka Vaiśāleya, to propitiate them for a good harvest or appropriate rainfall; and second, it lists various precautions that should be taken to avoid their fangs. The *Sarpabali* ritual is not restricted to brahmins, moreover, but could be practiced by anyone, for it does not rely on a sacrificial fire, "but merely the placing on the ground of the oblations destined for the divine powers."[51] As encompassed within this story, however, the *Sarpabali* is offered "to the Nāga king at great expense," it is offered in thanks for the bestowal of three kingdoms (one of which is the fabulously luxurious Nāgaloka) and it is accepted by the Nāga while all the people observed the Nāga king's splendor. This story thus marks not only the further development of Nāga worship as it now extends to the propitiation of the Nāga for earthly riches, but also the transformation of rituals redesigned to reflect this development.

Given the fact that the Nāgas are now associated with worldly fortune, it is not surprising that Nāga worship functions as stiff competition for these Buddhist redactors bent on disseminating a tradition of spiritual fortune and asceticism. The redactors, however, use a savvy tactic in dissuading Nāga worshippers from what they deem as wayward practices. For while they set up the world of the snakes as a paradise filled with precious gems and beguiling snake women, it is a world that a wise person, like the Nāga king himself, will reject in favor of following the Buddhist path.

The fact that the Nāga king is none other than the Buddha himself, who, in a former life wished for life as a Nāga, further emphasizes the seductive yet ultimately fruitless world of the Nāga. For after having been born as a Nāga king, this life-style does not satisfy him and he leaves the Nāgaloka regularly in order to pursue his vows, thus highlighting not only the spiritual poverty of the Nāga's world but also the idea that an association with the Nāgas is not conducive to being a good Buddhist.[52] This idea, as we will recall, is explicitly formulated in the prologue to this tale. Rather than being a life of luxury, moreover, the Buddha's stint as the Nāga King Campeyya is portrayed as a hellish nightmare as he is captured, tortured and humiliated by an evil brahmin snake-harmer. The fact that the perpetrator of such violence is portrayed as a brahmin again allows the redactors to take a swipe at brahminical Hinduism at the same time that they are denigrating the worship of Nāgas. Thus, in juxtaposing the many material and carnal pleasures of the Nāga's world against the Nāga king's/Buddha's rejection of these pleasures, the redactors are attempting to sway their listeners away from Nāga worship and toward the spiritual rewards awaiting the pious layperson.

These redactors do recognize, however, that Nāga worship involves more than the pursuit of a hedonistic life-style. Along these lines, it is interesting to note that while they denigrate the pursuit of riches, they preserve without criticizing the Nāga-centered fertility ritual. For as the Nāga king lay on his ant-hill observing the *Uposatha*, people coming and going on the highway spread sand under him, made a pavilion over him, and worshipped him with perfumes "in their desire for sons."[53] In this tale, those showing reverence to the Nāga king believe that he can aid in the process of human fertility. This is reminiscent of one of the boons accruing to brahmins who would reenact the late Vedic *Sarpasattra* ritual, for it is said that in addition to cattle, and snake-bite protection, sons will also be forthcoming. In fact, Nāga rituals designed to induce human fertility are practiced by women up to the present day in India, and a stone carving of a single Nāga or a plaque inscribed with a pair of entwined Nāgas (a *nāgakal*) is a customary gift for a new bride who indicates a desire to become pregnant.[54]

I would argue that the redactors preserve this ritual for the following reason: the incorporated Nāga in this story allows these Buddhist redactors to provide for a primary desire of their laypeople—their desire for children. In fact, the Nāga is crucial to the redactors in this regard, for while the Buddha and his saints can pose as rainmakers, these celibate ascetics cannot in any way pose as fertility deities. They can, however, function as the controllers of a fertility deity. Thus, by making use of an incorporated Nāga, one that continuously emphasizes the superiority of Buddhism, the redactors can accommodate this desire on the part of their laypeople. And again, the redactors use a very savvy strategy to contextualize the Nāga exclusively as a Buddhist, but one nevertheless capable of providing fertility treatments; for while these people are worshipping the Nāga "in their desire for sons," the Nāga king, abiding by the prologue's directive, has left the "fortune of the Nāgas" in order to "observe the *Uposatha* vows."[55]

While these redactors are clearly attempting to transfer Nāgas and Nāga-related sites and rituals from a central role within Nāga worship to a peripheral role within Buddhism, they take great pains along the way to recontextualize these items in order to insure the following: that these figures, sites, and rituals are dissociated as much as possible from Nāga worship to be reinterpreted by laypeople as belonging to the Buddhist tradition. However, through the very act of incorporating rituals such as the Nāga-centered fertility ritual from the *Campeyya Jātaka,* these redactors run the risk of sending an unintended message: that it is possible and permissible to be both a Buddhist layperson and a Nāga worshipper simultaneously. Given that these early Pāli redactors are trying not only to establish the boundaries of orthodoxy and orthopraxy but also to set up a community of true believers, such an unintended message would have been anathema. It is therefore not surprising that in addition to an explicit warning such as that encompassed within the prologue to the *Campeyya Jātaka,* these Pāli redactors would think it necessary to reiterate the fact that in order to pledge one's full allegiance to Buddhism, one must reject Nāga worship. The signature story in terms of demonstrating this idea tells the tale of a wretched Nāga, who, ashamed of his very being, attempts to transform himself into a Buddhist monk. But just as a Nāga worshipper cannot be a Buddhist, this Nāga cannot be a Buddhist monk, and he is summarily rejected from the saṃgha.

> At that time, there was a Nāga who was ashamed, troubled, and disgusted at his Nāga birth....The Nāga, having assumed the form of a young man, approached the monks and asked them for 'going forth.'[56] The monks conferred on him both the Pabbajja and the Umpasampāda ordinations. During that time, the Nāga lived together with a certain monk in a vihāra situated far away [from any others]. The monk, who had risen during the night, was still walking about in the open air by morning time. But the Nāga, feeling confident, had gone to sleep when the monk had gone out [and thus resumed his natural shape]. As a result, the entire vihāra was filled up with the snake and his coils protruded from the windows....Then the Blessed One said to the monks. 'Nāgas are not capable of growth in the dharma or in the discipline....There are two occasions, O Monks, when a Nāga will reveal his true form: when he indulges in sexual intercourse and when he falls asleep in confidence. So, O Monks, if an animal has not yet received the Umpasampāda ordination, it should not receive it, if it has received the Umpasampāda ordination, it should be expelled.'[57]

In relation to this story, Richard Gombrich notes that "in Sri Lanka candidates for the higher ordination (umpasampāda) are dressed in elegant lay clothes with a cloth so arranged over their heads as to resemble a cobra's hood, and are called 'nāga.'"[58] It would seem possible that this custom derives from this story as it plays upon the need to discern a candidate's status, both physical and spiritual, as a measure for ordination. Gombrich argues that the Theravādin incorporation of this term reflects that they were in competition with Nāga worship, for as they apply the word 'nāga' to ordinands, "the Buddhists are saying to the nāga worshippers, 'Our nāgas are better than yours.'"[59] I would certainly agree with this statement and point out that in addition to the Theravādin appropriation of the Nāga worshippers' terminology, the story itself serves as yet another attempt to assert Buddhism's superior status over Nāga worship as the Nāga declares his preference for life as a monk. This story also serves to illustrate the point that while Nāgas may be associated with Buddhists, they can never actually be Buddhists. I would argue, then, that this story functions primarily as an analogy; one that seeks to warn laypeople that if they are to progress along the Buddhist path, they must give up their worship of Nāgas. For the story implies that just as "Nāgas are not capable of growth in the dharma or in the discipline,"[60] neither are those who attempt to maintain their worship of the Nāga.

Conclusion: The Reversal of Ideological Fortunes

As we have seen, the redactors of both the *Mahāvagga* and the *Jātakas* do not hesitate to make use of the Nāgas when it suits their needs: first, as the Nāga's powers are transferred to the Buddha and the arhats; and second, as the Nāga is incorporated into the Buddhist symbolic framework in order to commemorate the absent Buddha, to prove Buddhism's superiority over Nāga worship as well as other competing traditions, and to bring in potential converts.

The fact that the redactors include practices associated with Nāga worship leads us back to an important point. While promoting Buddhism through the subordination of the sovereign snake, the redactors have also been preserving, while often denigrating, a number of snake-centered ritual practices: the Mucalinda story alludes to *caitya* worship, while the *Campeyya Jātaka* includes direct references to the late Vedic *Sarpabali* ritual as well as the Nāga king's regional connection. And at times, the redactors intentionally preserve, while resignifying, these rituals in order to provide for their laypeople's needs, as we saw in relation to the fertility ritual encompassed within the *Campeyya Jātaka.*

Stories such as the *Campeyya Jātaka*, moreover, expand our understanding of the ways in which Nāga worship developed over time: while the late Vedic Nāgas were devoted primarily to providing rainfall, sons, and a bountiful harvest, these early Pāli Nāgas are also capable of providing earthly riches. In addition, these stories have preserved a great deal of information about the supernatural snake, such as its luxurious home in the Nāgaloka, its various supernatural capabilities, its appearance, and its association with gems and other priceless objects.

Clearly, then, these redactors are walking a very fine line, for as they attempt to incorporate the Nāga into a Buddhist framework, they run the risk of positioning the Nāga not as a subordinate figure but rather as the preeminent figure. Not surprisingly, such a transposition actually occurs on occasion. As Lowell Bloss has noted, representations of the Buddha and the Nāgarāja Mucalinda particularly lend themselves to such reversals of ideological fortune, for far from highlighting the superiority of the Blessed One, representations at Amarāvatī and Nāgārjunakoṇḍa show a huge Nāga engulfing a barely visible Buddha, so that it is the Buddha who seems to occupy the subordinate role.[61] Thus, in incorporating the Nāga to increase the popularity of Buddhism, the Buddhists may have also given a boost to the popularity of Nāga worship, as every now and again the Nāga reassumes his central position.

As we turn to chapter 6, however, we encounter a group of Buddhist redactors who would not have objected to the Nāga's elevated role. In fact, the redactors of the *Mahāvastu* celebrate Nāga worship as they see it as a means for grounding their new and improved version of the Buddha: no longer an extraordinary man, the *Mahāvastu's* Buddha is transcendent, literally, *lokottara*, or "above the earth." Understood as such, the redactors of the *Mahāvastu* do not see the Nāga, a mere earth-god, as a competitor but rather as a friend; one whose sovereign role and ritual practices might be used to maintain an earthly context for this otherworldly Buddha.

6

The Mahāvastu: The Buddha Shares in the Snake's Largess

Unlike the Pāli redactors of chapter 5, some Buddhist redactors find Nāgas and Nāga worship to be compatible with the religious framework they are creating. In a similar fashion to the late Vedic redactors then, these Buddhist redactors promote various supernatural snakes and snake-centered practices as these figures and rituals complement their narrative agenda. This is clearly the case for the Lokottaravādin School, which, along with the Theravādins, is counted among the original 18 schools of early Buddhism. While this school is no longer in existence, they have left us their text, the *Mahāvastu,* which was redacted sometime during the period from 100-400 CE.[1]

The *Mahāvastu* states in the prologue that it is "the *Vinaya Piṭaka* according to the recitation of the noble Mahāsāṃghikās, the Lokottaravādins of the Middle Country."[2] In contrast to the Theravādin's Vinaya, the Lokottaravādin's Vinaya is more concerned with the life story of the Buddha than with monastic discipline or recruiting converts. As their name proclaims, the Lokottaravādin's *raison d'être* consists of presenting a new image of the Buddha. *Lokottara* means that which is 'above the world,' and thus the Lokottaravādins are those who taught that Siddhārtha Gautama, as well as all the Buddhas who preceded him,[3] were to be seen as transcendent figures; capable of manifesting 'in' this world but who are not 'of' this world. The *Mahāvastu* thus marks a fascinating moment in the history of Buddhism, for in this text we see the building of a contextual framework through which the Buddha is shifted from his role as an extraordinary man to that of a transcendent being.

J. J. Jones, one of the first translators of this text, saw this shift as reflecting an urge to glorify the founder of Buddhism. "As an example of how admiration for a great man and his teaching developed into the worship of that man as a divinity of infinite power and goodness, the *Mahāvastu* is worthy of careful study."[4] Given the prominent role of the noble Nāga king in this text, it is not surprising that the redactors include the Nāgas in this important passage about the transcendent nature of the Buddhas.

> The eye of the Buddhas with clear sight, those who crush old age and death as well as make the unrestrained restrained, is of many kinds and works in many ways.
>
> The conduct of the Blessed One is beyond the world and the root of its merit is beyond the world. The walking, standing, sitting, and laying down of the sage is beyond the world.
>
> The body of the Sugata, which causes our bonds to existence to be destroyed, that body is also beyond the world. There should be no doubt about that.
>
> The sage's wearing of the monk's robe is beyond the world. As to this there is no doubt. The eating of food by the Sugata is also beyond the world.
>
> *The teaching of Nāgas and of men* (italics mine) is to be thought of as beyond all worlds. And I will proclaim the power of those Buddhas, whose enlightenment is the best, as it really is. [5]

The redactors of the *Mahāvastu*, however, are not out to characterize their lokottara Buddha as an omnipotent, benevolent *deus otiosus*—a distant god residing in an other-worldly realm. Rather, they seem most interested in establishing Siddhārtha, as well as his predecessors such as Dīpaṃkara and Mangala, as transcendent, yet earthly figures; liminal, transformational beings who might illuminate the Buddhist path while exceeding the mundanity of the human condition. Interestingly, the Lokottaravādin's desire to construct a figure whose glory might be grounded within an earthly setting is demonstrated by the fact that they are credited with erecting the giant images of the Buddha in Bāmiyān, Afghanistan that were destroyed by the Taliban regime in March of 2001. For more than 1,500 years, these giant figures towered over the Bāmiyān Valley at 55 and 38 meters, respectively, reminding all those who passed of the Buddha's splendor.

Within the narrative framework of the *Mahāvastu*, the Nāga king is crucial for effecting the Lokottaravādin's agenda. For in constructing the Nāga king as a supernaturally powerful yet pious *bhūmya deva*, "earth-god," with whom the Buddha might be positively associated, the redactors construct a medium for situating their transcendent Buddha back on this earth. Their agenda is particularly clear as we revisit four Nāga kings from the Pāli texts: the Nāgarāja of Uruvelā, the Nāgarāja Kāla, the Nāgarāja Mucalinda, and the Nāgarāja Campeyya.[6] As we recall from chapter 5, the Pāli redactors were ruthless in their quest to stamp out Nāga worship while incorporating many elements of this grass-roots tradition into the Buddhist framework. In the *Mahāvastu*, however, the Nāga kings share in the riches of Buddhism while the Buddha shares in the Nāga kings' ritual practices, seasonal festivals, and sacred sites.

The Lokottaravādins construct this setting of mutual admiration as they recontextualize the relationship between the Buddha and the Nāga kings in the following ways: the Buddha affirms the Nāga of Uruvilvā's desire to become a Buddhist; the Buddha achieves enlightenment through the help of the Nāga King Kāla; the Buddha celebrates the sacred territory belonging to the Nāga King Mucilinda; and the Buddha delights in the life of a Nāga and honors the supernatural powers of the Nāga King Campaka. The Lokottaravādins, moreover, introduce us to three new Nāga kings: the Nāga Kings Vinipāta and Sudarśana, whom the Buddha goes out of his way to visit at their magnificent palatial abodes, and the Nāga King Elapatra, whom the Buddha joins on the occasion of the Nāga king's monthly treasure festival. Thus, within the pages of the *Mahāvastu*, the Nāga kings both share in and contribute to the Buddha's glory, and the sovereign snake is made to thrive along with its associated ritual tradition.

The Nāga of Uruvilvā and the Construction of the Noble Nāgarāja

In contrast to the Pāli texts, the Nāgas of the *Mahāvastu* are neither subservient nor malevolent. Rather, the Lokottaravādins consistently associate these figures with dharma—the enlightened state experienced by the Buddha and conveyed through his teachings. The Nāga kings are thus portrayed as recognizing the dharma, proclaiming the dharma, being like the dharma, and even instructing on the subject of dharma.[7] In fact, the redactors go so far as to highlight the Nāgas as an ontological goal to which those who keep to the Buddhist path might aspire:[8]

> Thus, the venerable Mahā-Kātyāyana said to the venerable Mahā-Kāśyapa: 'Bodhisattvas, O maintainer of the dharma, those who are not prone to turning back [from the path], they do not, over the course of these seven bhūmis, in any way, or at any time, go to hell, nor are they reborn as animals, nor do they become poor or weak. Rather, they become...Nāgas and kings of Nāgas.'[9]

As we will see throughout the *Mahāvastu*, the redactors are careful to contextualize Nāgas as peace-loving creatures. In certain tales where the story line calls for a malevolent serpent, the *Mahāvastu* takes pains to characterize this demonic figure as something other than a Nāga, such as a fork-tongued demon[10] or a water-dwelling monster.[11] For example, in the *Mahāvastu's* story of the brahmin youth Dharmapāla, three snake-like figures play a role: a black snake who is associated with chaos, a water-demon who has a reputation for destroying humans, and a noble Nāga king, whose son becomes friendly with the young Dharmapāla. When the water-demon threatens Dharmapāla's life, the Nāga prince saves Dharmapāla by carrying him away to the Nāgaloka.[12] The redactors' efforts to differentiate the Nāga from a mere animal thus reflects their desire not only to elevate the Nāga but also to strip the Nāga of its destructive powers; or in the words of the Lokottaravādins, to "make the unrestrained restrained."[13]

Transforming the Nāga into a peaceful being marks the crucial difference between the *Mahāvastu's* treatment of the supernatural snake and that of the late Vedas, which in all other ways share a similar affirmative orientation toward the supernatural snake and snake-centered rituals. It is certainly possible that this transformation of the Nāga from a venomously biting creature to a restrained non-biting creature reflects the redactors' use of an evolving tradition of snake worship; a natural development given not only that Nāga worshippers would probably want the Nāga to be as approachable as possible but also that an increasingly anthropomorphized Nāga might demonstrate an increasingly benevolent nature. Whatever the source of this change, it certainly works for the *Mahāvastu's* redactors, for it speaks directly to their goal of rendering the Nāga as a suitable associate of the Buddha; one who conforms to the dictates of ahiṃsā or non-harm.

The freeing of the Nāga from its savage reputation is nowhere clearer than in the *Mahāvastu's* treatment of the Nāga of Uruvilvā. As we will recall from the *Mahāvagga's* portrayal of this figure, one of the primary functions of that story was to render the Nāga as a demonic character who might be vanquished by the superior yet compassionate Buddha. In fact, as the demonization of the Nāga seemed to be the main point of that tale, it is hard to imagine how it might be presented in such a way as to depict the Nāga as a sympathetic character. That is precisely what occurs, however, in the following rendition found in the *Mahāvastu*; a rendition that constructs the Nāga as both a practicing Buddhist and a sovereign earth-god. The redactors effect this portrayal of the Nāga as it is first, rendered poisonless, second, presented as one who might join the Buddhist order, and third, allowed to maintain its supernatural capabilities.

Thus the Blessed One, in the presence of Uruvilvā-Kāśyapa, instructed the three brothers and their retinue by means of 500 miracles. This is the last miracle.

The Blessed One said to Uruvilvā-Kāśyapa, 'I wish to meditate privately. I will meditate here, Kāśyapa, in your sacrificial fire shelter.' Uruvilvā-Kāśyapa said: 'O Gautama, this fire shelter cannot be entered by either humans or non-humans, for a vicious Nāga lives in there. We should stay far away from there for fear of that malicious Nāga.' The Blessed One said: 'Grant me your consent Kāśyapa, and I will retire to that fire shelter.' Uruvilvā-Kāśyapa said: 'O Gautama, I will not grant your request to enter that fire shelter. Wickedness emanates from that place. There are many hundreds of huts of grass and leaves, so let the honorable Gautama retire to whichever one of these he likes.' Then, the Blessed One, having risen from his seat and entered the fire shelter of Uruvilvā-Kāśyapa, sat down to meditate. Once in the sacrificial fire shelter, the Blessed One attained the element of fire. The Nāga, not able to tolerate the flames of the Blessed One, descended into the bowl given by the four great kings. The Nāga, filled with loving kindness, was tamed and rendered poisonless by the Buddha, and he no longer displayed his anger. Because of the flames emitted by the Blessed One, the sacrificial fire shelter looked like one blazing mass. As that was how it looked to them, the brahmins thought that the mendicant Gautama had been burned by that vicious Nāga, for the fire-shelter was completely ablaze. Then, having taken up water they ran, thinking, 'We will extinguish the fire-shelter and we will rescue the mendicant Gautama.' The Blessed One, having subdued the Nāga and rendered him poisonless, took him up in the bowl and placed it before Uruvilvā-Kāśyapa. Upon seeing the Nāga in the Blessed One's bowl, Uruvilvā-Kāśyapa was amazed, as was his entire company. 'The Mendicant Gautama has great power and magic, for while it was said that the Nāga's dwelling place could not be entered by either humans or non-humans, it has been overcome by the flames of the mendicant Gautama.'

> Because of this last miracle in the presence of Uruvilvā-Kāśyapa, the three brothers, along with their retinue, were completely won over by the Blessed One.
>
> Having caused that king of snakes to be subdued in the fire-shelter of Uruvilvā-Kāśyapa, and having removed him from his bowl, he offered him to the honorable Kāśyapa. 'Look how the fire of the Nāga, whose dwelling place no one in the world could enter, has been overcome by my own fire O Kāśyapa.'
>
> Uruvilvā-Kāśyapa and his retinue were thrilled with delight when they saw that the Nāga had been subdued and made calm by that Nāga among men. For that Nāga, who had blocked the great ṛṣi's shelter had been tamed and rendered poisonless by the power of the Buddha.
>
> The Blessed One said:
> 'There are no faults in one instructed by me and no unrestrained ones to be found, O Kāśyapa. The sky could fall and the earth be torn apart, but one subdued by the Buddha will have nothing to do with poison.'
>
> Released by the Blessed One, this snake was called 'the restrained Nāga,' and having transformed himself into human form, he fell at the feet of the Buddha saying, 'Be my refuge, O best of men. There is no vice in me, O greatly wise one. My evil mind is visibly cast away. O ultimate of men, I have thrown away my sin and am now sinless. May I enter your refuge again, O best of gurus.'
> And having honored the one worthy of honor, and having bowed around him clockwise many times, thus showing great respect for the teacher, the Nāga left.[14]

Both versions of this story begin with the same scenario: a "vicious Nāga," yet a "rāja," has holed up in the fire-shelter, making it impossible for either "humans or non-humans" to enter this chamber. The fire shelter is literally an *agni-śariṇam*, which is defined as "a house or place for keeping the sacrificial fire."[15] As in the Pāli version, the Nāga king has blocked the entrance to the ritual space that operates as the *sine qua non* of brahminical Hinduism. Both renditions highlight the fact that while a Nāga is powerful enough to stop a brahmin in his tracks, he is not powerful enough to stop the Buddha. Thus, in subduing the Nāga, the Buddha proves his superiority in relation to both the brahmins and the Nāga king.

As with most comparisons, however, it is the differences rather than the similarities that are the most intriguing. First, the *Mahāvagga's* version of the Buddha's performance at Uruvilvā left the ascetics wanting more, and is only the first of five miraculous acts to be performed.[16] In contrast, the miracle of taming the Nāga in the *Mahāvastu* turns the trick, for as the best and last of 500 miracles, it succeeds in converting a whole hermitage full of brahmins to the Buddha's teaching. The ascetics' wholesale conversion to Buddhism is made clear as they declare themselves to be "completely won over by the Blessed One."

What is most curious about this version, however, is that the miracle enacted is not really the overcoming of the Nāga at all, for the Nāga neither becomes enraged nor blazes up as he does in the Pāli text. Rather, unable to tolerate the Buddha's fiery splendor,[17] the Nāga seeks refuge in the Buddha's begging bowl. The Lokottaravādins, moreover, do not burden the Nāga king with the name Caṇḍa, meaning one who is savage or fierce. Thus, while the redactors of the Pāli text chose to portray him as a savage snake who instigates a flame-throwing competition, the redactors of the *Mahāvastu* focus on the Nāga as a powerful yet reclusive snake who is over-awed by the Buddha's ascetic prowess.

The Pāli texts, in particular, characterize the Nāga as a fiery figure. While the late Vedic texts associate snakes twice with the natural element of fire[18] and the *Śatapatha Brāhmaṇa's Sarpanāma* ritual equates snakes with the sacrificial fire, the late Vedic redactors do not portray them as fiery creatures. In the *Ādi Parvan* these creatures display a strong antipathy toward fire and heat in general although, at times, Taksaka's venom is equated with fire. The Pāli texts, however, consistently portray the Nāga as a fiery creature, and one whose fire is used for destructive purposes. Such a portrayal has led Andrew Rawlinson to note that "the most important element in the Nāga make-up is fire."[19] This is certainly true of the Pāli texts reviewed in chapter 5 as well as other Pāli texts. As noted by Rawlinson, there is a story in the *Mahāvaṃsa*, in which Vāsuladatta, nephew to a Nāgarāja, swallows the relics of the Buddha in order to protect them and remains at the foot of Mt. Sineru emitting smoke and flames.[20] It is not true, however, of the *Mahāvastu*.[21]

Just as the *Mahāvastu's* redactors do not allow the Nāga to control fire as a destructive supernatural power, neither do they allow it to retain another destructive yet inherent power: its capacity to deliver a poisonous bite. Several times throughout this story it is said the Buddha rendered the Nāga poisonless. And at the conclusion of the story, the Buddha states the following: "The sky could fall and the earth be torn apart, but one subdued by the Buddha will have nothing to do with poison." Moreover, having been rendered poisonless, the Nāga is presented in the following ways: first, he takes refuge in the alms bowl, a primary symbol of Buddhism; second, he is "filled with loving kindness," a primary virtue for Buddhist monastics and laypeople alike; and third, the Nāga does these things as he is "instructed by me," the Buddha. Clearly, then, the redactors transform the supernatural snake into a "restrained Nāga," in order to obviate the one factor that would stand in the Nāga's way of becoming a Buddhist—his destructive capacity.

And with nothing standing in his way, the Nāga king is quick to join up, for having been subdued and rendered poisonless by the Buddha, the Nāga falls at the Buddha's feet and begs refuge in his teachings. As we will recall from our reading of chapter 5, this stance toward the Nāga king is wildly different from that encapsulated within the Pāli texts wherein the Buddha made the following proclamation: "Nāgas are not capable of growth in the dharma or in the discipline."[22] This statement seemed to be directed toward laypeople, moreover, as a warning to reject Nāga worship if they were to progress along the Buddhist path. What we see in this story, however, is an overturning of this injunction, for not only does the Nāga increase his dharmic stature, but more importantly, he is allowed to do so without dissociating himself from his role as a Nāga king. This point is made clear as the Nāga king, while rendered poisonless, retains his capacity to transform magically into a human being. It would seem that the redactors of the *Mahāvastu* are unconcerned with the potential dual religious citizenship not only of the Nāga but also of their laypeople, a point to which we will return in relation to the Nāga King Campaka and a new figure, the Nāga King Elapatra.

The Pāli version of the Nāga of Uruvilvā nowhere mentions the Nāga's magical transformation into a human being. Rather, in the *Mahāvagga's* rendition, the story ends with the Nāga King Caṇḍa being tossed and left to languish in the Buddha's alms bowl, his spirit broken but his skin and bones left intact. In fact, both the *Ādi Parvan* and the Pāli texts primarily depict the Nāga's transformative ability as a negative thing, for it is seen as a means for disguising the Nāga's real nature in an effort to gain entry into the forbidden realm of humans.[23] In contrast, the redactors of the *Mahāvastu* allow the supernatural snakes their full complement of magical abilities and present the transformed Nāga king as a noble being. The necessity of maintaining the Nāga king as a powerful, efficacious deity becomes particularly clear in our next set of stories wherein we revisit two Nāga kings from the Pāli texts, the Nāga Kings Kāla and Mucilinda, as well as meet two new Nāga kings, Vinipāta and Sudarśana.

The Nāgarājas Kāla, Mucilinda, Vinipāta, and Sudarśana: The Earthly Situating of the Lokottara Buddha

The theme of the noble Nāgarāja is continued as we shift our focus to the Nāga Kings Kāla, Mucilinda, Vinipāta, and Sudarśana, all of whom host the Buddha as he travels through northern India expounding the dharma. And as we examine our first set of stories featuring Kāla, it is evident that having contextualized the Nāga as a supernaturally powerful yet pious figure, the redactors are prepared to use him in the following ways: first, to model and reflect the splendid yet immanent nature of the Lokottaravādin's Buddhas; and second, to mark the serial presence on earth of innumerable, transcendent Buddhas. Like Uruvilvā, then, Kāla appears nothing like his name-sake from the Pāli texts, for rather than being discredited as a cowardly failure, he is hailed as a heroic protector—one who might assist both Buddhists and Nāga worshippers alike.

> O Monks, the Nāga king by the name of Kāla saw the Bodhisattva striding forth, and having seen him said 'Go Great Mendicant! By that path that you go, the Blessed One, the Great Mendicant Krakucchanda also went; and he is one who awoke to the unsurpassed true enlightenment. O Great Mendicant, go also by this path and you will awake today to the unsurpassed true enlightenment. The Blessed One, the Great Mendicant Konākamuni also went by this path and he awoke to the unsurpassed true enlightenment. O Great Mendicant, go also by this path, and today you will awake to the unsurpassed true enlightenment. The Blessed One, the Great Mendicant Kāśyapa also went by this path, and he awoke to the unsurpassed true enlightenment. O Great Mendicant, go also by this path, and today you will awake to the unsurpassed true enlightenment.
>
> This having been said, O Monks, the Bodhisattva said to the Nāga King Kāla, 'This is so, O Kāla, this is so, O Nāga. Today I will awake to the unsurpassed true enlightenment.'[24]

In the *Nidānakathā*, the Nāga King Kāla was made to cover his face in shame and descend to the depths of the Nāgaloka when confronted by Māra and his hordes. As depicted here, however, he attends faithfully to Siddhārtha and proclaims that the Bodhisattva will become a Buddha on that very day. The *Mahāvastu* tells the story of Śākyamuni's enlightenment three times, with certain variations, and the Nāga King Kāla appears to cheer Siddhārtha onward in all three episodes.

In the second, and longest, version of the enlightenment story in the *Mahāvastu*, the Nāga King Kāla is the only earth-god[25] not to join up with Māra's hordes against the Bodhisattva.[26] Instead, he stands with him and foretells the Bodhisattva's eventual defeat of Māra.

> 'Just as all of these gods have risen up for the purpose of worshipping you, there is no doubt, Great Hero, that today you will become a Buddha. Having grasped the weapon of wisdom in your hand, you will break the bonds of Māra. The snare (up to now) unconquered, namely, desire that leads to continued existence....'
> And the Buddha, having heard the speech spoken by the Nāgarāja Kāla, went to the root of the Bodhi tree, happy and content of mind.[27]

Shortly thereafter, the Nāga King Kāla adds the following:

> 'May these winds blow softly and gently with the pleasant fragrance of spring,
> Neither too hot, nor too cold.
> May the devas rain on you a shower of flowers. Thus, may you be tranquil, O Sugata, best of bipeds.
> Keeping to the right, go onwards, Lord, joyful, thrilled, rejoicing, glad, elated, radiating happiness.
> And just as a thousand musical instruments are played by the devas thronging the sky above, you, elated, glad, and eager, will be a Buddha who is distinguished from all others in the world.'[28]

Beyond helping the Bodhisattva to arm himself mentally against his coming ordeal, the Nāga king also manipulates the natural elements so as to be most conducive to the Bodhisattva's attaining of enlightenment. The Nāga king thus directs the winds to "blow softly and gently with the pleasant fragrance of spring." In contrast to the Pāli texts, the Nāga king retains his powers over the natural world. This is a crucial point, for contextualized in this manner, the Nāga king retains the primary supernatural powers for which he is worshipped. And while the Nāga king's powers are maintained in order to assist the Buddha, they remain within the purview of this autonomous earth-god. This motif recurs throughout the *Mahāvastu*: while the Buddhas are made to share in the benefits stemming from the Nāga's powers, they do not exclusively claim these powers. This is due to the fact that the redactors of the *Mahāvastu* are not attempting to engage in an ideological competition with Nāga worship, for as noted, their primary agenda involves advancing their new image of the Buddha; an agenda in which the efficacious Nāga king functions quite fruitfully. Thus, unlike the cooptation of the Nāga king's powers and subsequent incorporation of the Nāga as demonstrated by the redactors of the *Ādi Parvan* and Pāli texts, the redactors of the *Mahāvastu* allow the Nāga's powers to remain within the purview of the Nāga, and thereby accessible to all comers.

In the Nāga King Kāla's third appearance, his is the voice that testifies to the fact that the earth is responding to the Bodhisattva's enlightenment: the jet-black night is filled with radiance; the submerged Nāgaloka is fully illuminated; the air resounds as though a giant metal pan were being beaten; the winds are blowing without shaking the trees; the earth is completely covered with flowers; and all sorts of birds and animals are rising up to salute the Bodhisattva.[29] It is not just that the natural world is responding to the power of dharma, but also that the power of dharma is responding to the natural world, for as "the great Nāga [Kāla] looked, he saw the ultimate man like a blazing branch of fire, or like lightning among the clouds."[30] Or in other words, he is displaying the elemental powers of a Nāga. While in the Pāli texts, such displays demonstrated the exclusive cooptation of the Nāga's powers, here they serve to demonstrate something else entirely: that just as the Nāga is made to share in some aspects of the Buddha-nature, the Buddha is made to share in some aspects of the Nāga-nature.

This is the third time, moreover, that we have seen Buddhas either explicitly referenced as Nāgas or made to appear as Nāgas.[31] The redactors equate these two figures in order that the Nāga might function as both a model of and a model for the new image of the Buddha put forth by the Lokottaravādin's: one who is simultaneously superhuman yet immanent. And as a preestablished earth-god, the Nāga king is well prepared to model this duality. In the world of the *Mahāvastu*, then, the Nāga functions as the means for expressing the immanent power of the Buddhas just as the natural world functions as the means for expressing the immanent power of dharma.

An important focus of the Lokottaravādin's ideology is the serial presence on earth of innumerable, lokottara, "transcendent," Buddhas. This focus is alluded to in the first set of Kāla-related verses, as it tells how the path trod by former Buddhas functions to mark the way for Śākyamuni Buddha. This is hardly an isolated occurrence, for the redactors include page after page listing the names of various lokottara Buddhas;[32] they consistently bring up the existence of Buddhas such as Krakucchanda, Konākamuni, Kāśyapa,[33] and even such esoteric figures as Sikhin;[34] and they give us a full treatment of the history of other Buddhas such as Dīpaṃkara and Mangala. The Nāga King Kāla thus serves to testify to the earthly presence of these innumerable other Buddhas who had conquered impermanence.[35]

The redactors of the *Mahāvastu* constantly frame these transcendent Buddhas within natural, earthly settings, and Nāgas are an essential part of this recurring natural motif: Nāgas watch over their pregnant mothers,[36] Nāgas proclaim at the moment of the Buddhas' enlightenment,[37] and Nāgas receive the teaching from the Buddhas.[38] It was clearly important to the redactors to prove that the lokottara Buddha was not just a transcendent figure but also one who maintained an intrinsic connection with the earth.

While the necessity of situating the lokottara Buddhas within an earthly setting is a crucial component of the redactors' agenda, so too is the necessity of maintaining the Nāga as an efficacious earth-god; one who retains his central role within the context of snake worship. The combining of these two motifs is particularly apparent in our next set of stories wherein the Nāga Kings Kāla,

Mucilinda, Vinipāta, and Sudarśana act as local sovereigns who 'host' the Buddhas as they travel from place to place. Depicting them as regional ambassadors who witness the earthly appearance of numerous Buddhas, the redactors of the *Mahāvastu* capitalize on the Nāga kings' regional identity; an identity which has historically situated these Nāga kings as local earth-gods charged with insuring the prosperity of their regional domains. Thus, unlike the Pāli texts that resignified the homes of the Nāgas as Buddhist sites, the *Mahāvastu* maintains these sites as belonging to the Nāga and more importantly, to those who would worship the Nāga. The following comes from a section of the text that chronicles a series of visits by the Buddhas to the Nāga kings as they make their way from Bodhgaya to Sarnath.

> Then the Nāga King Kāla approached the Blessed One on his great walking tour. Having bowed down, with his head at the feet of the Blessed One, he arranged his robe over one shoulder and placed his hands together in a gesture of respect and said: 'O Blessed One, my palace was enjoyed by former enlightened ones, by the Blessed One Krakucchanda, by Konākamuni, and by Kāśyapa. O Holy One,[39] may the Blessed One also enjoy my palace, thus showing his compassion.' Therefore, the Blessed One spent the fourth week with pleasure and happiness at the home of the Nāga King Kāla.
>
> Then, with the passing of the fourth week, the Blessed One left the palace of the Nāga king.
> The Nāga King Mucilinda, as one who had recognized former Buddhas, approached the Blessed One.
>
> Having bowed down, with his head at the feet of the Blessed One, privately off to one side he placed his hands together in a gesture of respect and asked the Blessed One: 'My palace was enjoyed by former enlightened ones, O Blessed One, by the Blessed One Krakucchanda, by Konākamuni, and by Kāśyapa. O Holy One, may the Blessed One also enjoy my palace, thus showing his compassion.'

> The Blessed One spent the fifth week in the palace of the Nāga King Mucilinda, fasting well with pleasure and happiness.
>
> Now, during that week, unseasonable rainy weather arose. And day and night of that week it rained. The Nāga King Mucilinda, having thrown his coils around the Blessed one seven times and thus forming a protective layer half a yojana long, covered him with his extensive hood.
>
> So that no smell of poison or any offensive smell might injure the Blessed One, the Nāga King Mucilinda emerged from his own palace and covered him for seven days with his coils and with his blessed, well-made, thick hood, and thus generated extensive merit.
>
> And merit was generated by the Nāgarāja Vinipāta, for he threw his great coils around [him] for seven days.[40]

While the Nāga King Vinipāta is new to us, Mucilinda is familiar from our discussion of the *Mahāvagga*, and the association between the Nāga and the cobra remains in force. This version of the Mucilinda story, however, states that the Nāga King Mucilinda had the innate ability to "recognize" these Buddhas' enlightened state. The Buddhist-Hybrid Sanskrit word used is *purimbuddhadarśāvī*, a word that should be taken as "perceiving" or "intellectually realizing" the essence of these figures.[41] Thus, once again, the *Mahāvastu* emphasizes the almost symbiotic relationship between the Nāga kings and the Buddhas. The Nāga King Mucilinda also invites the Buddha to enjoy his hospitality, and the Buddha agrees to stay with him for the fifth week of his journey, but fasts "well with pleasure and happiness." This line in particular highlights how different the *Mahāvastu's* characterization is from the Pāli texts, for rather than establishing the Nāga realm as one that is incompatible with being a good Buddhist, the redactors portray the home of the Nāga king as a place where one might live according to the precepts.

At no point do the redactors of the Pāli texts portray the Nāga King Mucilinda as a kingly host of these Buddhas. Rather, in the

Mahāvagga's version, Mucilinda approaches the Buddha, who is sitting under the Mucilinda tree, and this story is situated between two others about trees. In the *Mahāvastu's* account, however, the action occurs in the context of the Buddha's visit to the palaces of these various Nāga kings, and the Buddha goes to the Nāga king's home rather than the Nāga king "having [to] come forth from his palace."[42] This difference is particularly indicative of the *Mahāvastu's* different orientation toward the Nāgas: in the *Mahāvagga,* the emphasis on trees probably indicates the redactors' attempt to resignify those sacred sites traditionally associated with Nāgas—*caityas*—so that they might be solely associated with Buddhism. In contrast, the redactors of the *Mahāvastu* allow the Buddhas to share space that is explicitly described as belonging to the Nāga kings without attempting to coopt it in any way. The redactors of the *Mahāvastu* maintain the Nāga kings in this way for the following reason: as the Lokottaravādins' primary focus involves the establishment of the Buddhas' transcendent nature, resignifying the Nāga's home as the Buddhas' home would serve only to compromise the Buddhas' 'above the world' status. In contextualizing the Buddhas as visitors to these sites, however, these lokottara figures are provided with a temporary earthly setting that does not compromise their superhuman status. And while the Buddhas reside at these various Nāga sites for only a short time, both the sites and the stories about the sites serve to testify to the Buddhas' earthly presence at these regional domains.

Therefore, we can see that the Lokottaravādins have a very different orientation toward Nāga worship than the Theravādins; for while the Theravādins narratively took over Nāga sites as they wished to assert Buddhism over Nāga worship, the Lokottaravādins narratively maintain these sites as they wish to coexist with Nāga worship in order to share in the Nāga's largess. This largess is demonstrated in the above passages as the Buddhas share the Nāgas' homes without dissociating the Nāgas from them.

Both the Nāga Kings Mucilinda and Vinipāta are made to shelter the Buddha with their hoods in this story. However, unlike the

Pāli version wherein the Nāga king acts as an umbrella to shield the Buddha from rain—a strange situation, indeed, given that the Nāga kings are worshipped for their control over the natural elements—the redactors of the *Mahāvastu* offer an alternative context for protecting the Buddha:

> So that no smell of poison or any offensive smell might injure the Blessed One, the Nāga King Mucilinda emerged from his own palace and covered him for seven days with his coils and with his blessed, well-made, thick hood, and thus generated extensive merit.

Rather than stripping the Nāga King Mucilinda of the very powers for which he is worshipped, the Nāga king is depicted here as shielding the Buddha from bad smells and poison gasses. This verse also notes that the Nāga king gained merit from hosting the Buddhas.[43] Thus, in contrast to the *Mahāvagga's* version of this story which emphasizes the disempowered status of the Nāga king, the *Mahāvastu* uses the Nāga to demonstrate how a devoted Buddhist might gain merit: through the act of giving. In highlighting the Nāga in this manner, the redactors emphasize that it is possible and permissible to be both a Buddhist layperson and a Nāga king simultaneously; leading one to extrapolate that they are also condoning the simultaneous practice of Buddhism and Nāga worship.

After leaving the homes of the Nāga Kings Kāla, Mucilinda, and Vinipāta to continue on his way to the deer park outside of Banāras, Śākyamuni Buddha makes one final visit to the palace of the Nāga King Sudarśana.

> When the Blessed One departed from the Bodhi Tree to the deer park at Ṛṣipatana in Banāras in order to turn the unsurpassed wheel of dharma, the path had already been attended to by the Śuddhāvasa Devas, who had created a great army of four branches: a great troop of elephants, a great troop of horses, a great troop of chariots, and a great troop of foot-soldiers. They accompanied the Blessed One on his journey to Vārāṇasī. Meanwhile, the sovereign lords

> and kings of the Suvarṇas: those born of eggs, those born of embryos, those born of sweat, and those who were self-produced, created from their magical powers a great army of four branches, and they also accompanied the Blessed One on his journey. Just as among the Nāgas, the sovereign lords and kings, those born of eggs, those born of embryos, those born of sweat, and those who were self-produced, created from their magical powers a great army of four branches, and they too accompanied the Blessed One on his journey to Vārāṇasī. The Cāturmahārājika devas, the Trāyastriṃśa devas, the Yāma and Tuṣita Devas, the Nirmāṇarati and Paranirmitavaśavarti devas and the devas belonging to the multitude of the Brahmā-class, created from their magical powers a great army of four branches and they also accompanied the Blessed One on his journey to Kāśi. Then the Blessed One honored and accompanied by a great entourage of several hundreds, several thousands, and several hundreds of thousands, went from Uruvilvā to Gayā, and from Gayā to Aparagayā.
>
> In Aparagayā, there was a Nāga king by the name of Sudarśana. The Blessed One was invited by the Nāga king to stay over and eat in Aparagayā. Then the Blessed One, having stayed and eaten at the palace of the Nāga King Sudarśana, went on to Vaśālā.[44]

The *Mahāvastu* delights in the transcendence of classificatory categories presented by the Nāga as it reiterates a version of the above verse not less than four times: "the Nāga lords and kings, [are] born of eggs, born of an embryo, born of sweat, and self-produced."[45] This verse is usually used to refer to the various means by which *all* of the creatures in the universe are created, but as all four forms are applied here to the Nāga, it shows that the *Mahāvastu's* Nāga transcends all classificatory systems. In relation to this verse, Rawlinson notes that "[n]o level of the cosmic hierarchy is wholly without the influence of the nāgadeva."[46] As depicted here, the Suvarṇa—synonymous with the garuḍa bird—is not only endowed with the same multi-form nature as the Nāga but also portrayed as working in tandem with the Nāgas in order to effect the Buddha's safe passage.

Such a brotherhood between the Nāgas and the Suvarṇas goes against all of the previous texts reviewed, for the animosity between the bird and the snake, as first established in the Vedas, was greatly elaborated in the *Mahābhārata* as a means for keeping the multitude of malevolent Nāgas in their place. The Pāli texts, moreover, took the existence of one snake-eating bird (Garuḍa) and expanded it into a whole flock of such creatures. In the *Mahāvastu*, however, the redactors portray this voracious enemy as a friend and colleague of the Nāga because the Nāga is no longer portrayed as a destructive being. As such, it is not necessary to provide him with an enemy to check his malevolent proclivities. In some ways, this alteration in the relationship between the snake and the bird reflects the circumstances which brought Brahmā to offer Garuḍa to Śeṣa as a friend in the *Ādi Parvan*. However, as seen here there is one crucial difference: while Śeṣa was completely disempowered as he was forced to stand immobile bearing the earth on his head, the *Mahāvastu's* Nāgas retain their supernatural powers.

The Pāli texts do not highlight the Buddha's trip to Aparagayā or his subsequent stay with the Nāga King Sudarśana. According to the *Mahāvastu*, the only reason that the Buddha goes to Aparagayā at all is to enjoy the hospitality of the Nāga king, for having lodged and eaten with Sudarśana, he and his entire entourage move on to Vaśālā. As we will recall from the late Vedas, the great snake kings were consistently portrayed as localized sovereigns responsible for insuring the prosperity of specific regional domains.[47] The *Mahāvastu's* emphasis on the particular location of these Nāgarājas echoes the late Vedas, and thereby maintains the snakes' regional identities as a crucial component of their make-up. Thus, while the *Mahāvastu's* Nāgas have very little in common with those in either the *Ādi Parvan* or the Pāli literature—texts that are attempting to subordinate the supernatural snake and the practices with which it is associated—they have a great deal in common with the snakes in the late Vedas. For as the redactors of both the *Mahāvastu* and the late Vedas construct a contextual framework that complements that of snake worshippers, their texts serve to revere the snake and preserve its rituals. This is clear as both sets of texts emphasize the Nāgas' regional identity, multi-form nature, supernatural powers, and kingly nobility to characterize the Nāga as an efficacious deity worthy of reverence.

The Nāgarāja Campaka: The Merging of Power and Piety

The unique conflation of non-violence, piety, and supernatural powers that characterizes the *Mahāvastu's* Nāga kings is particularly apparent in the redactors' prose version of the Nāga King Campaka.[48] In this version, the redactors not only accentuate the Nāga king's capacity to be both a good Nāga and a good Buddhist simultaneously but also highlight the equal status of the Nāga king with the human king, as well as the Nāga king's capacity to protect the human king and his family. Moreover, the *Mahāvastu's* version of this tale omits several of the narrative elements employed by the Pāli redactors to demote the Nāga king and Nāga worship. This includes the omission of the violent abuse of the Nāga king by the brahmin snake harmer; the transference of the Nāga king's territory to the human king; and most tellingly, the cautionary prologue instructing the faithful to abandon "the fortune of the Nāgas."[49]

> Then the Bhikṣus said:
> The Blessed One was rescued by Yaśodharā while he was being led away to his death.
> Did Yaśodharā do things for the sake of the Blessed One as he was transmigrating through mundane existence as a Bodhisattva?
>
> The Blessed One said:
> Indeed Monks, Yaśodharā did many deeds for the sake of

the Tathāgata as he transmigrated through mundane existence. I was also rescued another time by Yaśodharā when I had fallen into the hands of an enemy.
The Bhikṣus said:
Was there another time Blessed One?

The Blessed One said:
Yes Monks, there was also another time.

In a previous time, Monks, in the city of Vārāṇasī in the kingdom of Kāśi, there ruled a king named Ugrasena who acquired merit, who was called 'Great Lord,' who controlled his retinue well, who was in the habit of giving, and who possessed great wealth as well as a great army. This kingdom was prosperous, bountiful and secure, had abundant alms, and was well-populated. Violence and punishment were equally controlled, and the activities of thieves was easily restrained. Now, in that kingdom, there lived a Nāga king by the name of Campaka who had acquired merit, had an abundant mass of goodness, and who had a retinue of several thousand Nāgas. The palace of the Nāga King Campaka resembled that of the Gods. There were mansions made of the seven jewels. Everywhere and in every season there were flowers and fruits, as well as lotus pools encrusted with jewels and enveloped with every kind of lotus flower. Not far from these lotus pools, there was a jeweled hall with columns of cats-eye gems and with a floor made of coral. The female apartments of this king held sixteen thousand snake women. He enjoyed himself in that Nāga palace just like a king of the devas.

He keeps the three days of the first half of the lunar month, the 8th, the 14th, and the 15th, and observes the *Uposatha* at the cross-roads. Furnished with the eight precepts of the Buddhist layperson, he abides in a state of remove. Now, while the Nāga king was observing the *Upavāsa* at the cross-roads, he was seen by a snake-harmer. Thus, the Nāga King Campaka, having been seized from the cross-roads by the snake-harmer, was thrown into the snake basket in which he sits. However, he was not angry with the snake-harmer and even though he was covered up, the Nāga king of great power and brilliance did not want to turn Vārāṇasī to ashes along with the whole kingdom. So there he stayed in his basket, observing his vow. However, certain portents had been pointed out by the Nāga king to his retinue. He said, 'If while I am in the cross-roads observing the *Upavāsa* someone should injure me, then these signs will appear in the palace grounds of the Nāgas. If here in the palace grounds of the Nāgas, the great trees and all of the lotus flowers should become wilted, then know that the Nāga king is caught. If all of the leaves on the great trees should become desiccated and the lotus pools should dry-up, then know that the Nāga king has been killed.'

When Campaka, king of the Nāgas, was bound in that snake basket, then in the home of the Nāgas these portents became manifest. Having seen these signs appear in their home, all the Nāga men and women were choked-up: the king was captured!

What next?!
Each and every one of them was able to free the Nāga king from the hands of the snake-harmer, but they did not free him. Because at an earlier time the following had been stipulated by the Nāga king to his retinue: 'If while participating in the *Upavāsa* someone should capture or kidnap me, none of you are to do anything unfriendly or hateful, because this is my ultimate vow.'

Then, having gone to Vārāṇasī, the first queen of the Nāga king, among those sixteen thousand snake women, reported the capture of the Nāga king along with its circumstances to King Ugrasena who was residing in his best palace. King Ugrasena, having heard the proclamation of the qualities of the Nāga King Campaka from the Nāga queen, became favorably inclined. The king said to her, 'Either rest or go to your own palace until the good messengers return from their search for the Nāga king.' The Nāga queen said: 'Great king, free the Nāga king after having satisfied the snake-harmer with a village or with coined gold, but not by royal command.' The king said: 'Let it be so. Having satisfied the snake-harmer with a village or with coined gold, I will free Campaka, the Nāga king.' Then the Nāga queen said to Ugrasena, ruler of Kāśi, 'O Great King, Campaka the king along with these sixteen thousand women take refuge in your protection.' And having spoken, the Nāga queen vanished.

Ugrasena sent messengers out all over the neighborhood, who said, 'Campaka the Nāga king, while engaging in the *Upavāsa* was seized by a snake-harmer. Bring him!'

Gods [accomplish all] by the mind, kings, by speech, the wealthy, by speed, the poor, by work.

By the mere words of King Ugrasena, the snake-harmer and the Nāga king were brought by the royal messengers. After having satisfied the snake-harmer with a village and coined gold, Campaka, the Nāga king, was freed by the king. Immediately upon his release, Campaka, the Nāga king, turned into one who was comparable to a deva-king, and the palace of the Nāgas became like a palace of the gods just as it was before. And having seen the palace returned to its former glory, the retinue of the Nāga king became happy and joyful. The Nāga king was free!

Then the Nāga king along with Ugrasena, king of Kāśi, sat together as one on a couch. And he announced to the king of Kāśi: 'I wish, Great King, that you could see my palace along with your retinue.' The king said, 'You Nāgas are sharply venomous and wrathful, I am not able to go to your Nāga palace.' The Nāga king said to him: 'Anyone who would harm you after you have done us such a great service should fall bodily into a great hell, he should fall alive into hell! May the earth along with the moon and the stars fall, and may the rivers flow upstream; truly, I should not speak false words and not forget your action.' The king said: 'Let the desire of the Nāga king be realized. I will see your palace.' King Ugrasena then ordered his ministers: 'Let the chariots, elephants, horses, and various vehicles be prepared. We will see the palace of the Nāga king.'

Immediately following this speech, the ministers attended to everything. Along with his ministers, retinue, paired horses, armies, and carriages, the king, having mounted into the same vehicle together with the Nāga King Campaka, left the city of Vārāṇasī. And with great royal power and great royal splendor along with the great roar of the drum and conches and hoorahs from the populace, he went to the home of the Nāga King Campaka. Having gone as far as the ground was prepared for vehicles, he along with his retinue entered the palace of the Nāga king on foot. As he saw the palace of the Nāga King Campaka, it seemed like the palace of the gods: beautified by thousands of trees bearing fruits and flowers and suffused with a variety of garlands, and splendid with jewel encrusted lotus pools amassed with a variety of lotus flowers, with bejeweled upper rooms and halls with columns of cats-eye gem and floors made of coral. There the king of Kāśi was seated close by the Nāga King Campaka on a couch made of jewels. The sixteen thousand Nāga women, having approached the Nāga King Campaka, asked him: 'How was your stay in the midst of enemies? How did you eat and drink? How were you freed?' The Nāga king said: 'The drink and the food obtained for me were just as they should be, and I was freed by this king of Kāśi here.' Then the Nāga king's sixteen thousand Nāga women became happy and joyful. The Nāga King Campaka gave 500 cart-loads of pearls mixed with cats-eye gems to King Ugrasena, and he watches-over the palace of King Ugrasena all the time, which was like a palace of the devas.[50] There was continuous protection for the royal family, and when a fire broke out, the Nāga King Campaka extinguished it.[51]

The presentation of this tale in the *Mahāvastu* is completely different from its presentation in the Pāli texts. As noted, the introductory verses which target an audience of Buddhist laypeople in order to caution them against Nāga worship are missing entirely. The redactors of the *Mahāvastu* leave out such a warning because they are not trying to win and maintain the exclusive allegiance of laypeople and as such, they have no need to discredit Nāga worship. Rather, as we have seen throughout the *Mahāvastu*, the redactors present Nāga worship and Buddhism as compatible modes of religiosity in order that they might associate the Buddhas with the Nāga kings, their sites, and their rituals. As such, they go out of their way in the preceding story to stress the compatible lifestyles of the Nāga king and the Buddhist layperson as it is stated in back-to-back verses that while the Nāga king (the future Buddha—Śākyamuni) "enjoyed himself in that Nāga palace just like a king of the devas" he was still prepared to go out on "the 8th, the 14th, and the 15th, and observe the *Uposatha* at the crossroads [f]urnished with the 8 precepts of the Buddhist layperson."

As far as the *Mahāvastu's* redactors are concerned, then, the piety of the Nāga king need never conflict with his basic nature, for this version portrays him as neither dissatisfied with his life as a Nāga nor as wishing to escape the Nāgaloka in order to become a human being.[52] In fact, this version states that the entire Nāga kingdom has taken up Buddhist vows against violence as they were first adopted by the Nāga king. This narrative emphasis on the Nāga's piety also occurs in two other *Jātaka* tales presented in the *Mahāvastu*, namely, the stories of the Nāga King Ugra and and the Nāga King Atula. In each story, the Nāga king *cum* Bodhisattva is able to act as both a proper Buddhist layperson and a Nāga.[53]

There are several other telling omissions within this version that also help to reveal the text's narrative agenda. For example, the *Mahāvastu* leaves out the portion of the story in which the Nāga king hands over his own watery realm to the rescued ruler of Magadha. In the *Mahāvastu*, then, the regional sovereignty of the

Nāga King Campaka, whose name denotes his territorial association with the Campā River region, remains sacrosanct. The *Mahāvastu* also omits the violent mishandling of the Nāga king as well as all allusions to the Nāga king being forced to appear as a dancing snake. These omissions allow the text to frame the Nāga king in an entirely different way from the Pāli text's version of this *Jātaka*: at no point is he made to appear as a ridiculous and pathetic character, rather even when covered up in the snake-harmer's basket, the Nāga king is said to be a figure of "great power and brilliance."

In this version, the Nāga king's fertility ritual is also absent; a fertility ritual that was incorporated and resignified as a Buddhist ritual within the Pāli text. Given the fact that the *Mahāvastu's* redactors are not attempting to recruit converts from Nāga worship, however, they need neither incorporate nor resignify Nāga centered ritual practices. In fact, as far as the redactors of this text are concerned, supernatural powers over both earthly and human fertility are far better left to those snake sovereigns originally charged with their dispatchment.

The *Mahāvastu's* redactors add several things to the preceding story which are missing from the Pāli version. While the redactors of the Pāli texts removed the Nāgas' beneficial association with water in order to associate them with the destructive force of fire, the redactors of the *Mahāvastu* take the opposite tack, as the last line of the text states that "[t]here was continuous protection for the royal family, and when a fire broke-out, the Nāga King Campaka extinguished it." Moreover, the redactors go out of their way to portray the two royal sovereigns, Campaka and Ugrasena, as equals:

> In a previous time, Monks, in the city of Vārāṇasī in the kingdom of Kāśi, there ruled a king named Ugrasena who acquired merit, [and] who was called 'Great Lord.'
>
> Now, in that kingdom, there lived a Nāga king by the name of Campaka who had acquired merit, [and] had an abundant mass of goodness.

In the above passages, not only do the two kings rule over almost identical kingdoms, but also both are depicted as having "acquired merit," a Buddhist value that we also saw highlighted in relation to the Nāga Kings Mucilinda and Vinipāta. Moreover, the two kings are seen to move between each other's realms, enjoy each other's hospitality, and even, in a sweetly evocative moment, sit together as one on a couch. The text even calls Campaka at one point the rāja Campaka (not *Nāga* rāja Campaka).[54] However, the Nāga King Campaka has one attribute that King Ugrasena lacks: he has the supernatural "power and brilliance" of a devatā. The praise of the Nāga's supernatural powers is reminiscent of the late Vedic texts, the only other set of texts in our series to recognize the Nāga as an object of religious devotion.

The Nāga King Elapatra and the Festival of the Four Treasures

The reverential treatment that this text accords the Nāgas is seconded only by their treatment in the late Vedas. And like the late Vedas, the *Mahāvastu's* sanctioning of the snake as an efficacious, autonomous deity has led not only to the elevation of the Nāga and the narrative preservation of its sites, but also to the preservation and formalization of certain snake-centered rituals. This is particularly clear in the *Mahāvastu's* story of the Nāga King Elapatra—who also made a brief appearance in the *Ādi Parvan*[55]—for in this story we learn something about the development of snake worship during this historical period as the text tells us of the monthly festivals designed to celebrate the Nāga kings and their earthly treasures.

> In Vārāṇasī, there were six self-alleged teachers: Kāśyapa Purāṇa, Maskari Gośālikāputra, Ajita Keśamkambalin, Kakuda Kātyāyana, Sañjayin Veraṭṭikāputra and Nirgrantha Jñātiputra. Nālaka went to them, but his mind was not gratified. There are four great treasures: the conch in Vārāṇasī, the lotus in Mithilā, the piṃgala in Kaliṃga, and the elapatra in Takṣaśīla. In Vārāṇasī, there is a monthly

festival of the shell. And there, the Nāga kings come as invited guests for they are the guardians of the treasures. There, by the Nāga King Elapatra, questions were posed, and to the one who could answer the questions, 1,000 pieces of gold as well as Elapatra's daughter would be given.

The Nāga King Elapatra said:

Of what is a king the ruler? How does one become passionate? How does he become purified? And for what reason is he called a child?

The Blessed One said:

The king is the ruler when the sixth sense is sovereign. He becomes tainted[56] with passion when he is excited. When unexcited he is untainted. He is called a child when he is excited.

Elapatra said:

By what is a child carried away? What does the wise one push away? How does a man destroy his bonds? This I ask, let it be told to me.

The Blessed One said:

The child is carried off by bonds of attachment. The wise one pushes away those bonds. The one who is not tied up by any bonds at all is one who has destroyed the bonds of attachment.

Elapatra said:

You are called Buddha, Buddha. How do you appear in sleeping dreams and waking sight? Do you speak the truth? Having seen it, speak! And cut away doubt.

By a Deva it was said:

Like a lion in a mountain cave he is seen proclaiming the best of dharmas. Ah, at last we will see the brilliant limbs with marks that are like the stars of the Buddha with the best intelligence. Ah, at last we will hear the voice that

> resembles that of Lord Brahmā[57] speaking of impermanence, suffering, and selflessness, and tearing apart all afflictions. Having heard the voice that resembled Lord Brahmā's, we will obtain release at these *tīrthas* having approached that bull among men.[58]

The redactors of the *Mahāvastu* have purposefully chosen to highlight the role of the Nāgas on the occasion of a Nāga festival, thereby emphasizing the fact that these occasions are conducive to the teaching of the dharma. Their teaching of dharma, moreover, focuses not only on the liminal nature of the lokottara Buddhas, those who appear both in "sleeping dreams and waking sight," but also on the inferior nature of Brahminism as the story begins with the fact that Nālaka went to a variety of brahmin ascetics "but his mind was not gratified." Taking a swipe at brahmin ascetics while preserving and even elevating the Nāga is reminiscent of the Uruvilvā story.

The *Mahāvastu*'s presentation of a Nāga king who is a noble spiritual sojourner, and who is wise enough in the ways of dharma to engage the Buddha in a doctrinal discourse, is by far the most elevated characterization that we have seen of the Nāga. In portraying the Nāga King Elapatra and the Buddha as dialogue partners, the Buddha is explicitly equated with this earthly figure. This passage, moreover, particularly associates the Buddha with the Nāga not as a Nāgarāja but as a *bhūmya deva*, one who is celebrated along with the riches of the earth. The fact that the Nāga is specifically contextualized as an earth-god rather than a king, allows the redactors to critique the role of the king and to realign this role in keeping with Buddhist ethics: "The king is the ruler when the sixth sense is sovereign. He becomes tainted with passion when he is excited." More importantly, highlighting the Nāga as an earth-god also allows the Buddha to share the stage with the Nāga King Elapatra on the occasion of the Nāga kings' monthly festival. [59] Clearly, a highly desirable venue from the perspective of the redactors as it allows them a setting whereby Buddhist practices might be perceived as more generally accessible and relevant to the needs of the people.

The section of the text extolling the Nāga kings and their four treasures is perhaps the most interesting part of the tale in terms of telling us something about snake worship during this period. And as we saw in relation to the Pāli texts, the Nāga kings are well identified at this point in time with earthly riches. Apparently, there are four Nāga kings who are the guardians of four treasures. And these four are so identified with these treasures that their very names derive from them: *saṃkha* is easy enough for it means simply "conch" or "shell;" *paduma* is also clear, for it is a common variety of lotus; *piṃgala* and *elapatra*, however, are a bit more difficult. *Piṃgala*, literally, means nothing more than reddish-brown in color, and Edgerton tells us little more than the fact that it is "one of the four 'great treasures,' or of the 'king' who guards it."[60] *Ela* itself merely signifies a high number; thus the name Elapatra, like Piṃgala, yields little in the way of clues.[61]

These treasures and the Nāga kings who guard them are the principle foci of a monthly festival, and the Nāga kings themselves show up as "invited guests" at each of these four festivals. At the time of our story, all of the Nāga kings have repaired to Banāras to celebrate the festival of the shell and the Nāga King Saṃkha. Banāras has several ancient sites dedicated to the worship of Nāgas: there are two Nāga kuāns—elaborately constructed stone-work pools—one inside the city that is used for Nāga worship up to the present time, and another in ruins outside of the city. Also, at the top of Caukī Ghāt in Banāras, there are several Nāga statues that were established there by Nāga rulers.[62]

While the name of the Nāga King Saṃkha is not referenced specifically in relation to the Nāga temples in Banāras, the name of the Nāga King Elapatra does show up in historical documents. Hsuan Tsang, the 7th century monk who made a pilgrimage from China to India in search of Buddhist scriptures, tells of a Nāga tank dedicated to the Nāga King Elapatra:

> Northwest of the capital [Takṣaśila] about 70 li is the tank of the Nāgarāja Elapatra; it is about 100 paces round, the waters are pure and sweet; lotus flowers of various colors, which reflect different tints in their common beauty, garnish the surface....[63]

Given that the Pāli redactors explicitly warned against worshipping the Nāgas for their "fortune," it is telling that the *Mahāvastu's* redactors highlight a celebration of the Nāga kings' treasures. Clearly, the *Mahāvastu's* redactors are not looking to illuminate potential incompatibilities between Nāga worship and Buddhism. Rather, it would seem that they highlight the pragmatic aspects of Nāga worship, such as the Nāga's control over earthly riches, in order to make Buddhist practices appear more generally relevant. This desire to situate Buddhist practices within the confines of Nāga worship is particularly demonstrated as this story highlights *tīrthas*, those places where one might *tṝ* or "cross" a body of water and thereby gain access to the supernatural snakes living below the waters. For in relation to these sacred Nāga sites, the text states explicitly that those who come to worship the Nāgas at *tīrthas* "will obtain release at these *tīrthas* having approached that bull among men." Like the stories of Kāla, Mucilinda, and Campaka, then, this story preserves the Nāga king's regional sites in order that the Buddha might share them, indicating that the redactors of the *Mahāvastu* were well aware that just as the Nāga complements the Buddha, Nāga worship might very well complement the practice of Buddhism. Thus, in contrast to the redactors of the Pāli texts, who perceived the Nāga king as a competitor and denigrated both the sites and practices associated with him, the redactors of the *Mahāvastu* perceive the sovereign snake differently: as a revered ally whose sites, rituals, and festivals might be used both to amplify the redactors' distinctive vision of the lokottara Buddhas and to render Buddhism and Buddhist practices more generally accessible.

Conclusion: Lokottara Buddhas and Earthly Nāgas

As noted by J.J. Jones in his translation of the *Mahāvastu*: "Indeed, if the translator has not gained a wrong impression, the divinities of the lower culture play a rather more prominent part in the *Mahāvastu* than in other Buddhist works."[64] I would have to agree. For while the redactors of the Pāli texts demonized the Nāga in an attempt to stamp out Nāga worship, the redactors of the *Mahāvastu* seem to appreciate Nāga worship as it provides them with an opportunity to present their new version of a glorified yet grounded Buddha. The redactors of this text are thus doing something quite different than their Theravādin brethren with the Nāga Kings Kāla, Mucilinda, Campaka, and Uruvilvā. First, they are using the Nāga to model the fabulous attributes of a liminal being. In so doing, these redactors are able to reconfigure the significance of the Buddha indirectly, as the Nāga is made both to affirm and to reflect the unique nature of these transcendent, transformative beings, who successively reside upon the earth. Second, the redactors are maintaining the Nāga as an accessible figure within its own tradition of snake worship so that the lokottara Buddhas might be seen as similarly accessible as they appear at the Nāga kings' homes, sites, and festivals. Thus, within the pages of the *Mahāvastu*, Nāga worship and Buddhism coexist as compatible contextual frameworks, and ideological competition is kept at a minimum, reserved as it is to the redactors' infrequent jabs at Brahminism.

The lokottara Buddhas portrayed within this text are figures who are "distinguished from all others in the world."[65] They are "distinguished," moreover, because they exemplify a relational dynamic between transcendence and earthliness; a dynamic demonstrated by the *Mahāvastu's* Nāga kings as well. Just as a powerful earthly figure will inspire deification, a deified figure demands an earthly platform, a solid foundation from which its glory might be made manifest. And as far as the redactors of the *Mahāvastu* are concerned, the Nāga king, through his noble bearing, regional sites, and colorful festivals, provides the best support for that earthly platform. An earthly platform, moreover, that unlike the giant Buddha statues in Afghanistan, cannot be destroyed as long as Nāga worship endures, for while the statues were engraved in stone, the Nāga king is engraved in the hearts and minds of worshippers.

7

Conclusion: It Is Hard to Keep a Good Snake Down

Throughout this book, I have attempted to provide a comprehensive analysis of the role of the supernatural snake as it has been featured within orthodox texts of both the Hindu and Buddhist traditions. And what I have argued from the beginning of this analysis is that these orthodox redactors are not constructing the supernatural snake *ex nihilo*, but rather are sometimes borrowing and at other times stealing this figure, its powers, its sites, and its rituals from a preestablished tradition of snake worship. As a result of this borrowing/stealing process, these orthodox texts provide us with a tremendous resource for viewing the development of snake worship over the centuries.

While orthodox texts provide a valuable chronicle of older, non-literary traditions, scholars, for the most part, have not viewed or used them as such. This is due to the fact that, historically, grass-roots traditions were held to be inferior to canonical traditions. Monier-Williams, one of the great Indologists of the 19th century, speaks eloquently of this bias when speaking of Hinduism: "[I]n no other system of the world is the chasm more vast which separates the religion of the higher, cultured, and thoughtful classes from that of the lower, uncultured, and unthinking masses."[1] Given the fact that the orthodox redactors of "the higher, cultured, and thoughtful classes," appear to have been constantly borrowing from "the lower, uncultured, and unthinking masses," it would appear best to reverse the roles assigned to his respective subjects of analysis.

In focusing our attention on the figure of the supernatural snake, we have been able not only to re-think the role that non-literary traditions play in providing the building blocks of a larger religious sensibility, but also to focus on the process by which both literary and non-literary traditions come to be. This process is one of constructing a contextual framework. Snake worshippers have been actively involved for millennia in building up a contextual framework around the snake that allows this figure to speak to their fears and experiences, hopes and dreams. The elements comprising this contextual framework include all of the details that render this figure as an efficacious deity: its range of supernatural powers, its appearance, its friends, its enemies, its title, its home, the degree of honor it commands, and the means for honoring it. These snake worshippers thus act as 'context constructors,' for it is through their efforts in building up a contextual framework around the snake that this object of religious devotion, as well as its accompanying ritual and discursive modalities, come to be.

We have also seen throughout these chapters that the efforts of those 'context constructors' involved in creating a tradition of snake worship have been either stymied or supported by other sets of 'context constructors': various orthodox redactors from both the Hindu and Buddhist traditions who were bent on either stealing the snake's powers and eradicating this tradition or borrowing the snake's powers and preserving this tradition. Moreover, as we have applied the phrase, 'context constructor' to both snake worshippers and orthodox redactors, understanding both parties to be engaged in the construction of contextual frameworks which reflect their respective fears and desires, we are able to see the process by which these religious traditions come to be, and the motivations of those engaged in the construction of a religious tradition as well as the contextualizing strategies employed to assert one tradition over another. Thus, while we might substitute the terms 'redactor' or 'worshipper' for 'context constructor,' as well as 'tradition,' or 'movement' for 'contextual framework,' the latter term in each case has forced our attention not only to the *process* of building up these religious structures but also to the *agents* engaged in this process.

Competing Contextual Frameworks

The orthodox redactors most threatened by snake worship and thereby most concerned with asserting their contextual framework over snake worship have included the brahmin redactors of the *Ṛg Veda* and the *Ādi Parvan*, as well as the Buddhist redactors of the Pāli texts. Each of these sets of redactors found snake worship to be threatening because it compromised their ability to construct a contextual frame wherein they or their champions are perceived as embodying the highest religious authority. In each set of texts wherein the supernatural snake was perceived as a threat, however, it was also perceived as an opportunity; for having subordinated the snake and the ritual tradition with which it is associated, the redactors would take over the snake's powers, rituals, and sites in order to transfer them to their chosen champions.

In terms of the brahmin redactors, their specific narrative agenda might be stated quite simply: to achieve the hierarchical elevation of brahmins over all others. While enacting the same agenda, however, each set of brahmin redactors did so in the midst of very different historical moments. In terms of the *Ṛg Veda*, those brahmin redactors were engaged in the process of establishing the Āryan people on the Indian sub-continent and establishing the brahmin class at the top of the Āryan social order. Confronted with the indigenous phenomenon of snake worship wherein a supernatural snake was positioned as a powerful earthly sovereign, the brahmin redactors were faced with the challenge of demoting the supernatural snake from its preestablished religious role in order to replace this figure with a brahmin-controlled god. This process was made particularly clear as Vṛtra—the *Ṛg Veda's* serpentine antagonist—was set up as a rival sovereign only to be conquered by Indra—the brahmins' divine champion. And having been conquered, Vṛtra was immediately divested of those elements which would have elevated him originally to divine status: his sovereign authority, power over water and other earthly elements, as well as control over cows and various earthly resources. Upon overcoming Vṛtra, moreover, the supernatural snake's authority, power, and control were transferred to Indra who became known as the King of the Gods.

> No use was the lightning and thunder, rain and hail that he [Vṛtra] scattered about, when the *ahi* and Indra fought. Indra the Generous was made the victor both for now and for the future....Indra, who raises up the thunderbolt in his hand, is the king of those that journey and those that rest, of the tame and of the horned. He rules over the people as king, encompassing everything as a rim encompasses spokes.[2]

Thus, we see in the *Ṛg Veda* a moment in which the redactors of an orthodox text must respond to a preestablished contextual framework; one which constructs the snake as a supernaturally powerful sovereign who controls the earthly and atmospheric resources upon which agrarian peoples are so dependent. As the brahmin redactors wish to replace this accessible snake sovereign with their chosen champion and thereby elevate their class to the role of divine intermediaries, they dismantle the sovereign snake's contextual framework and use the pieces to construct their own: one which centralizes the brahmin-controlled Indra as a supernaturally powerful sovereign.

Like the *Ṛg Veda*, the *Ādi Parvan* is redacted at a time when brahmins are again required to consolidate their religious authority. This is not surprising given that approximately eight to ten centuries have elapsed since the proclamation of the *Ṛg Vedic* social order which positioned brahmins as the first class. In the intervening centuries, moreover, the supernatural snake and its accompanying ritual practices only grew in stature, especially with the narrative assistance of the late Vedic redactors. As a result, the redactors of the *Ādi Parvan* perceive snake worship as both a tremendous threat and a tremendous opportunity. In terms of the former, they not only divest the snake of all the powers for which it is worshipped but also dismantle the ritual tradition with which it is associated. In terms of the latter, the redactors coopt the snake's powers as well as its sacred sites and reserve them for the exclusive use of brahmins and brahmin-like figures. Thus, in the same manner as the *Ṛg Veda*, the *Ādi Parvan* deconstructs the contextual framework within which the supernatural snake is centered in order to reconstruct a new framework within which brahmins are centered.

The redactors of the *Ṛg Veda* and the *Ādi Parvan* might both be seen as having enacted a political agenda through a religious agenda, as the hierarchical elevation of brahmins occurred through the hierarchical elevation of Brahminism. In contrast, the Buddhist redactors of the Pāli texts are not motivated by political concerns but rather by ideological concerns; for these redactors are attempting to promote Buddhism not as a means to a political end, but rather as an end in itself. In the Pāli texts, then, the brahminical agenda is reversed as the hierarchical elevation of Buddhism occurs through the hierarchical elevation of the Buddha. As seen previously, however, snake worship is still very much perceived as a threat. This derives from the fact that as far as the Pāli redactors are concerned, the prominence of snake worship compromises their ability to construct a contextual frame wherein the Buddha and various Buddhist saints are perceived as embodying the highest religious authority. These redactors, moreover, are very interested in recruiting converts to this nascent tradition of Buddhism. They therefore launch a three-pronged attack whereby they demonize the snake, coopt its powers, and incorporate this figure, its sites, and several of its rituals into the Buddhist contextual framework.

Each of the three chapters featuring these texts clearly documents a struggle between competing forms of religiosity: Brahminism and Nāga worship on the one hand and Buddhism and Nāga worship on the other. And as such, they demonstrate a contest over not only which contextual framework but also which system of values is to be granted preeminent status: those associated with the experiences and desires of respective sets of orthodox redactors or those associated with the experiences and desires of Nāga worshippers. In terms of the textual preservation of snake worship, moreover, this ongoing ideological competition has an interesting side-effect; for while the redactors are subordinating the supernatural snake in order to transfer its powers to their various champions, they are also preserving, while usually denigrating, a number of snake-centered ritual practices. Additionally, having incorporated the supernatural snake and its ritual tradition to stand on the limen of orthodoxy, the supernatural snake remains poised—always ready to spring—at the juncture of competing contextual frameworks. Both Śeṣa and Mucilinda demonstrate this ideological reversal of fortunes as they loose the redactors' bonds to spring back to their preestablished positions as objects of religious devotion. Thus, while doing their best to subordinate the supernatural snake as well as the sites and ritual practices with which it is associated, these redactors certainly preserved many aspects of this rival tradition and may have advanced its development.

Compatible Contextual Frameworks

While the redactors of the *Ṛg Veda*, the *Ādi Parvan* and the Pāli texts engaged in a contextual tug-of-war with snake worshippers, some redactors were involved in the construction of contextual frameworks that were compatible with this grass-roots movement. This is particularly clear as we turn to the late Vedas and the *Mahāvastu*, for in neither case were the redactors threatened by the phenomenon of snake worship. Rather, both sets of redactors sought to preserve the supernatural snake and the ritual tradition with which it is associated because it was seen to complement their own respective narrative agendas.

The late Vedas, more than any other texts in our survey, preserved and formalized the figures, sites and rituals central to snake worship. The redactors did this for two reasons: first, various snake-centered ritual practices such as the *Sarpasattra* and the

Sarpanāma function to empower brahmins and help them to carry out their own ritual activities. Second, one of the primary jobs of these learned brahmin priests was that of sorting out and recording the correct manner in which rituals were to be performed, thereby establishing an orthodox canon of ritual activities. Toward that end, the late Vedic redactors were interested in compiling all of the various means available for controlling nature, and as such they valorize the supernatural snake and its accompanying ritual tradition as one of those means.

The *Mahāvastu* also preserves the snake as well as snake-centered sites and ritual practices. However, the redactors of this text do so for their own very particular reasons: they believe that the supernatural snake might function not only as a means for situating their transcendent Buddha back on this earth but also as a model through which their audience might apprehend their new image of a transcendent yet immanent Buddha. As the redactors borrow the Nāga king, his sites, and his festivals, without dissociating these things from their original context, they advance not only their distinctive image of the Buddha but also the snake in the grass-roots movement. The redactors of this text enact their narrative agenda, moreover, through altering the contextual details of four snake stories previewed in the Pāli texts. And as a result, the *Mahāvastu* provides us with a marvelous occasion for seeing the double-edged nature of the contextual weapon.

Snake Worshippers as Context Constructors

Through these orthodox texts we have seen myriad snake kings come to life such as Vṛtra, Arbuda Kādraveya, Takṣaka Vaiśāleya, Dhṛtarāṣṭra Airāvata, Vāsuki, Kāla, Mucilinda, Campaka, and Elapatra. We have been allowed visions of the luxurious Nāgaloka, examined *tīrthas* and *caityas*, learned of the snake kings' regional connections, and enjoyed their colorful festivals. And finally, we have read about snake-centered rituals that could insure a good harvest, purify a building site, provide one with sons, protect one from biting snakes, and grant one untold riches. However, even without the direct help of like-minded redactors and the inadvertent support of those less well-inclined, I would argue that it is hard to keep a good snake down. And as far as snake worshippers are concerned, the figure that they have custom-designed through the construction and constant updating of their contextual framework is a very good snake indeed. It has sovereign control over all earthly elements, it enjoys possession of all earthly riches, it responds to all manner of human desires, and most importantly, it is endlessly accessible to all human beings.

I would argue that it is this last issue, moreover, that has caused snake worship to persevere throughout the ages. For as the supernatural snake might be accessed at river crossings, ponds, kuans, and small shrines all across India, anyone with a desire to do so might approach this powerful sovereign and propitiate him to secure their heart's desire. In fact, most of the snake-centered rituals encompassed within these texts are not restricted to select humans such as kings or brahmins, but rather might be practiced by anyone who desires something from the supernatural snake. For example, in the late Vedic *Sarpabali,*[3] any human could ask the supernatural snake kings to protect them from poisonous snakes, as the ritual merely requires "the placing on the ground of the oblations destined for the divine powers."[4] This is also the case in rituals like the late Vedic *Vāstupraśamana*, in which King Vāsuki is propitiated to insure the propitious setting of a new foundation stone.[5] Additionally, the *Jātaka Tales* state that anyone "who came and went by the highway" could worship the Nāgarāja Campeyya "in their desire for sons."[6] In the *Mahāvastu*, none were barred from attending the various festivals of the Nāga kings and worshipping "at these *tīrthas*."[7] Thus, I would argue that snake worship has continued to thrive throughout the centuries because it offers something to its worshippers that they are loathe to give up: direct access to a sovereign figure perceived to be able to influence the prosperity of its regional domain.

Because the supernatural snake is accessible to all, its ritual tradition is enjoyed by those most often disenfranchised by orthodox traditions in India: women. The freedom of worship engendered by the snake's accessibility was particularly clear to me when visiting those sites devoted to the worship of supernatural snakes in Banāras, for I observed that women account for a large percentage of the practitioners.[8] In present times, women desiring to become pregnant particularly worship Nāgas; a contemporary ritual practice that can be linked back to the *Campeyya Jātaka*. Women, moreover, dominate the ritual spaces associated with these practices. The most popular temple devoted to snakes situated in the northwest sector of Banāras operates both as a place where women might propitiate these divine sovereigns and as a place where women would gather together on Saturday evenings to sing, tell stories, and socialize.

While first-hand observation is one means for identifying those groups involved in the worship of the supernatural snake, that method does not help us compose a historical picture of these various practitioners. These orthodox texts, however, provide us with another means. For just as the contextual frame constructed around the supernatural snake allows us to see the processes by which various traditions come to be, a further analysis of these contextual frames has allowed us to glimpse a larger context: the lived reality of those groups actively involved in the construction of these contextual frames. In terms of those who have constructed the snake as an object of religious devotion, their contextual framework most likely reflects the lived reality of various groups including farmers hoping for a good harvest; women concerned with giving birth; average citizens desirous of riches; families involved in building homes; and parents worried about poisonous snakes. Seen in this light, those men and women who constructed and maintained the supernatural snake as an object of religious devotion did so in order to create a sacred being relevant and responsive to their fears and hopes, experiences and desires.

Of course, the contextual framework constructed around the snake by the orthodox redactors also provides us with a glimpse into their larger reality: the desire on behalf of the *Ṛg Vedic* priests to advance the place and position of the brahmin-led Āryans; the late Vedic redactors' urge both to compile a complete canon of ritual activities and to avail themselves of a snake deity who might enhance their ritual efficacy; the epic priests' fear that their stature would be diminished by this local snake sovereign; the Theravādins' hope to recruit converts away from ideological competitors; and the Lokottaravādins' dream of a transcendent yet accessible Buddha.

Throughout this book I have been most interested in the snake worshippers and the alternative religious tradition of which they are the authors. For in responding to the mysterious, ubiquitous snake and constructing such a rich contextual framework around this creature, snake worshippers act as the primary agents of their own religious life. This religious life not only empowers the worshipper in very pragmatic ways, but also elevates particular modes of religious sensibility: recognizing the sacrality and power of the natural world; staking a claim but not a hegemonic claim within the natural world; promoting the importance of immanent divinity; and maintaining the sanctity of a world-view rich with mystery and grace.

Clearly, the goal of all context constructors is to center themselves in a context that works for them; to create a context wherein both the world and their place in the world makes sense. As noted, Charles Long sees this as a religious task and he feels that it is often necessary to look beyond conventional settings, for while "the church is one place one looks for religion...the church [is] not the only context for the meaning of religion."[9] While I agree with this statement, this textual analysis has demonstrated that one does not have to resort to non-conventional locations to see non-conventional modes of religiosity. In fact, viewing snake worship through the narratives of these orthodox redactors has allowed us to mount a methodological strategy through which we have been able to use a conventional religious setting to provide evidence of alternative avenues of religious agency. These orthodox redactors thus provide us with an opportunity to view alternative "cultural narratives and to define the terms of another perspective—a view from 'elsewhere.'"[10]

Of course this "view from 'elsewhere'" is not readily apparent in most of these texts, for it has been ensconced within these institutional settings as a buried discourse. Moreover, when examining an orthodox text, such as those featured within this analysis, if the issue of context is seen to pertain only to the internal logic of the text itself, then buried discourses will not be brought to light. This book, however, offers a strategy for exhuming these buried discourses through the medium of contextual analysis. This strategy highlights the fact that both orthodox redactors and grass-roots practitioners such as snake worshippers are engaged in the construction of a contextual framework within which each group will center its chosen divine champion amidst a matrix of contextual details. When a grass-roots tradition is perceived as a threat, however, the orthodox redactors may move to counter this threat by mounting a narrative attack. This occurs as the redactors deconstruct the contextual framework centralizing the grass-roots figure in order to use the pieces to help bolster their own framework: one which centralizes their own divine champion. Moreover, if the redactors of an orthodox text are employing such a strategy, their agenda becomes easier to see as one utilizes a comparative methodology, because it is in the spaces in between—in the shifting or recontextualizing process perceived as we compare one text to another—that the redactors allow us to see their various reactions to alternative modes of religiosity. Thus, as scholars focus on the fact that these redactors oftentimes use context to achieve narrative goals that extend well beyond the limits of the page, we are positioned to unearth these buried discourses and thus reveal a "view from 'elsewhere.'"

This has certainly been apparent as we have examined these texts for the alternative mode of religiosity defined by snake worshippers, for as various orthodox redactors perceived snake worship as both a threat and an opportunity, they struggled to suppress its efficacy while consistently highlighting its figures, sites, and rituals. Paradoxically, then, those Hindu and Buddhist redactors most interested in eradicating this tradition of snake worship have been extremely helpful in making it visible. I would therefore assert that it is important for scholars to analyze religious texts as sources of preservation not only for orthodox ideologies but also for buried discourses that centralize figures such as the supernatural snake, for oftentimes it is the latter rather than the former that have the most direct impact on the day-to-day lives of devout people.

Bibliography

Aitareya Brāhmaṇa. With the Commentary of Sāyaṇa. Ed. S. Samasrami. Calcutta: Asiatic Society of Bengal, 1897.

Aitareya Brāhmaṇa. 2 vols. Anandasrama-samskrta-granthavalih, granthannkha 32. Poona: Anandasrama, 1931.

Āpastamba Śrauta Sūtra. 3 vols. Ed. Garbe. Calcutta: Royal Asiatic Society of Bengal, 1882-1902.

Aśvaghoṣa's Buddhacarita or Acts of the Buddha. Trans. E.H. Johnston. Delhi: Munshiram Manoharlal, 1972.

Āśvalāyana Gṛhya Sūtra. With the Commentary of Nārāyaṇa. Eds. Vidyaratna and Vedantavagisa. Calcutta: Asiatic Society of Bengal, 1869.

Āśvalāyana Śrauta Sūtra. Ed. Vidyaratna. Calcutta: Asiatic Society of Bengal, 1874.

Atharva Veda. With the Commentary of Sāyaṇa, Ed. Vishva Bandhu and others. Hoshiarpur: Visveshvaranand Indological Series, 1960-1964.

——. Trans. W.D. Whitney. Cambridge: Harvard Oriental Series, 1905.

——. Trans. Maurice Bloomfield. Delhi: Motilal Banarsidass, 1964.

Auboyer, Jeannine. "Le caractere Royal et Divine du Trône dans l'inde Ancienne." In *The Sacral Kingship*, Vol. IV of *Studies in the History of Religion.* Leiden: E.J. Brill, 1959.

——. *Le Trône et son symbolisme dans l'Inde Ancienne.* Paris: Presses Universitaires de France, 1949.

Baudhāyana Gṛhya Sūtra. Ed. Shama Sastri. Mysore: Government Branch Press, 1920; reprint New Delhi: Meharchand Lachhmandas, 1982.

Baudhāyana Śrauta Sūtra. 3 vols. Ed. W. Caland. Calcutta: Asiatic Society of Bengal, 1904-24; reprint New Delhi: Munshiram Manoharlal, 1982.

Bareau, Andre. "The Superhuman Personality of Buddha and its Symbolism in the Mahāparinirvāṇasụtra of Dharmaguptaka." In *Myths and Symbols: Studies in Honor of Mircea Eliade.* Eds. Kitagawa and Long. Chicago: University of Chicago Press, 1969.

———. "Les récits canoniques des funérailles du Buddha et leurs anomalies: Nouvel essai d'interprétation." Bulletin de l'Ecole Française d'Extreme-Orient 62 (1975): 151-189.

———. "Hināyāna Buddhism." Article in Volume 2 of *The Encyclopedia of Religion.* Ed. Mircea Eliade. New York: Macmillan Publishing Company, 1987.

Basham, A.L. *The Wonder that was India.* New York: Grove Press, 1964.

Beal, Samuel, trans. *Travels of Fah-hian and Sung-yun: Buddhist Pilgrims from China to India (400A.D. and 518 A.D.).* London: Trubner and Co., 1869.

Bhāgavata Pūraṇa. With the commentary of Sridhara. Bombay: 1832.

Biardeau, M. *Études de mythologies Hindoue.* Paris: École des Hautes Études of the Sorbonne, 1969.

———. "Purāṇic Cosmogony." In *Asian Mythologies.* Comp. by Yves Bonnefoy. Chicago: University of Chicago Press, 1993.

Bloss, L. *Ancient Indian Folk Religion as Seen through the Symbolism of the Nāga.* University of Chicago Dissertation, 1971.

———. "The Buddha and the Nāga: A Study in Buddhist Folk Religiosity." *History of Religions* 13 (1973): 36-53.

———."The Taming of Māra: Witnessing to the Buddha's Virtues." *History of Religions* 18 (1978): 156-176.

———. "Nāgas and Yakṣas." Article in Volume 10 of *The Encyclopedia of Religion.* Ed. Mircea Eliade. New York: MacMillan Publishing Co., 1987.

Bṛhadāraṇyaka Upaniṣad. Eds. Limaye and Vadekar. *In Eighteen Principal Upaniṣads.* Poona: Vaidika Samsodhana Mandala, 1958.

Burkert, W. *Creation of the Sacred: Tracks of Biology in Early Religions.* Cambridge: Harvard University Press, 1996.

Cabezon, J.I., ed. *Buddhism, Sexuality, and Gender.* Albany: State University of New York Press, 1992.

Coedes, G. "La Legend de la Nāgī." *Bulletin de L'École française d'Extreme Orient.* XI (1911): 391-93.

Conze, E. *Buddhist Thought in India.* Ann Arbor: University of Michigan Press, 1967.

Coomaraswamy, A. *Yakṣas, Essays in the Water Cosmology.* New York: Oxford University Press, 1993.

Craven, Roy. *Indian Art.* London: Thames and Hudson, 1976.

Daly, Mary. *Beyond God the Father: Toward a Philosophy of Women's Liberation.* Boston: Beacon Press, 1973.

Dange, S.A. *Myths from the Mahābhārata.* Delhi: Aryan Books International, 1997.

Das Kanjabihari. "The Plant in Orissan Folklore," *Tree Symbol Worship in India: A New Survey of a Pattern of Folk-religion.* Ed Sankar Sen Gupta. Calcutta: Indian Publications, 1965.

de Lauretis, Teresa. *Technologies of Gender: Essays on Theory, Film, and Fiction.* Bloomington: Indiana University Press, 1987.

Denis, E. *La Lokapaññatti et les idées cosmologiques du boud-dhisme ancien.* 3 vols. Lille, 1977.

de Souza, J.P. "The Serpent as a Symbol of Life and Immortality," *Indian Historical Congress,* Pt. I (1966): 101-8.

de Visser, M.W. *The Dragon in China and Japan.* Amsterdam: Johannes Muller, 1913.

Dhammapada. Trans. Narada Thera. London: J. Murray, 1954.

Dīgha Nikāya. Eds. Rhys Davids and J. Estlin Carpenter. London: Pāli Text Society, 1890.

Dikshitar, V.R. "Origin and Early History of Caityas". *Indian Historical Quarterly,* XIV, No. 3 (1938): 440-51.

Dimock, E.C. "The Goddess of Snakes in Medieval Bengali Literature." *History of Religions* 1 (1962): 307-321.

———. "Manasā, Goddess of Snakes: The Ṣaṣṭhī Myth." *Myths and Symbols.* Eds. Kitagawa and Long. Chicago: University of Chicago Press, 1969.

Dimock, E.C. and Ramanujan, A.K. "The Goddess of Snakes in Medieval Bengali Literature, Part II." *History of Religions* 3 (1964): 300-322.

Dīpavaṃsa. Trans. Hermann Oldenburg. London: Williams and Norgate, 1879.

Divyāvadāna. Ed. P.L. Vaidya. Buddhist Sanskrit Texts, no 20. Darbhanga: Mithila Insitute, 1959.

Doniger, Wendy, ed. *Textual Sources for the Study of Hinduism.* Chicago: University of Chicago Press, 1988.

Dumezil G. *The Destiny of a Warrior.* Trans. Alf Hiltebeitel. Chicago: University of Chicago Press, 1970.

——. *The Destiny of a King.* Trans. Alf Hiltebeitel. Chicago: University of Chicago Press, 1973.

Dutt, S. *The Buddha and the Five After-Centuries.* London: Luzac and Co, 1957.

——. *Buddhist Sects in India.* Calcutta: Calcutta Oriental Press, 1970

Eck, Diana. *Banāras: City of Light.* Princeton: Princeton University Press, 1982.

Edgerton, Franklin. *Buddhist Hybrid Sanskrit Grammar and Dictionary.* Delhi: Motilal Banarsidass, 1953.

Eliade, M. *The Quest: History and Meaning in Religion.* Chicago: University of Chicago Press, 1969.

——., ed. *The Encyclopedia of Religion.* New York: Macmillan Publishing Co., 1987.

Falk, N. & Gross, R., eds. *Unspoken Worlds: Women's Religious Lives.* Belmont: Wadsworth Publishing Co., 1989.

Faure, B. "Space and Place in Chinese Religious Traditions." *History of Religions* 26 (1987): 337-356.

——. *The Rhetoric of Immediacy: A Cultural Critique of Chan/ Zen Buddhism.* Princeton: Princeton University Press, 1991

Fausboll, V. *Indian Mythology.* London: Luzac and Co., 1903.

Fernandes, W., ed. *The Indigenous Question: Search for an Identity.* Delhi: Indian Social Institute, 1993.

Fergusson, J. *Tree and Serpent Worship.* Delhi: Indological Book House, 1868.

Foucault, M. *The Order of Things: An Archaeology of the Human Sciences.* New York: Vintage Books, 1970.

Foucher, A. *The Life of the Buddha: According to the Ancient Texts and Monuments of India.* Trans. Simone Brangier Boas. Middleton, Conn: Wesleyan University Press, 1963.

———. *Beginnings of Buddhist Art.* Varanasi: Indological Book House, 1972.

Geertz, C. *The Interpretation of Cultures.* Basic Books, 1973.

Glucklich, A. *The Sense of Adharma.* Oxford: Oxford University Press, 1994.

Gobhila Gṛhya Sūtra. Ed. Bhattacharya. Calcutta: Metropolitan Printing and Publishing House, 1936.

Gombrich, Richard. *How Buddhism Began.* London: Athlone Press, 1996.

Gomez, L. "Buddhism in India." In *The Encyclopedia of Religion.* Ed. M. Eliade. New York: MacMillan Publishing Co., 1987.

Gonda, Jan. *Ancient Indian Kingship from the Religion Point of View.* Leiden: E.J. Brill, 1969.

———. *The Ritual Sūtras.* Wiesbaden: Otto Harrassowitz, 1977.

Goodwin-Raheja, G. *The Poison in the Gift.* Chicago: University of Chicago Press, 1988.

Grunwedel, Albert. *Buddhist Art in India.* New Delhi: S. Chand, 1972.

Heisig, J. "Symbolism." In *The Encyclopedia of Religion.* Ed. Mircea Eliade. New York: MacMillan Publishing Co, 1987.

Heras, Henry. *Studies in Proto-Indo-Mediterranean Culture.* Bombay: Indian Historical Research Institute, 1953.

Hopkins, E. Washburn. *The Great Epic of India.* Delhi: Motilal Banarsidass, 1993.

Hsuan Tsang. *Si-Yu-Ki: Buddhist Records of the Western World.* Trans. Samuel Beal. London: Kegan Paul, 1906.

The Jātaka Together with its Commentary. Ed. V. Fausboll. London: Luzac and Company Ltd.,1963.

The Jātaka: Or Stories of the Buddha's Former Births Translated from the Pāli by Various Hands. Ed. E.B. Cowell. 7 vols. Cambridge: Cambridge University Press, 1895-1913.

Jayal, S. *The Status of Women in the Epics.* Delhi: Motilal Banarsidass, 1966.

Journey to the West. 4 vols. Trans. Anthony C. Yu. Chicago: University of Chicago Press, 1977.

Kālidāsa. *Raghuvaṃśa.* Delhi: Motilal Banarsidass, 1971.

Kauśika Sūtra. Ed. Bloomfield. Reprint Delhi: Motilal Banarsidass, 1972.

Kauṣītaki Brāhmaṇ a. Ed. Bhattacharya. Calcutta Sanskrit College Research Series, no. 73. Calcutta: Sanskrit College, 1970.

Keith, Arthur Berriedale. *The Religion and Philosophy of the Vedas and Upanishads.* 2 vols. London: Harvard University Press, 1925.

Kersenboom, Saskia. "The Traditional Repertoire of the Tiruttaṇi Temple Dancers." In *Roles and Rituals for Hindu Women.* Ed. Julia Leslie. Delhi: Motilal Banarsidass, 1992.

Kitagawa, Joseph, Cummings, Mark, eds. *Buddhism and Asian History.* New York: Macmillan Publishing Company, 1987.

Knipe, David. "The Heroic Theft: Myths from Ṛg Veda IV and the Ancient Near East." *History of Religions* 6 (1967): 328-360.

——. *Hinduism, Experiments in the Sacred.* Prospect Heights, Illinois: Waveland Press, Inc., 1991.

Kosambi, D.D. "The Authochthonous Element in the Mahābhārata." *Journal of the American Oriental Society* 84, 1946.

——. *Ancient India.* London: Routledge and K. Paul, 1965.

Law, B.C. *A Study of the Mahāvastu.* Delhi: Bharatiya Publishing House, 1978.

Levi-Strauss, C. *The Savage Mind.* Chicago: University of Chicago Press, 1966.

Long, C. *Significations: Signs, Symbols, and Images in the Interpretation of Religion.* Aurora, CO: The Davies Group, 1995.

MacDonell, A.A. *Vedic Mythology.* New York: Gordon Press, 1974.

Mackay, Ernest. *The Indus Civilization.* London: Dickerson and Thompson, Ltd., 1935.

Mahābhārata, Text as Constituted in its Critical Edition, Ed. Vishnu S. Sukthankar. Poona: The Bandarkar Oriental Research Institute, 1927-1966.

Mahābhārata. 3 vols. Trans. and Ed. by J.A.B. van Buitenen. Chicago: The University of Chicago Press, 1973.

Mahalingam, T.V. "Nāgas in Indian History and Culture." *Journal of Indian History* 43 (1965): 1-69.

Mahathera, Buddhadatta. *Concise Pāli-English Dictionary.* Delhi: Motilal Banarsidass, 1994.

Mahāvagga. Ed. Hermann Oldenberg. Vol. I of the Pāli Text Society *Vinaya Pitakam.* London: Luzac & Company, Ltd., 1969.

Mahāvaṃsa. Ed. Geiger. London: Pāli Text Society, 1908.

The Mahāvastu. Trans. J.J. Jones. 3 vols. London: Luzac and Co., 1949-56.

Mahāvastu. Ed. Emile Senart. Paris: Imprimerie Nationale, 1897.

McCrindle, J.W. *Ancient India as Described in Classical Literature.* Amsterdam: Philo Press, 1971.

Minkowski, Christopher. "Snakes, Sattras, and the Mahābhārata." In *Essays on the Mahābhārata.* Ed. Arvind Sharma. New York: E.J. Brill, 1991.

Monier-Williams. *A Sanskrit-English Dictionary.* Oxford: Clarendon Press, 1992.

——. *Brahmanism and Hinduism.* London: J. Murray, 1891.

Nattier J. and Prebish C. "Mahāsāṃghika Origins: The Beginnings of Buddhist Sectarianism." *History of Religions* 16 (1977): 237-72.

Nidānakathā. Vārānasī: Chowhamba Sanskrit Series Office, 1970.

Oldenberg, H. Trans. Shrotri, S. *The Doctrine of the Upaniṣads and the Early Buddhism.* Delhi: Motilal Banarsidass, 1991.

Oldham, C.F. *The Sun and the Serpent.* London: Archibald Constable and Co., 1905.

Ortner, S. *Making Gender: The Politics and Erotics of Culture.* Boston: Beacon Press, 1996.

Otto, Rudolf. *The Idea of the Holy.* Oxford: Oxford University Press, 1958.

Pañcaviṃśa Brāhmaṇa. 2 vols. Eds. Cinnaswami Sastri and Pattachirama Sastri. Kashi Sanskrit Series, no. 105. Benares: Sanskrit Series Office, 1935.

Pañcaviṃśa Brāhmaṇa. Trans. W. Caland. Calcutta: Asiatic Society, 1931.

Pāraskara Gṛhya Sūtra. Ed. Bakre. Bombay: Gujarati Printing Press, 1917; reprint Delhi: Munsirama Manoharalala, 1982.

Prebish, C. "A Review of Scholarship on the Buddhist Councils." *Journal of Asian Studies* 33 (1974): 239-254.

Pritchard, James B., ed. *Ancient Near Eastern texts relating to the Old Testament.* Princeton, N.J.: Princeton University Press, 1969.

———. *Ancient Near East in Pictures Relating to the Old Testament.* Princeton, N.J. : Princeton University Press, 1969.

Przyluski, J. "La Princess A L'odeur de Poisson et La Nāgī dan les Tradition de l'Asie Orientale." *Etudes Asiatique*, II, 1925.

———. "Harmika and the Origin of Buddhist Stūpas," *Indian Historical Quarterly,* XI, 1935.

Rahula, T. *A Critical Study of the Mahāvastu.* Delhi: Motilal Banarsidass, 1978.

Ramanujan, A.K., ed. and trans. *Folktales from India.* London: Penguin Books, 1991.

Rawlinson, Andrew. "Nāgas and the Magical Cosmology of Buddhism," *Religion* 16 (1986): 135-153.

Ray, Reginald. *Buddhist Saints in India: A Study in Buddhist Values and Orientations.* Oxford: Oxford University Press, 1994.

Ṛg Veda. With the commentary of Sāyaṇa. Eds. N.S. Sontakke and C.G. Kashikar. Poona: Vaidika Samsodhana Mandala, 1933-1951.

———. Ed. Wendy Doniger O'Flaherty. London: Penguin Books, 1981.

Ruether, Rosemary Radford. *Sexism and God-Talk: Toward a Feminist Theology.* Boston: Beacon Press, 1983.

Sāmavidhāna Brāhmaṇa. Tirupati: Kendriyasamskrtavidyapitham, 1964.

Śāṃkhāyana Gṛhya Sūtra. Ed. Ganga Sagar Rai. Vārāṇasī: Ratnā Pablikeśansa, 1995.

Śāṃkhāyana Śrauta Sūtra. 2 vols. Ed. Hillebrandt. Reprint New Delhi: Meharchand Lachhmandas, 1981.

Śatapatha Brāhmaṇa of the White Yajurveda in the Mādhyandina Recension. Ed. A. Weber. Vārāṇasī: Chowkamba Sanskrit Series Office,1964.

Śatapatha Brāhmaṇa. New Delhi: The Research Institute of Ancient Scientific Studies, 1967.

Śatapatha Brāhmaṇa. Trans. Julius Eggeling. Delhi: Motilal Banarsidass, 1966.

Schopen, G. *Bones, Stones, and Buddhist Monks*. Honolulu: University of Hawaii Press, 1997.

Sharma, Arvind. "The Significance of Viṣṇu Reclining on the Serpent." *Religion* 16 (1986): 101-114.

Singh, Rana P.B. *Cultural Symbols and Literary Images of Vārāṇasī*. Vārāṇasī: Tara Book Agency, 1989.

Sinha, N.K.P. *Political Ideas and Ideals in the Mahābhārata*. New Delhi: Oriental Publishers and Distributors, 1976.

Skilton, Andrew. *A Concise History of Buddhism*. Birmingham: Windhorse Publications, 1994.

Smith, J.Z. *Map is not Territory*. Leiden: E.J. Brill, 1978.

———. *Imagining Religion: From Babylon to Jonestown*. Chicago: University Chicago Press, 1982.

Strong, J. "The Legend of the Lion-Roarer: A Study of the Buddhist Arhat Pindola Bhāradvāja." *Numen* 26 (1979): 50-88.

———. *The Legend of King Aśoka: A Study and Translation of the Aśokāvadāna*. Princeton: Princeton University Press, 1983.

———. *The Legend and Cult of Upagupta*. Delhi: Motilal Banarsidass, 1992.

———. *The Experience of Buddhism: Sources and Interpretations*. Belmont: Wadsworth Publishing Company, 1995.

Tabick, J. “The Snake in the Grass: The Problems of Interpreting a Symbol inthe Hebrew Bible and Rabbinic Writings.” *Religion* 16 (1986): 166-168.

Taittirīya Saṃhitā. 8 vols. Anandasrama-samskrta-granthavalih, granthankha 42. Poona: Anandasrama, 1978.

———. Trans. Arthur Berriedale Keith. Delhi: Motilal Banarsidass, 1967.

Tavakar, N.G. *New Light Thrown on the History of India, The Historical Nāga Kings of India.* Bombay: Tavkar Prakashan, 1984.

Trautmann, Thomas. *Aryans and British India.* Berkeley: University of California Press, 1997.

Trawick, M. *Notes on Love in a Tamil Family.* Berkeley: University of California Press, 1992.

Turner, V. *The Forest of Symbols: Aspects of Ndembu Ritual.* Ithaca: Cornell University Press, 1967.

Vinaya Texts. Trans. Rhys Davids and Hermann Oldenberg. Vol. XIII of *Sacred Books of the East.* Delhi: Motilal Banarsidass, 1965.

Viṣṇu Purāṇa. With the commentary of Sridhara. Calcutta: 1972.

Vogel, J. PH. *Indian Serpent-Lore or The Nāgas in Hindu Legend and Art.* London: Arthur Probsthain, 1926.

Wadley, Susan. “Hindu Women's Family and Household Rites in a North Indian Village.” In *Unspoken Worlds: Women's Religious Lives.* Eds. Nancy Falk and Rita Gross. Belmont: Wadsworth Publishing Company, 1989.

Waghorne, J.P., Cutler, N., Narayanan, V., eds. *Gods of Flesh, Gods of Stone, The Embodiment of Divinity in India.* New York: Columbia University Press, 1996.

Warder, Anthony. *Indian Buddhism.* Delhi: Motilal Banarsidass, 1980.

Weber, M. *The Sociology of Religion.* Boston: Beacon Press, 1922.

Winternitz, M. “Asceticism in Ancient India.” *Some Problems in Indian Literature.* Calcutta: University of Calcutta, 1925.

——. "The Serpent Sacrifice Mentioned in the Mahābhārata." *Journal of the Asiatic Society of Bengal,* (New Series) 2 (1926): 74-91.

——. *A History of Indian Literature,* Vol. 2. Delhi: Motilal Banarsidass, 1983.

Zimmer, H. *Myths and Symbols in Indian Art and Civilization.* Washington, D.C.: Bollingen Foundation, 1946.

——. *Philosophies of India.* New York: Pantheon Books, 1951.

Chapter 1 Notes

1. Observance of the 8 Buddhist precepts.
2. *Campeyya Jātaka* in *The Jātaka Together with its Commentary*, V. Fausboll, ed., (London: Luzac and Company Ltd., 1963), 454, 1-5.
3. Nāga Pañcamī (Snake's Fifth).
4. Diana Eck, *Banaras: City of Light* (Princeton: Princeton University Press, 1982), 264.
5. In post-BCE narratives and representations, Nāgas are depicted specifically as cobras.
6. I received these first-hand reports during my 1997 visit to Banāras.
7. J.W. McCrindle, *Ancient India as Described in Classical Literature* (Amsterdam: Philo Press, 1971), 145. I am grateful to J. PH. Vogel, *Indian Serpent-Lore or The Nāgas in Hindu Legend and Art* (London: Arthur Probsthain, 1926), for directing me to this source.
8. Lowell Bloss, "Nāgas and Yakṣas," in *The Encyclopedia of Religion* 10 (New York: MacMillan Publishing Co., 1987), 293-294.
9. Charles H. Long, *Significations: Signs, Symbols, and Images in the Interpretation of Religion* (Fortress Press, 1986; reprint, Aurora, Colorado: The Davies Group, 1995), 7.
10. Given that most of these rituals center around the management of natural events such as childbirth and rainfall, one might surmise that women and farmers make up two of the primary groups of practitioners.
11. *Ādi Parvan,* of the *Mahābhārata, Text as Constituted in its Critical Edition,* Vishnu S. Sukthankar, ed. (Poona: The Bandarkar Oriental Research Institute, 1927-1966), 1.3.135-177.
12. Ibid., 1.3.139-142.
13. Ibid., 1.32.1-25.
14. *Campeyya Jātaka*, 10., 454, 1-5.
15. *Ṛg Veda-Saṃhitā, With the Commentary of Sāyaṇa*, N.W. Sontakke and C.G. Kashikar, eds., (Poona: Vaidika Samsodhana Mandala, 1933-1951) 1.32.8.

16. *Ādi Parvan*, 1.18.2-11.
17. As is further explained in chapter 2, the term Āryan denotes a language affinity rather than a discrete ethnicity and refers to those people who established themselves in India between 2000 and 1500 BCE. The top class within Āryan society was that of the brahmins or priests.
18. In Buddhist-Hybrid Sanskrit, Uruvelā is rendered Uruvilvā, Campeyya is rendered Campaka and Mucalinda is rendered Mucilinda.

Chapter 2 Notes

1. See *Ṛg Veda* 10.90 for the myth of the Cosmic Giant Puruṣa or *Puruṣa-Sūkta*, which chronicles, among other things, the creation of a hierarchical social order—the mouth of the giant becomes the brahmin or priestly class, his arms become the warrior class, his thighs become the producer/commoner class, and his feet become the servant class.
2. Ibid., 1.32.15.
3. Ibid., 1.32. The stakes involved in this fight for sovereignty include control over land, water, and other crucial resources such as cattle.
4. Ibid., 1.52.2, 1.52.6, 2.14.2, 6.30.4, 7.21.3, 8.12.26. In the *Śatapatha Brāhmaṇa of the White Yajurveda in the Mādhyandina Recension* (Vārāṇasī: Chowkamba Sanskrit Series Office, 1964), 1.1.3.4. the etymology of Vṛtra's name is made explicit: "Vṛtra lay there, having covered up all that was between sky and earth, and since he lay there having covered up all of this, he is named Vṛtra."
5. Ibid., 1.32.13.
6. Ibid., 1.32.2.
7. Ibid., 1.32.12.
8. A. A. MacDonell, *Vedic Mythology* (New York: Gordon Press, 1974), 158.
9. Ibid., 153. Both MacDonell and James Fergusson in *Tree and Serpent Worship* (Delhi: Indological Book House, 1868) have argued that the indigenous peoples of India were snake worshippers. And while the work of both scholars is dated (*Vedic Mythology* was originally published in 1897 and Fergusson's *Tree and Serpent Worship*, 1868) their conclusions are supported by later literary and archaeological scholarship such as that carried out by Richard

Gombrich and Herbert Hartel. For a further discussion of this issue, see Richard Gombrich's *How Buddhism Began*, (London: Athlone Press, 1996), 74.

10. The hymns in the *Ṛg Veda* that reinforce the idea that the ascendancy of Indra represents the promotion of the brahmin-led Āryans while the demonization of Vṛtra represents the demotion of the indigenous peoples of India are 1.32, 2.12, and 4.18. In addition, in hymn 10.102, Indra is implored to stop the missiles of the Dāsas, Dāsas defined by Doniger as "the native enemies of the Āryans" in *The Rig Veda*, 329.
11. *Ṛg Veda*, 1.32.5. Literally, his *vṛtratara*; for as noted by Monier-Williams, Vṛtra's very name denotes an "enemy, foe...[or] malignant influence." Monier-Williams, *A Sanskrit-English Dictionary* (Oxford: Clarendon Press, 1992), 1007.
12. In hymn 1.2 and 1.32 the terms *ahi* and Vṛtra are used interchangeably.
13. Monier-Williams, *Sanskrit-English Dictionary*, 1.
14. *Ṛg Veda*, 1.32.3.
15. Ibid., 1.51.6, 2.11.20, 2.14.4.
16. Ibid., 7.34.16.
17. Ibid., 5.41.16, 7.34.17.
18. Ibid., 1.32.8.
19. Ibid., 1.85.8. Viṣṇu, who is only briefly mentioned in the *Ṛg Veda* is associated with the sun while the Maruts, literally the "shining ones," are portrayed as companions of Indra.
20. Ibid., 1.32.13 and 15.
21. Ibid., 1.32.13.
22. Ibid., 1.32.15.
23. Ibid., 1.32. 10.
24. In the *Purāṇic* texts, which date from c. 250 - 1700 CE, the killing of Vṛtra is no longer applauded but rather condemned, for the snake has been shifted from a negative supernatural force to a powerful object of worship.
25. *Ṛg Veda*, 1.32.1.
26. Ibid., 10.90.
27. Ibid., 1.32.13.
28. These dates are based on carbon-14 datings, documented in Craven, *Indian Art* (London: Thames and Hudson, 1976).
29. Mahalingam, "The Nagas in Indian History and Culture," *Journal of Indian History* 43 (1965),4.

30. Ernest Mackay, *The Indus Civilization* (London: Dickerson and Thompson, Ltd., 1935), 83; Henry Heras, *Studies in Proto-Indo-Mediterranean Culture* (Bombay: Indian Historical Research Institute, 1953), 364.
31. This relationship is further suggested as noted by Minkowski in "Snakes, *Sattras*, and the *Mahābhārata*," in *Essays on the Mahābhārata* (New York: E.J. Brill, 1991), 388,as the terms *daśa* (ten) and *daṃś* (bite) are often put together in various word play scenarios featuring snakes.
32. *Ṛg Veda,* 10.90, *Puruṣa-Sūkta.*
33. MacDonell, *Vedic Mythology,* 157.
34. *Ṛg Veda,* 4.18.9.
35. Vṛtra is referred to as *anaṃsa* in *Ṛg Veda* 1.32 and as *viaṃsa* in *Ṛg Veda* 4.18. This descriptor recurs across space and time, for in present-day Mississippi—another region abounding in snakes—I have often heard snakes referred to as 'Mr. No-Shoulders.'
36. *Ṛg Veda,* 1.32.11.
37. Ibid., 1.85.8.
38. Ibid., 1.32.5.

Chapter 3 Notes

1. Gonda, *The Ritual Sūtras* (Wiesbaden: Otto Harrassowitz, 1977), 467.
2. *Textual Sources for the Study of Hinduism*, Wendy Doniger O'Flaherty, ed. (Chicago: University of Chicago Press, 1988), 2.
3. *Ṛg Veda*, 1.32.10.
4. J.W. McCrindle, *Ancient India as Described in Classical Literature,* 145.
5. Gombrich, *How Buddhism Began* (London: Athlone Press, 1996), 72.
6. Bloss, "Nāgas and Yakṣas," 293-294.
7. See chapter 2.
8. *Śatapatha Brāhmaṇa*, 10.5.2.20.
9. Literally, *simidā,* a female demon of some sort.
10. *Śatapatha Brāhmaṇa*, 7.4.1.25-30.
11. *Atharva Veda, With the Commentary of Sāyaṇa*, Vishva Bandhu, ed. (Hoshiapur: Visveshvaranand Indological Series, 1960-1964), 6.56.

12. Rudolf Otto, *The Idea of the Holy* (Oxford: Oxford University Press, 1958), 25-27.
13. *Śatapatha Brāhmaṇa*, 10.5.2.21.
14. Susan Wadley, "Hindu Women's Family and Household Rites in a North Indian Village," in *Unspoken Worlds: Women's Religious Lives* (Belmont: Wadsworth Publishing Company, 1989), 74.
15. Evidence for the worship of the snake in the 4th C. BCE comes to us from Greek sources documenting Alexander the Great's visit to India.
16. *Śatapatha Brāhmaṇa*, 5.4.1.2. The long-haired man referred to in this passage is a Keśin who figures in the *Ṛg Vedic* hymn 10.136: "The long-haired ascetic (Keśin), an early precursor of the *Upsaniṣadic* yogi, drinks a drug (probably some hallucinogen other than soma) in the company of Rudra, the master of poison and a god who is excluded from the *Soma* sacrifice." *The Rig Veda*, Doniger O'Flaherty, trans. (London: Penguin Books, 1981), 137.
17. Ibid., 11.2.7.12.
18. Commentary by the Mādhyandhinas to *Śatapatha Brāhmaṇa*, 11.2.7.12.
19. J.W. McCrindle, *Ancient India as Described in Classical Literature,* 145.
20. *Āśvalāyana Gṛhya Sūtra with Sanskrit Commentary of Nārāyaṇa,* Vidyaratna and Vedantavagisa, eds. (Calcutta: Asiatic Society of Bengal, 1869).
21. Ibid.
22. *Atharva Veda,* 8.8. and 8.10.
23. *Ṛg Veda,* 2.11.20.
24. Ibid., 1.51.6, 2.14.4.
25. *Śatapatha Brāhmaṇa*, 13.4.3.9.
26. I owe this insight about ritual merging to Saskia C. Kersenboom as she discusses it in the context of *devadāsīs* in "Tiruttaṇi Temple Dancers," in *Roles and Rituals for Hindu Women* (Delhi: Motilal Banarsidass, 1992), 136.
27. *Śāṃkhāyana Śrauta Sūtra,* Alfred Hillebrandt, ed., 2 vols. (reprint, New Delhi: Meharchand Lachhmandas, 1981), 16.2.13-14.
28. Minkowski, "Snakes, *Sattras*, and the *Mahābhārata*," 394.
29. *Śatapatha Brāhmaṇa*, 11.2.7.12.
30. Two other snakes listed here in this Vedic *Sarpasattra*, namely, Cakra and Piśaṅga, reappear as snakes in the snake sacrifice of the *Mahābhārata*, verses 1.52.1-20.

31. Minkowski, "Snakes, *Sattras*, and the *Mahābhārata*," 387.
32. Ibid., 388.
33. *Baudhāyana Śrauta Sūtra*, Willem Caland, ed., 3 vols. (Calcutta: Asiatic Society of Bengal, 1904-24; reprint, New Delhi: Munshiram Manoharlal, 1982),17.18 as noted in Minkowski, "Snakes, *Sattras*, and the *Mahābhārata*," 387.
34. Ibid., 388.
35. *Baudhāyana Gṛhyasūtra,* Shama Sastri, ed. (Mysore: Government Branch Press, 1920; reprint, New Delhi: Meharchand Lachhmandas, 1982), 3.10. I appreciate Christopher Minkowski's work in his article, "Snakes, *Sattras*, and the *Mahābhārata*," 394, for bringing this passage to my attention.
36. Minkowski, "Snakes, *Sattras*, and the *Mahābhārata*," 392.
37. *Śatapatha Brāhmaṇa,* 3.6.2.2. As noted in this verse, Arbuda's mother, is said to be "*iyam*" or "this" world as contrasted with "*asau,*" or "that" world. Kadrū is also denoted in this way in Taittirīya Samhitā, 6.1.6. Monier-Williams states the following on page 165 of the Sanskrit-English Dictionary in regard to this standardized distinction: "*idam; ayam, iyam, idam*...this earthly world, this universe; *ayam agnih*, this fire which burns on the earth; but *asāv agnih*, that fire in the sky, i.e. the lightning; so also *idam* or *iyam* alone sometimes signifies 'this earth'."
38. *Atharva Veda,* 11.9.4-5.
39. *Ṛg Veda*, 1.32.8-13.
40. *Hymns of the Atharva Veda,* Maurice Bloomfield, trans. (Delhi: Motilal Banarsidass, 1964), 633.
41. *Atharva Veda*, 11.9.4-5. We see snakes constructed as war-lords again in hymn 8.8 of the Atharva Veda, wherein snakes in the company of the mythic Gandharvas and Apsarasas are called upon to protect the king's army, and in hymn 11.10, where they are called upon to help demolish the enemy on the battlefield.
42. Monier-Williams, *Sanskrit-English Dictionary*, 168.
43. *Karṇa Parvan* of the *Mahābhārata, Text as Constituted in its Critical Edition,* Vishnu S. Sukthankar, ed. (Poona: The Bandarkar Oriental Research Institute, 1927-1966), 8.63.37.
44. *Pañcaviṃśa Brāhmaṇa,* C. Sastri and P. Sastri, eds. (Benares: Sanskrit Series Office, 1935), 25.15.3.
45. For more on the snake priest, Timirgha Daureśruta, see Caland, trans., *Pañcaviṃśa Brāhmaṇa*, 641, and Monier-Williams, *Sanskrit-English Dictionary*, 499.

46. *Dūre* "far" or "far-reaching," *śruta* "hearing."
47. *Tīrtha-Yatra Parvan* of the *Mahābhārata, Text as Constituted in its Critical Edition,* Vishnu S. Sukthankar, ed. (Poona: The Bandarkar Oriental Research Institute, 1927-1966), 3.80-3.153.
48. Lowell Bloss, *Ancient Indian Folk Religion as Seen through the Symbolism of the Nāga* (Ph.D. diss., University of Chicago, 1971), 37.
49. *Śāṃkhāyana Gṛhya Sūtra*, Ganga Sagar Rai, ed. (Vārāṇasī: Ratnā Pablikeśansa, 1995), 4.18.1.
50. *Pāraskara Gṛhya Sūtra,* Mahādevaśarmā Bākre, ed. (New Delhi: Munsirama Manoharalala, 1982), 2.14.
51. *Śāṃkhāyana Gṛhya Sūtra,* 4.15.
52. Gonda, *The Ritual Sūtras*, 547.
53. Ibid., 547.
54. Bloss, "Nāgas and Yakṣas," 294.
55. Gonda, *The Ritual Sūtras*, 547.
56. *Sāmavidhāna Brāhmaṇa,* Bellikoth R. Sharma, ed. (Tirupati: Kendriyasamskrtavidyapitham, 1964), 3.3.7.
57. *Gobhila Gṛhya Sūtra,* Chintamani Bhattacharya, ed. (Calcutta: Metropolitan Printing and Publishing House, 1936-1940), 4.7.41.
58. In rituals that are performed at the laying of foundation stones in present times, it is Śesnāg who is invoked as the deity who resides within and thereby supports the earth. However, since Śesnāg does not appear in these early texts, the task belongs to Vāsuki. Moreover, in the *Bhagavad Gītā*, 10.28-29, Vāsuki is described as the king of the *sarpas*—the designation used for snakes in these early texts, whereas Śesnāg is described as the king of the Nāgas—the later designation.
59. *Kauśika Sūtra*, Maurice Bloomfield, ed. (Delhi: Motilal Banarsidass, 1972), 74.8.
60. Minkowski, "Snakes, *Sattras*, and the *Mahābhārata*," 394.

Chapter 4 Notes

1. *The Book of the Beginning* in *The Mahābhārata,* J.A.B. van Buitenen, ed. and trans., 3 vols. (Chicago: The University of Chicago Press), xxiii.
2. Ibid., J.A. B. van Buitenen endorses the later dating of the *Ādi Parvan*.
3. For example, the redactors characterize kings such as King Janamejaya and his father King Parikṣit as immature and

destructive beings, see especially 1.3.178-195 and 1.36.9-1.37.25. And in the *Puloman* section of the *Ādi Parvan* there is a passage critiquing kṣatradharma, which at the same times functions to exalt the brahmin's dharma of non-injury, 1.11.12-17.

4. *Ādi Parvan*, 1.24.3. See *Ṛg Veda* 10.90 for the myth of the Cosmic Giant Puruṣa in which the four social classes are arranged hierarchically: the Brahmins first, the Kṣatriyas second, the Vaiśyas third, and the Śūdras fourth.
5. J.A.B. van Buitenen lists four minor books in total: *Lists of Contents, Summaries, Pauṣya, and Puloman.* J.A.B. van Buitenen, ed. and trans., *The Mahābhārata*: *The Book of the Beginning*, 2.
6. He goes for water in order to purify himself, for having just come from the house of Pauṣya, in which Pauṣya's wife was invisible to him due to his impure state, he thinks that the mendicant's [in actuality, Takṣaka's] invisibility also stems from his own impure condition.
7. *Ādi Parvan*, 1.3.135-138.
8. Ibid., 1.3.139-144.
9. Ibid., 1.3.172-174. Interestingly, while Dhātā and Vidhātā are presented as goddesses in this passage, they are in fact male gods as the declension of their names implies.
10. Ibid., 1.3.152.
11. Ibid., 1.3.155-165.
12. This motif is repeated, for example, in relation to the brahmin Ruru, 1.8.15ff, and the brahmin Kāśyapa, 1.38.30ff.
13. The term Vaiśāleya re-surfaces in the *Karṇa Parvan* of the *Mahābhārata* to indicate a tribe of Nāga people—those who took the divine snake as a totem. (*Karṇa Parvan* 8.63. 37.) Moreover, supernatural snakes in the Buddhist texts within our survey also have names that tie them to specific regional areas.
14. *Ādi Parvan*, 1.31.1 ff.
15. The epic Dhṛtarāṣṭra loses his place name altogether, and the epic Airāvata does not play a role at all in this text, but rather is mentioned by name, usually as part of a long list of snakes, on five different occasions: 1.3.139, 1.3.174, 1.31.5, 1.33.1, 1.52.10.
16. In fact, it may be the first extant textual reference ever, for while some of the Buddhist *Jātaka Tales* discuss the Nāgaloka, their period of redaction is later than that of the *Mahābhārata.*
17. *Sāmavidhāna Brāhmaṇa*, 3.3.7.
18. *Ādi Parvan*, 1.3.175.

19. Ibid., 1.3.172. Vidhātā also shows up in the book of Āstīka as one who ordains that the snakes will be Garuḍa's food supply: 1.14.23.
20. Monier-Williams, *Sanskrit-English Dictionary*, 514.
21. *Atharva Veda,* 6.56, 8.8 and 8.10; *Āśvalāyana Gṛhya Sūtra,* 3.4.1
22. *Ṛg Veda*, 1.32.8.
23. *Soma* is a plant extract used in sacrificial rituals. This tale of two sisters is melded together with an even earlier tale, the stealing of the *soma*, as recounted in the *Ṛg Veda*, 4.26 and 4.27.
24. My translation of Sanskrit passage located in the *Taittirīya Saṃhitā,* Arthur B. Keith, trans., 2 vols. (Delhi: Motilal Banarsidass, 1967) 6.1.6.
25. *Ādi Parvan,* 1.14.5-23.
26. David Knipe, "The Heroic Theft: Myths from *Ṛg Veda* IV and the Ancient Near East," in *History of Religions* 6 (1967) 347.
27. *Ādi Parvan*, 1.21.1-15.
28. *Ṛg Veda*, 2.38.
29. *Atharva Veda,* 4.6.3.
30. *Śāṃkhāyana Gṛhya Sūtra*, 1.22.15.
31. *Ādi Parvan*, 1.28.1.
32. Ibid., 1.32.25.
33. Ibid., 1.27.13.
34. Ibid., 1.24.3.
35. Ibid., 1.15.1-3.
36. Long ā, in the name Kāśyapa indicates Kaśyapa's direct descendent.
37. *Ādi Parvan*, 1.18.1-13.
38. *Baudhāyana Gṛhya Sūtra*, 3.10. Also noted in Minkowski, "Snakes, *Sattras,* and the *Mahābhārata*," 394.
39. *Ādi Parvan*, 1.3.188-192.
40. *Śatapatha Brāhmaṇa*, 5.4.1.2.
41. *Ādi Parvan,* 1.39.29-33.
42. Ibid., 1.3.136-137.
43. Agni is the god of fire.
44. *Ādi Parvan*, 1.38. 35-38.
45. Ibid., 1.11.12.
46. *Sāmavidhāna Brāhmaṇa*, 3.3.7, *Gobhila Gṛhya Sūtra,* 4.7.41.
47. *Ādi Parvan*, 1.33.3.
48. Ibid., 1.18.11.
49. Ibid., 1.33.23-28.

50. While we cannot say for certain that Śeṣa is a brand new character, as he may have a previous life in either oral sources or in a textual source that has since disappeared, we can say that this is his first appearance in any extant text.
51. *Ādi Parvan*, 1.32.1-4.
52. Ibid., 1.32.5-17.
53. Ibid., 1.32.18-25.
54. *Śatapatha Brāhmaṇa,* 7.4.1.25-30.
55. *Sāmavidhāna Brāhmaṇa,* 3.3.7 and *Kauśika Sūtra,* 74.8.
56. Vogel, *Indian Serpent Lore*, 192.
57. Bloss, *Ancient Indian Folk Religion*, 32-33. Bloss gives the date of the Nāga statue at "about 100 AD."
58. *Tīrtha-Yātra Parvan*, 3.80-3.153. The *Tīrtha-Yatra Parvan* is positioned directly after the story of Nala, which features the episode of the Nāga King Karkoṭaka, 3.63ff.
59. Ibid., 3.80.119 and 3.81.12.
60. This refers to a protracted sacrificial ritual, the *Agniṣṭoma*, that requires the services of sixteen brahmin priests.
61. *Tīrtha-Yatra Parvan*, 3.80.40.
62. *Ādi Parvan*, 1.34.4-15.
63. Ibid., 1.11.17.
64. The most usual term for a female supernatural snake in both Hindu and Buddhist texts is Nāgī—declined like any feminine stem ending in ī. I am grateful to Vogel, *Indian Serpent Lore*, 34, for having drawn my attention to these stories.
65. *Ādi Parvan*, 1.206.1ff.
66. Kalidāsā, *Raghuvaṃśa* (Delhi: Motilal Banarsidass, 1971) 16.72-88.
67. *Bhūridatta Jātaka* in *The Jātaka Together with its Commentary*, V. Fausboll, ed., (London: Luzac and Company Ltd., 1963).
68. This is particularly true of the *Bhūridatta Jātaka*, no. 543, in which the Nāgī is actually depicted as a widow whose lust drives her to remarriage with a mortal man.
69. Ananda Coomaraswamy, *Yakṣas, Essays in the Water Cosmology* (New Delhi: Oxford University Press, 1993), 98. I disagree with Coomaraswamy's argument that Yakṣas, rather than Nāgas, are more often identified with life-giving waters.
70. I am grateful to Vogel, *Indian Serpent Lore*, 35-37, for having catalogued these various dynasties.

71. See especially, Przyluski, "La Princesse a` l'odeur de poisson et la Nāgī dans les traditions de l'Asie Orientale," in *Etudes Asiatique* II (1925).
72. For a further look at the black magic nature of the *Mahābhārata's Sarpasattra*, see Christopher Minkowski's "Snakes, *Sattras,* and the *Mahābhārata.*"
73. *Ādi Parvan*, 1.47.17-24.
74. Ibid., 1.47.15.
75. Ibid., 1.50.17.
76. Ibid., 1.50.10.
77. Knipe, "Hinduism," 39.
78. The *hotṛ* is an officiating priest at a sacrifice.
79. *Ādi Parvan*, 1.51.16-23.
80. Ibid., 1.53.24.
81. Ibid., 1.53.10.
82. Ibid., 1.53.13.
83. Ibid., 1.36.3.
84. Ibid., 1.41.3.
85. Ibid., 1.41.12-13.
86. Ibid., 1.42.5-9.
87. Ibid., 1.43.1ff.
88. Ibid., 1.53.24.
89. *Ādi Parvan,* 1.11.12-17.
90. Ibid., 1.53.17-21.
91. *Baudhāyana Gṛhya Sūtra*, 3.10. Also noted in Minkowski, "Snakes, *Sattras,* and the *Mahābhārata*," 394.
92. *Ādi Parvan*, 1.18.11
93. A gotra is a descent group from the father's family line.
94. Gloria Goodwin-Raheja, *The Poison in the Gift* (Chicago: University of Chicago Press, 1988), 55.
95. Ibid., 55-56.
96. *Sāmavidhāna Brāhmaṇa* 3.3.7 and *Gobhila Gṛhya Sūtra,* 4.7.41.

Chapter 5 Notes

1. The founder of Buddhism is Siddhārtha Gautama, the historical Buddha. We will place his birth at c. 485 BCE.
2. The Sthaviravādins and the Mahāsaṃghikas were the first two schools or sects of early Buddhism. The name, Theravādin, is the Pāli derivative of the Sanskrit Sthaviravādin, and the Theravādin

school is the only extant representative of the Sthaviravādin's primary doctrines and practices. The Theravādin school probably formed in the mid-third century BCE and is one of the original 18 schools of early Buddhism.

3. The two main parts of the *Vinaya Piṭaka* are the *Sūtravibhaṃga* and the *Skandhaka.* Sometimes a third part is included, the *Appendices.* The *Mahāvagga* is part of the *Skandhaka.* The *Mahāvagga,* Hermann Oldenberg, ed., in Vol. I of the *Vinaya Piṭakam* (London: Luzac & Company, Ltd., 1969).
4. Preserved orally for several centuries, the Pāli tradition maintains that it was King Vaṭṭagāmaṇī of Sri Lanka who ordered that these oral transmissions be written down between 35 and 32 BCE, for fear that they might be lost due to the pressures of internecine strife and famine. The Theravādins also claim that the extant version of the Pāli canon represents a fairly direct transmission of the Buddha's teaching as compiled at the First Buddhist Council immediately following the Buddha's parinirvāṇa. (According to the tradition, at the Second Council only minor adjustments in the Vinaya were made and at the Council at Pāṭaliputra only Moggaliputtatissa's *Kathāvatthu* was added.) It is said that Mahinda then transmitted these teachings to Sri Lanka where they were preserved orally up until the beginning of the Common Era. The Theravādins thus maintain that the Pāli canon is written in the original language of the Buddha. The majority of western scholars, however, disagree not only with this claim but also the claim that the Pāli canon maintains a direct discursive line from the First Council forward. Luis Gomez asserts the following: "Although the Theravādin tradition claims that the language of its canon, Pāli, is the language spoken by the Buddha, Western scholars disagree. Evidently, the Pāli canon, like other Buddhist scriptures, is the creation, or at least the compilation and composition, of another age and a different linguistic milieu.... Some of the earliest Buddhist scriptures may have been translations from logia or sayings of the Buddha that were transmitted for some time in his own language. But even if this is the case, the extant versions represent at the very least redactions and reworkings, if not creations of a later age." Luis Gomez, "Buddhism in India," in *The Encyclopedia of Religion* 2 (New York: MacMillan Publishing Co., 1987), 360.
5. The verses of the *Jātakas* are considered canonical while the commentaries and the introduction to the commentaries, the

Nidānakathā, are not for the following reason: according to the Pāli tradition, only the verses remained true to an original Pāli redaction, while the commentary was translated from the Pāli and preserved in Sinhalese (and later returned to Pāli) and the *Nidānakathā* was probably redacted in Sinhalese and later translated into Pāli.

6. Andrew Skilton, *A Concise History of Buddhism* (Birmingham: Windhorse Publications, 1994), 74.
7. For more on this idea see Bloss, *Ancient Indian Folk Religion*, 199-227. This early tradition of Buddhism is usually referred to by scholars as the Nikāya tradition.
8. *Ādi Parvan,* 1.27.13.
9. Literally, Jaṭilas, which signifies a type of ascetic with matted hair.
10. *Mahāvagga*, I.15.1-5.
11. Reproductions of this bas-relief can be seen in Fergusson's *Tree and Serpent Worship*, Grunwedel's *Buddhist Art in India* (New Delhi: S. Chand, 1972), and Foucher's *Beginnings of Buddhist Art* (Varanasi: Indological Book House, 1972).
12. *Atharva Veda,* 12.3.
13. *Ādi Parvan*, 1.47.23-24.
14. As we will see when we turn to the *Mahāvastu*, the specification of the supernatural snake as a Nāga, a rāja, and a cobra is maintained (as it is throughout the Buddhist textual tradition) despite the *Mahāvastu*'s contrasting narrative agenda. *Mahāvastu,* Emile Senart, ed., (Paris: Imprimerie Nationale, 1897).
15. Of course between the Hindu and the Buddhist texts, the significance of the term dharma has been shifted. In the Hindu texts, in broad terms, the term dharma is equated with religiously prescribed social duty, while in the Buddhist texts, in broad terms, it is equated with the Buddha's experience of a non-dualistic reality and his dissemination of that experience.
16. Rawlinson, "Nāgas and the Magical Cosmology of Buddhism," *Religion* 16 (1986), 145.
17. See *Mahāvagga*, I.20-I.21.
18. Gombrich, *How Buddhism Began*, 74. This is an important point and one that we will return to as the *Campeyya Jātaka* functions primarily as a cautionary tale against Nāga worship.
19. See Bloss, *Ancient Indian Folk Religion*, 199-227.
20. The Buddha became enlightened, or in other words, achieved nirvāṇa, at the age of 35. However, his ultimate nirvāṇa or

pārinirvāṇa occurred when his physical body wore out, allowing him to become fully dispersed into everything.

21. A cakra is literally a wheel, but in this context it denotes the Buddha as a "wheel-turning" or "ruling" sovereign.
22. Rawlinson, "Nāgas and the Magical Cosmology of Buddhism," 147.
23. *Śatapatha Brāhmaṇa,* 13.4.3.9.
24. Māra is the king of desire, and thus functions as the antithesis of the Buddhist spiritual ideal of enlightenment.
25. In these early Pāli texts, the term Bodhisattva is used exclusively to identify the Buddha prior to his enlightenment.
26. *Jātaka* I. 70-72, the *Nidānakathā.*
27. *Mahāvagga,* I.3.1-3.
28. Vogel, *Indian Serpent Lore,* 94.
29. Reginald Ray, *Buddhist Saints in India: A Study in Buddhist Values and Orientations* (Oxford: Oxford University Press, 1994), 75.
30. The Ajapāla tree is the focus of the previous story, and the Rājāyatana tree is the focus of the following story. *Mahāvagga,* I.2 and I.4.
31. Vogel, *Indian Serpent Lore,* 103.
32. *Atharva Veda,* 8.8 and 8.10.
33. *Āśvalāyana Gṛhya Sūtra,* 3.4.1.
34. For more on the Yakṣas, see Coomaraswamy, *Yakṣas, Essays in the Water Cosmology.*
35. See chapter 4.
36. For more on this idea, see Bloss "The Buddha and the Nāga: A Study in Buddhist Folk Religiosity," *History of Religions* 13 (1973) 51-53.
37. See Fergusson, *Tree and Serpent Worship,* plate XXIV, fig. 1.
38. See reproduction in Fergusson, *Tree and Serpent Worship,* plate LXXVI.
39. See especially the *Saṃkhāpala Jātaka* and the *Vidhūrpaṇḍita Jātaka* in *The Jātaka Together with its Commentary* , V. Fausboll, ed., (London: Luzac and Company Ltd., 1963).
40. Observance of the 8 Buddhist precepts.
41. *Campeyya Jātaka,* 10., 454, 1-5.
42. Ibid., 455, 1-5.
43. Ibid., 456, 17-22.
44. Ibid., 456, 6-11.

45. Ibid., 467, 1-5.
46. Ibid., 454, 1-5.
47. *Jātaka* 1, 121; 3, 378; 4, 445; 5, 520; 5, 529; and 6, 539.
48. See Bloss, "The Buddha and the Nāga: A Study in Buddhist Folk Religiosity," 38-40.
49. This is the primary motif in the *Bhūridatta Jātaka*, in which a heedless brahmin and his son leave a Nāga's gift of magic ornaments on a lake bank. Upon their return, they find that these gifts have vanished into the Nāgaloka.
50. *Campeyya Jātaka*, 10., 454, 1-5.
51. Gonda, *The Ritual Sūtras*, 547.
52. This is also the dominant theme of *Mahāvagga* I. 63, in which a Nāga is expelled from the Buddhist order. This story will be discussed shortly.
53. *Campeyya Jātaka* 10, 456, 6-11. As in all patriarchal cultures, including that of the contemporary United States, ancient Indian culture elevates males over females.
54. See Bloss, *Ancient Indian Folk Religion*, 48.
55. *Campeyya Jātaka* 10, 454, 1-5.
56. Pabbajjam, literally, to proceed or go forth into the life of a Buddhist monk.
57. *Mahāvagga*, I.63. Verses 1, 2, 4, and 5.
58. Gombrich, *How Buddhism Began*, 73.
59. Ibid., 74-75.
60. *Mahāvagga*, I.63. Verse 4.
61. For more on this, see Bloss article "The Buddha and the Nāga: A Study in Buddhist Folk Religiosity," 52.

Chapter 6 Notes

1. While older scholarship, such as that done by Winternitz, *History of Indian Literature*, (Delhi: Motilal Banarsidass, 1983), Vol. 2, 233, claims that the meter of certain sections of poetry indicate an early origin of c. 200 BCE, Jones, the original translator of the *Mahāvastu*, asserts that the metrical portions of the text were composed prior to its compilation, and thus inserted into the text rather than produced for the text. For more on this subject see *Mahāvastu*, J.J. Jones, trans. (London: Luzac and Co., 1949-1956), Vol. III, x. Moreover, the numerous critiques of the Yogācārins present in the *Mahāvastu* had to post-date the foundation of that School,

which is thought by most scholars to have occurred c. 250-300 CE. Also, linguistic evidence, such as the fact that the 10 "stages" of the Bodhisattva are signified by the word *bhūmi*—claimed by the Mahāyāna schools—rather than the word *magga*—used by the Theravādins—points to a later dating.

2. E. Senart, ed., *Mahāvastu*, Vol. I, 2. All further references to this text will state only *Mahāvastu*. As noted in our previous discussion from chapter 5, the two earliest Buddhist sects or schools were the Mahāsāṃghikās and the Sthaviravādins, both of which sub-divided along the following lines. From the Mahāsāṃghikās there formed the Gokulika, the Caitika, the Ekavyāvahārikas, and from the Ekavyāvahārikas, the Lokottaravādins. From the Sthaviravādins there formed the Haimavata, the Vātsīputrīya, the Sarvāstivādin, the Vibhajyavādin, and from the Vibhajyavādin, the Theravādins. For more on this see Andre Bareau, "Hīnayāna Buddhism," in *The Encyclopedia of Religion* 2 (New York: MacMillan Publishing Co., 1987), 444-456.
3. The redactors include page after page listing the names of various lokottara Buddhas who preceded Śākyamuni, such as Krakucchanda, Konākamuni, Kāśyapa, and even such esoteric figures as Sikhin; and they give us a full treatment of the history of Buddhas such as Dīpaṃkara and Mangala.
4. *Mahāvastu*, J.J. Jones, Vol. II, xiii.
5. *Mahāvastu*, Vol. I, 167-170.
6. In Buddhist-Hybrid Sanskrit, Uruvelā is rendered Uruvilvā, Mucalinda is rendered Mucilinda, and Campeyya is rendered Campaka.
7. *Mahāvastu*, Vol. II, 77-80 and 143.
8. The term Bodhisattva, as it is used here, refers to the lives of the previous Buddhas prior to their enlightenment. This passage describes that these Bodhisattvas have respective yet identical trajectories as they follow the template that leads to enlightenment. As noted by T. Rahula, "The striking dissimilarity between the eight stages of spiritual development in the Theravādin Path (magga) and the ten stages (bhūmi) of the *Mahāvastu* is that the former does not leave room for the backslide from the stage once attained, whereas the latter reiterates the possible danger of lapsing from the stages occupied by the aspirant," Telwatte Rahula, *A Critical Study of the Mahāvastu* (Delhi: Motilal Banarsidass, 1978), 63.
9. *Mahāvastu*, Vol. I, 102-103.

10. Ibid., Vol. II, 11.
11. Ibid., Vol. I, 93.
12. Ibid., Vol. II, 78.
13. Ibid., Vol. I, 167.
14. Ibid., Vol. III, 428-430.
15. Monier-Williams *Sanskrit-English Dictionary*, 5.
16. *Mahāvagga*, I.20-I.21.
17. A splendor that is manifested, just as it was in the *Mahāvagga,* as the Buddha is said to be "*tejodhatum samapanno*," or one who has attained the element of fire.
18. *Atharva Veda* 10.4, and *Pāraskara Gṛhya Sūtra,* 2.14.
19. Rawlinson, "Nāgas and the Magical Cosmology of Buddhism," 143.
20. See Rawlinson, "Nāgas and the Magical Cosmology of Buddhism," 139.
21. While some Nāga kings are said to be able to cause fiery destruction, such as the Nāga kings Ugra and Campaka, they never in fact do so.
22. *Mahāvagga*, I.63.4
23. While the concluding verse of the Pāli tale recounting the story of the Nāga King Mucalinda tells of the snake's transformation into a human, the broader context of this tale so disempowers the Nāga—forced as he is to function as an animate umbrella—that we cannot count his transformation as a boon for the Nāga. Gombrich notes in relation to this story that "we cannot tell why he takes human form; but this episode too has the air of being an allegory of religious rivalry" (*How Buddhism Began*, 72).
24. *Mahāvastu,* Vol. II., 265.
25. *Bhūmya deva* or 'earth-god' is the generic term used by the redactors for supernatural earthly figures such as Nāgas and Yakṣas.
26. *Mahāvastu,* Vol. II, 307-348.
27. Ibid., Vol. II, 307-308.
28. Ibid., Vol. II, 308.
29. Ibid., Vol. II, 401-402.
30. Ibid., Vol. II, 397.
31. Ibid., Vol. I, 102-103 as those who stay fixed on the Buddhist path "become...Nāgas and kings of Nāgas," and Vol. III, 428-430 as the Buddha is called a "Nāga among men."
32. Ibid., Vol. I, 46ff, 58ff, and 136ff.
33. Andre Bareau notes in "Les recits canoniques des funerailles du Buddha et leurs anomalies: Nouvel essai d'interpretation," *Bulletin*

de l'Ecole Francaise d'Extreme-Orient 62 (1975), 187-188, that stūpas dedicated to the worship of former Buddhas Konākamuni and Kāśyapa, as well as Śākyamuni, can be dated from the middle of the third century BCE according to the inscription of Nigālī Sagar.

34. *Mahāvastu*, Vol. III, 94.
35. Ibid., Vol. I, 62.
36. Ibid., Vol. I, 204, 208, 211-212, 214; II, 8, 10-11, 15-17.
37. Ibid., Vol. II, 25, 243, 249.
38. Ibid., Vol. 1, 167-170, 257; II, 294-295
39. I want to thank Lawrence McCrea for his suggestion that "sadhu" be translated as a vocative rather than an exclamatory.
40. *Mahāvastu*, Vol. III, 300-301.
41. Edgerton, *Buddhist Hybrid Sanskrit Dictionary* (Delhi: Motilal Banarsidass, 1953), 262.
42. *Mahāvagga,* I.3
43. Jones offers a different explanation, and states that "one would expect a different name here, for the action is more or less a repetition of the preceding one." J.J. Jones, *Mahāvastu*, Vol. III, 288.
44. *Mahāvastu*, Vol. III, 324-325.
45. Ibid., Vol. I, 211; II, 15 and 163; III, 324.
46. Rawlinson, "Nāgas and the Magical Cosmology of Buddhism," 151.
47. The late Vedic snake kings Taksaka Vaiśāleya and Dhṛtarāṣṭra Airāvata both had names that linked them to specific regions.
48. Portions of the prose tale are retold in verse immediately following the prose version.
49. *Campeyya Jātaka*, 10., 454, 1-5.
50. On the helpful suggestion of Lawrence McCrea, I am reading *paśyati*, in the sense of watching over and protecting rather than regarding, as this gives more emphasis to the last line which suggests that the Nāga king, in addition to giving the king jewels, also protected his family. This also avoids the problem that Jones refers to in the following footnote: "A lame ending to the prose story, containing, as it does, but a feeble allusion to the riches conferred on the king of Kāśi by the Nāgas as described in the Pāli version...." J.J. Jones, *Mahāvastu*, Vol. II, 175.
51. *Mahāvastu*, Vol. II, 177-181.
52. In the only real departure from the prose version, the partial verse version found in the *Mahāvastu* corresponds more closely to the Pāli texts as the Nāga states a desire to be reborn as a human.

53. Both of these stories can be found in the *Mahāvastu,* Vol. I: the Nāga King Ugra on 131ff; the Nāga King Atula on 249ff.
54. *Mahāvastu,* Vol. II, 179.
55. There is a slight difference in the names as rendered in the *Ādi Parvan* versus the *Mahāvastu,* for in the former one finds Elāpatra while in the latter one finds Elapatra.
56. I wish to thank Lawrence McCrea for his suggestion that *rakta* incorporate the idea of being smeared/stained with passion.
57. Edgerton says the Lord Brahmā referred to here is a former Buddha. *Buddhist Hybrid Sanskrit Dictionary,* 404.
58. *Mahāvastu,* Vol. III, 382ff. Nālaka is the nephew of Asita. However, the Asita of the *Mahāvastu* is different than the Asita of the Pāli texts, for the latter Asita was priest to Siṃhahanu and tutor to Simṃahanu's son Śuddhodana, whereas in the *Mahāvastu,* Asita is an ascetic recluse who has sequestered himself in the wilds of the Vindhya mountains.
59. Neither the *Dhammapada,* Narada Thera, trans. (London: J. Murray, 1954), Aśvaghoṣa's *Buddhacarita,* E. H. Johnston, trans., (Delhi: Munshiram Manoharlal, 1972), nor the *Divyāvadāna,* P.L. Vaidya, ed., (Darbhanga: Mithila Institute, 1959), elevate the Nāga king to this degree nor give us information relating to the Nāga kings to the extent that the *Mahāvastu* does. In fact, neither the *Dhammapada Commentary* 3.231, nor the *Buddhacarita,* 17.3 portray the Buddha and the Nāga king as dialogue partners, and in the *Divyāvadāna,* 61, Elapatra is portrayed as a human being, not a Nāga. Also, while the *Ādi Parvan* briefly mentions the Nāgarāja Elāpatra, 1.31.6, and Hsuan Tsang, *Si-Yu-Ki,* Samuel Beal, trans. (London: Kegan Paul, 1906), 137, also mentions this figure along with a short description of some ritual practices with which the Nāga king is associated, neither of these sources mentions anything about either the monthly festivals or the Nāgas' treasures.
60. Edgerton, 1993, 344.
61. Pingala is one of the names of the chief Nāgas from the *Ādi Parvan,* (1.31.8).
62. According to Rana P.B. Singh, author of *Cultural Symbols and Literary Images of Vārāṇasī* (Vārāṇasī: Tara Book Agency, 1989) and a specialist in the study of sacred sites at Banāras Hindu University, Banāras has had a long historical association with Nāga rulers. The oldest Nāga dynasty, for instance, the Śiśunāgas of Magadha, ruled Banāras.

63. Beal, *Si-Yu-Ki*, 137. Interestingly, Hsuan Tsang goes on to describe the Nāga King Elapatra as having been a Buddhist monk in a previous life, thus adding another layer to an ongoing contextual tug-of-war.
64. J.J. Jones, *The Mahāvastu*, Vol. I, xix.
65. *Mahāvastu*, Vol. II, 308. The social/hierarchical implications of the Lokottaravādin's Buddhas represent an ideological middle ground between the Pāli literature's exclusive path of the arhat and the *Mahāyāna* literature's inclusive path of the Bodhisattva. The *Mahāvastu's* redactors mark this middle ground as they blur the line between the arhat and the layperson, not by touting an inclusive soteriological path, but rather by setting the whole of humanity apart from these lokottara Buddhas.

Chapter 7 Notes

1. Monier-Williams, *Brahmanism and Hinduism* (London: J. Murray, 1891), xi.
2. *Ṛg Veda*, 1.32.13 and 15.
3. *Pāraskara Gṛhya Sūtra*, 2.14.
4. Gonda, *The Ritual Sūtras*, 547.
5. *Sāmividhāna Brāhmaṇa*, 3.3.7.
6. *Campeyya Jātaka*, 10, 6-11.
7. *Mahāvastu*, Vol. III, 385.
8. I collected this information during my 1997 visit to Banāras.
9. Charles H. Long, *Significations: Signs, Symbols, and Images in the Interpretation of Religion*, 7.
10. Teresa de Lauretis, *Technologies of Gender: Essays on Theory, Film, and Fiction* (Bloomington: Indiana University Press, 1987), 25.

Index

Ādi Parvan of the *Mahābhārata*, 8, 11, 12, 18, 41, 46, 48, 49-80, 83, 85, 95, 99, 114, 116, 119, 126, 134, 143, 144, 146
Agrahāyaṇa, month of, 44
Ahi, 'snake,' 16, 27, 32, 144
Ahi Budhnya, 16, 20
Ahiṃsā, non-injury, 88, 111
Airāvata, 53, 54, 55
Aitareya Brāhmaṇa, 38
Alexander the Great, 3, 26, 32
Amarāvatī, 95, 105
Ananta, 66-71; name defined, 66; *see also* Śeṣa
Anga, kingdom of, 96, 99
Anthropomorphization, of snakes, 35, 37-38, 45, 55-56, 64, 79, 93, 111, 116, 181n. 23
Aparagayā, 125, 126
Āpastamba Śrauta Sūtra, 38
Apsarasas, 33, 58, 170n. 41
Arbuda Kādraveya, 16, 20, 22, 26, 33-41, 43, 45, 46, 55, 58, 147
Arbudi, son of Arbuda, 38-41
Arjuna, 72
Aruṇa, 59
Āryan people, 10, 13-20, 40, 143, 150, 166n. 17
Āstīka, 71-78, 88
Āstīka, book of, 52, 73; *see also Ādi Parvan* of the *Mahābhārata*
Āśvalāyana Gṛhya Sūtra, 32, 45, 95
Atharva Veda, 24, 29, 33, 39, 42, 60, 95

Bakabrahma Jātaka, 85
Banāras, 2, 86, 97, 98, 124, 125, 128, 129, 131, 133, 134, 137, 149
Bareau, Andre, 181n. 33
Baudhāyana Gṛhya Sūtra, 37, 62
Baudhāyana Śrauta Sūtra, 37
Bhogāvatī, 56, 99; *see also* Nāgaloka
Bhūridatta Jātaka, 72, 91, 179n. 49
Bloomfield, Maurice, 40, 170n. 40
Bloss, Lowell, 7, 43, 95, 105, 165n. 8, 169n. 6, 171nn. 48, 54, 174n. 57, 177nn. 7, 19, 178n. 36, 179nn. 48, 54, 61
Bodhgaya, 121
Bodhisattva, 110, 117, 118, 119, 127, 178n. 25, 180n. 8
Bṛhatkathā, 72
Brahmā, 61, 62, 65, 66-68, 79, 92, 126
Brahmin, 9, 10, 13-18, 20-21, 37, 50-51, 76-77; ascetics, 75-76, 82, 86, 90, 100, 114, 136 [*see also* Jaratkāru]; brahminic agenda, 10-11, 23-24, 50-52, 78, 143-146, 150; dharma, 64-65, 76-77; sacrificial activities, 51, 65, 71

Buddha, 9, 81-106, 107-140, 145, 175n. 1, 177n. 20, 178n. 21, 181n. 33; Buddha as Nāga, 110, 113, 119-120, 181n. 31; Buddha statues, Bāmiyān, 109, 140; Buddhist saints, *arhats*, 9, 83, 85, 87, 145

Caitya, 4, 26-27, 95, 99, 104, 123, 147
Campā River, 96, 97, 98, 133; *see also* Supernatural snake, regional place names
Campeyya [Campaka], *see* Nāgarājas
Campeyya Jātaka, [Campaka Jātaka], 96, 99, 102, 104, 149; *see also* Nāgarāja Campeyya [Campaka]
Caukī Ghāt, 3, 137
Classes (four) of Hindu society, *varṇas*, 13, 19, 50-51, 166n. 1, 172n. 4; *see also* Puruṣa, Brahmin, Kṣatriya
Cobras, 87, 122, 165n. 5, 177n. 14
Comparative method, 7, 151
Coomaraswamy, A., 72, 174n. 69, 178n. 34
Contextual analysis, definition of, 5-6, 142, 151
Craven, Roy, 167n. 28

Dānu, Vṛtra's mother, 15
Dāsas, 19-21, 167n. 10, 168n. 31
deLauretis, T., 184n. 10
Dharma, 64-65, 67, 69, 88, 110, 116, 119, 136, 177n. 15
Dharmapāla, 110
Dhātā, 54, 57, 172n. 9
Dhṛtarāṣṭra, 53, 55
Dhṛtarāṣṭra Airāvata, 26, 34, 37, 38, 41-43, 47, 49, 54, 55, 68, 98, 147, 182n. 47
Dīpaṃkara, previous Buddha, 108, 120, 180n. 3
Doniger, Wendy, 6, 24

Earth-god, *see* Nāga as bhūmya deva
Eck, Diana, 2, 165n. 4
Edgerton, F., 182n. 41, 183nn. 57, 60
Elapatra, *see* Nāgarājas

Fergusson, James, 166n. 9, 177n. 11, 178nn. 37, 38
Fertility, snakes' power over, 2, 18, 37, 72, 96, 97, 101-102, 104, 133, 148
Fire: brahmins' relationship with, 60; Buddha's power over, 86, 87, 88, 91, 112, 181n. 17; snakes' relationship with, 54, 58, 60, 61, 63, 66, 73-74, 85, 87, 88, 114-115, 131, 133, 181n. 21

Gandharvas, 33, 58, 170n. 41
Garuḍa bird, 52, 59, 69, 85, 91, 126
Garutmat, 60; *see also* Garuḍa
Gāya, 125
Gems, snakes' power over riches, 1, 98, 99-100, 105, 131, 137, 148, 182n. 50
Ghatāsana Jātaka, 85
Gobhila Gṛhya Sūtra, 46, 80
Goodwin Raheja, Gloria, 80, 175nn. 94, 95

Gombrich, Richard, 26, 90, 103, 166n. 9, 168n. 5, 177n. 18, 179n. 58, 181n. 23
Gomez, Luis, 176n. 4
Gonda, Jan, 45, 168n. 1, 171nn. 52, 53, 179n. 51, 184n. 4
Gṛhya Sūtras, 24, 44, 60, 100

Hsuan Tsang, 137-138, 183n. 59, 184n. 63

Indra, 9, 10, 13-22, 23, 33, 39, 40, 41, 52, 54, 57, 58, 60, 68, 74, 85, 88, 92, 143, 144
Indus Valley Civilization, 18
Irāvatī River, 42; *see also* Supernatural snake, regional place names

Jains, 82, 90
Janamejaya, king, 50, 61, 65, 73-74, 77, 171n. 3
Jaratkāru, brahmin, 71-72, 75-76
Jaratkāru, Nāgī, 72, 76
Jātaka Tales, 8, 11, 12, 72, 82, 92, 104, 132, 133, 148, 176n. 5
Jones, J.J., 108, 139, 179n. 1, 180n. 4, 182nn. 43, 50, 184n. 64

Kadrū, 39, 53, 58-62, 66, 170n. 37
Kāla, see Nāgarājas
Kaṃlinga, location of the piṃgala treasure, 134; *see also* Nāga treasures
Karṇa Parvan of the *Mahābhārata*, 42, 170n. 43, 172n. 13
Kāśi, see Banāras
Kassapa, 86-87, 89
Kaśyapa, 59
Kāśyapa, brahmin in the *Ādi Parvan*, 61, 63
Kāśyapa, brahmin in the *Mahāvastu*, 112-113, 173n. 36
Kāśyapa, previous Buddha, 117, 120, 121, 180n. 3, 181n. 33
Kauśika Sūtra, 46, 69
Kauṣītakī Brāhmaṇa, 38
Kharaputta Jātaka, 91
Knipe, David, 59, 173n. 26, 175n. 77
Konākamuni, previous Buddha, 117, 120, 121, 180n. 3, 181n. 33
Krakucchanda, previous Buddha, 117, 120, 121, 180n. 3
Kṣatriya, 50, 171n. 3
Kumudvatī, Nāgī, 72
Kurus, 53, 64
Kuśa, 72

Late Vedic redactors, agenda of, 10-11, 23-26, 146-147, 150
Lincoln, Bruce, 6
Lokottaravādin School, 107, 120, 123, 180n. 2
Lokottaravādins' agenda, 12, 108-109, 123, 139, 147, 150, 184n. 65
Long, Charles, 6, 150, 165n. 9, 184n. 9

McCrea, Lawrence, 182nn. 39, 50, 183n. 56
McCrindle, J. W., 165n. 7, 168n. 4, 169n. 19
MacDonell, A.A., 15, 166nn. 8, 9, 168n. 33

Magadha, kingdom of, 96-99, 132

Mahābhārata, 39, 42, 50, 54, 69, 70, 72, 126

Mahalingam, T.V., 18

Mahāvagga, 8, 11, 12, 81-82, 86, 93, 94, 104, 114, 122, 123

Mahāvaṃsa, 115

Mahāvastu, 4, 8, 12, 84, 88, 105, 107-140, 146, 148, 179n. 1

Mangala, previous Buddha, 108, 120, 180n. 3

Māra, king of desire, 92, 117, 178n. 24

Maruts, 16, 20, 167n. 19

Matronymics, 39, 42, 54

Minkowski, Christopher, 7, 35, 37, 38, 47, 73, 169n. 28, 170nn. 31, 36, 60, 173n. 38, 175nn. 72, 91

Mithilā, location of the lotus treasure, 134; *see also* Nāga treasures

Monier-Williams, M., 16, 57, 141, 167nn. 11, 13, 170nn. 37, 42, 45, 173n. 20, 181n. 15, 184n. 1

Mucalinda [Mucilinda], *see* Nāgarāja

Nāga, 1-2, 27, 32-33, 36, 55, 70, 79, 103, 108, 125; as *bhūmya deva*, 109, 119, 120, 121, 136, 181n. 25; Buddhists warn against, 1, 96, 102, 127; kuān, 2, 70, 137, 148; statues, 70, 137, 174n. 57; temples, 26; textual debut, 32; who is also a monk, 102-103; *see also* Supernatural snake

Nāgaloka, 2, 53, 54, 55, 56, 57, 71, 79, 92, 96, 99, 100, 105, 111, 117, 147, 172n. 16; *see also* Bhogāvatī

Nāgarājas, 180n. 6; Atula, 132; Campeyya [Campaka], 12, 84, 96-102, 109, 116, 127-134, 138, 139, 147, 148; Caṇḍa, 85, 86, 87, 114, 116; Elapatra, 109, 116, 134-138, 147, 183n. 55, 184n. 63; Ganges, 85; Kāla, 12, 84, 92-93, 109, 116-121, 124, 138, 139, 147; Mucalinda [Mucilinda], 12, 84, 93-96, 105, 109, 116, 121-124, 134, 138, 139, 146, 147; Paṇḍara, 91; Saṃkha, 137; Sudarśana, 109, 116, 121, 124, 125, 126; Ugra, 132; Uruvelā [Uruvilvā], 12, 84, 85-91, 94, 96, 109, 111-116, 136, 139; Vinipāta, 109, 116, 121, 122, 123, 124, 134

Nāga festival, 134-138, 147

Nāga Pañcamī, 2

Nāga people, 42, 137, 172n. 13, 183n. 62

Nāga treasures, the conch, the lotus, the piṃgala, and the elapatra, 134, 137

Nāgārjunakoṇḍa, 105

Nāgī, 72, 96, 99, 100, 128, 129, 130, 174n. 64; matrimonial union, 72-73

Nālaka, 134, 183n. 58

Nidānakathā, 82, 92, 117; *see also Jātaka Tales*

Nyarbudi, son of Arbuda, 39-41

Otto, Rudolf, 30, 169n. 12

Pāli canon, 81, 88, 176n. 4
Pañcaviṃśa Brāhmaṇa, 24, 42
Paṇḍara Jātaka, 91
Pāṇḍavas, 61, 64
Pāraskara Gṛhya Sūtra, 44, 45
Parikṣit, king, 63, 64, 171n. 3
Parjanya, 54, 57; *see also* Indra
Patronymics, 42
Pauṣya, book of, 52; *see also Ādi Parvan* of the *Mahābhārata*
Puloman, book of, 52; *see also Ādi Parvan* of the *Mahābhārata*
Puruṣa, the Cosmic Giant, 14, 19, 166n. 1

Raghuvaṃśa, 72
Rahula, T., 180n. 8
Rāmāyana, 42
Rawlinson, Andrew, 7, 88-89, 92, 115, 125, 177n. 16, 178n. 22, 181n. 19, 182n. 46
Ray, Reginald, 94
Ṛg Veda, 4, 7, 10, 11, 12, 13-22, 23, 24, 25, 27, 33, 34, 38, 39, 40, 41, 46, 47, 48, 50, 51, 58, 60, 72, 88, 143, 144, 145, 146
Sāma Veda, 24
Sāmavidhāna Brāhmaṇa, 24, 46, 63, 69, 80
Śāṃkhāyana Gṛhya Sūtra, 44, 45
Śāṃkhāyana Śrauta Sūtra, 38
Sāñchi, 87, 91, 95
Sārnāth, 86, 94, 121
Sarpa, 27, 32, 33
Sarpabali ritual, 41, 44-45, 96, 97, 99-100, 104, 148
Sarpanāma ritual, 23, 27-29, 36, 43, 48, 69, 147
Sarpasattra ritual, 9, 11, 23, 33, 36-38, 48, 61-62, 72, 73-75, 77, 101, 146
Sarpavid, 30, 34-36, 92
Sarpavidyā, 33, 34-36, 38, 45, 47
Śatapatha Brāhmaṇa, 24, 27, 30, 31, 32, 33, 34-36, 69, 114
Senart, E., 180n. 2
Śeṣa, 66-71, 72, 79-80, 83, 95, 126, 146; name defined, 66; *see also* Ananta
Sikhin, previous Buddha, 120, 180n. 3
Singh, Rana, 183n. 62
Skilton, Andrew, 82, 177n. 6
Smith, J.Z., 6
Snake bite: loss of poison, 115; ritual formulas to counteract, 77-78, 148
Snake charmer/harmer, *ahi-tuṇḍika*, 92, 97, 99, 101, 127, 128, 129, 130
Snake women, see Nāgī
Soma, 58, 74, 173n. 23
Śrauta rituals, 24
Śrauta Sūtras, 24, 44
Śrāvana, month of, 2, 44
Sumanā, Nāgī queen, 97
Suparṇa, 60, 68, 97, 125, 126; *see also* Garuḍa
Suparṇī, 59; *see also* Vinatā
Supernatural snake, definition of, 7-8; as *deva-jana* or 'god-people,' 30, 46, 58; guardians of the four quarters, 29; hybrid nature of, 10-11, 31, 55, 63, 64, 79, 125; regional place names,

42, 52, 54-55, 78, 98, 104, 147, 172n. 15, 182n. 47 (*see also* patryonymics and matronymics); *see also* Nāga
Suvarṇa, *see* Suparṇa

Takṣaka, 53, 54, 56, 58, 63-65, 74
Takṣaka Vaiśāleya, 26, 33-34, 37, 38, 41-43, 44, 49, 54-55, 60, 68, 98, 100, 147, 182n. 47
Takṣaśīla, location of the elapatra treasure, 134; *see also* Nāga treasures
Taliban, 109
Theravādin School, 81, 107, 175n. 2, 180n. 2;
Theravādins' agenda, 11-12, 82-83, 87-88, 101-102, 103-104, 123, 139, 145-146, 150
Timirgha Daureśruta, 42-43, 170n. 45
Tīrtha, 4, 8, 26, 43, 66, 70-71, 95, 136, 138, 147
Tīrtha-Yatra Parvan, 70; *see also* Mahābhārata
Tutelary deities, snakes as, 83, 91-96

Uccaiḥśravas, horse, 61
Ugrasena, king, 98, 99, 128, 129, 130, 131, 133
Ulūpī, Nāgī, 72
Umpasampāda, Buddhist ordination, 103
Upavāsa, 128, 129
Uposatha, 1, 96, 97, 98, 101, 102, 128, 132, 163n. 1, 178n. 40
Uruvelā [Uruvilvā], Nāga king, *see* Nāgarāja
Uruvilvā, place, 125
Utanka, brahmin, 53, 56, 57, 64

van Buitenen, J. A. B., 171nn. 1, 2, 172n. 5
Vaśālā, 125, 126
Vaiśālī, 42, 54-55; *see also* Supernatural snake, regional place names
Vārāṇasī, location of the conch treasure, 134; *see also* Nāga treasures, Banāras
Vāstupraśamana ritual, 41, 46, 47, 80, 148
Vāsuki, 26, 41, 46, 49, 54, 56, 65, 68, 69, 75, 80, 147, 148
Vāsuladatta, 115
Vidhātā, 54, 57, 172n. 8, 173n. 19
Vinatā, 60-61, 68, 85
Viśāla, 42; *see also* Supernatural snake, regional place names
Viśālā river, 42; *see also* Supernatural snake, regional place names
Viṣṇu, 16, 20, 167n. 19
Vogel, J.Ph., 7, 69, 73, 94, 95, 174nn. 56, 64, 70, 178nn. 28, 31
Vṛtra, 10, 13-22, 23, 25, 33, 39, 40, 46, 54, 58, 85, 88, 143, 147; definition of name, 14, 166n. 4; as shoulderless, 19, 168n. 35

Wadley, Susan, 31, 169n. 14
Water: Buddha's and Buddhist saints' power over, 94, 102;

Indra's power over, 17, 54, 57, 60; snakes' power over, 14, 16, 17, 18, 19, 29, 39, 42, 52, 53, 70, 72, 78, 83, 85, 94, 105, 124, 133, 143
Winternitz, M., 179n. 1

Yakṣas, 33, 95, 178n. 34
Yaśodharā, 127-128
Yajur Veda, 24, 58, 60

11462074R0012

Made in the USA
Lexington, KY
05 October 2011